Britain and Arab Unity

Britain and Arab Unity

A Documentary History from the Treaty of Versailles to the End of World War II

Younan Labib Rizk

I.B.Tauris Publishers
In Association With
The Centre for Arab Unity Studies

مركز دراسات الوحدة العربية
CENTRE FOR ARAB UNITY STUDIES

مؤسسة محمد بن راشد آل مكتوم
MOHAMMED BIN RASHID
AL MAKTOUM FOUNDATION

The translation and publication of this book was made possible by the generous financial support of the Mohammed Bin Rashid Al Maktoum Foundation.

New paperback edition published in 2015 by I.B.Tauris & Co. Ltd
6 Salem Road, London W2 4BU
175 Fifth Avenue, New York NY 10010
www.ibtauris.com
Published in association with the Centre for Arab Unity Studies

Centre for Arab Unity Studies
'Beit Al-Nahda' Bldg. – Basra Street – Hamra
PO Box: 113-6001 Hamra
Beirut 2034 2407 – LEBANON
www.caus.org.lb

First published in 2009 in hardback by I.B.Tauris & Co. Ltd

ISBN: 978 1 78076 651 5
eISBN: 978 0 85773 754 0

A full CIP record for this book is available from the British Library
A full CIP record is available from the Library of Congress

Library of Congress Catalog Card Number: available

Designed and Typeset by 4word Ltd, Bristol, UK

Contents

Foreword vii

1 Britain's Divisive Role Prior to 1919 1
Indianisation of the Gulf
The Isolation of Egypt
The Judaisation of Palestine

2 The Arab Kingdom 1919–23 31
Arab Unity during World War I
The Arab Kingdom
The Arab Confederation

3 The Arab Conference 1931–3 53
The Islamic Conference in Jerusalem
The Arab Conference in Baghdad

4 Between Arab Unity and Pan-Arabism 1936–41 77
Pan-Islamism-Arabism
Pouring over the Concepts
The Impact of the War

5 British Policy Towards Arab Unity During World War II 1941–3 105
New Planning
Economic Cultural Unity
Convening the Arab Conference

Foreword

'The known and the unknown' is likely the most apt description of this study which addresses Great Britain's position towards Arab unity. Historians have taken the general view that Foreign Secretary Anthony Eden's declaration, at Mansion House on 29 May 1941,[1] regarding the need to adopt a positive view of Arab unity, marked the beginning of the embodiment of Pan-Arabism in an institutional form, known today as the Arab League. In other words, it is a view that suggests that the London Government was behind the establishment of this regional organisation, in 1945. It is, however, a notion fraught with misconceptions.

No state, regardless of its ability to dominate politically in a given historical period, can create something out of nothing. The concept of Pan-Arabism had been there all the time, as far back as the establishment of the very first Arab societies and political parties in the pre-war period such as "Arabīyah al-Fatāh', 'al-'Ahd' and the Decentralisation Party founded in Cairo. We should also not forget the Great Arab Revolt, the uprisings against the imperialist Britain and France, and rebellions against Zionist aspirations during which the concept of Arabism was ignited. At no time were these revolts free of nationalist sentiment, especially in the cases of Syria, Iraq and Palestine.

Thus Britain faced what was essentially a *fait accompli* and sought to contain it; and the embarrassment of the Allies at the hands of the Central powers, in the early years of World War I, gave it the opportunity to unfurl its containment policy. We might say, therefore, that, in one sense, the British Foreign Secretary's famous declaration was a product of nationalism and, in another, a product of circumstance.

On the other hand, to accept such a notion means simply ignoring British policies over the preceding decades, policies that harboured animosity towards Arab attempts to unite and, for obvious reasons, since such a union would inevitably pose a threat to the Empire's interests in the region. Nevertheless, it was not so strange for Great Britain to attempt, at times, to utilise various situations to sow division among the Arabs, and at most others, to work at consolidating its handiwork.

Thirdly, British documents reveal that in the four years intervening between Eden's declaration at Mansion House and the establishment of the Arab League, the British did their best to *obstruct* efforts to forge Arab unity. They used all possible methods at their disposal, from issuing warnings to Arab governments, to actually threatening them, to attempting to actively incite conflict between them. Finally, it worked arduously to confine efforts towards Arab unity to the cultural and economic domains.[2]

The present study attempts to make Britain's position towards Arab unity 'a fact well known', rather than a 'not such well known fact', by relying almost entirely on official British documents on Arab issues – mainly from the Foreign Office, the Colonial Office, the India Office and the World War II War Cabinet.

This overwhelming reliance on British official documents, and the minute details they contain, helped bring the full picture of Britain's attitude towards Arab unity to light. This compels us to describe the present work as a 'documentary study', a fact the reader will not help but notice from the very first pages to the last. It was not possible to include only footnotes in this documentary work. While pouring over these documents, we found several which we thought should be annexed to the text, not only to add authenticity to the narrative, but also to help the reader understand the underpinnings of British policy towards Arab unity, at that important junction in Arab contemporary history.

We decided to limit the period of research to the years 1919 to 1945, not only because the Centre for Arab Unity Studies has already published a considerable amount of material on the subject and the period,[3] but for other objective reasons, as well.

The first year of the post-World War I era was a settling-of-affairs period – mainly at the Versailles Conference; a period during which the policies of the London Government became all too evident. They became quite clear once Great Britain emerged as the greatest power ever to dominate the world, and began drawing the map of the Arab world in a manner that suited its own interests, rather than according to one that would honour the promises it made during the war.

On the other hand, the final year of the study not only witnessed the establishment of the Arab League, it symbolised the entry of the United States of America, the new and youthful Western power, into the world of Arab politics. The appearance of the United States on the scene came either as the result of its fast developing international policy, crystallised by the famous Truman Doctrine in 1947, or as a result of its growing interests in the region, especially in oil. While the American role in the region was on the increase, the British role was waning, a fact made all the more evident, and definite, when Britain had to relinquish its control over India in 1947, the jewel in the British Crown.

In our opinion, the authentic and scientific material at the root of this study that we were first to use, and its analyses of both the motives and development of British policies towards Arab unity, has culminated in a worthy and beneficial documentary work.

And unto God is the intent of the path.
Dr Younan Labib Rizk, Cairo

Notes

1. See Chapter 4 of this book
2. See Chapters 5 and 6 of this book.
3. In 1985 the Centre for Arab Unity Studies published a book by Dr Ali Muhafza, entitled *The Positions of France, Germany and Italy towards Arab Unity, 1919–1945.*

Chapter 1

Britain's Divisive Role Prior to 1919

At the end of May 1920, the London *Daily Express* raised an important case with very serious implications regarding the nature of Britain's role in fostering Arab divisions prior to 1919.

The *Daily Express* called the series 'The Muddle in the Middle East' and opened it, on the 27th of that same month, with an article strongly critical of the fact that many British Government departments were dealing with the Middle East at the same time, and of the relationship between these departments. It described it as a relationship fraught with contradictions that sometimes degenerate into open conflict, conflicts the price of which is shouldered ultimately by the British taxpayer. The newspaper cited, as an example, the situation in the Arabian Peninsula, where the Kingdom of the Ḥijāz, ruled by King Ḥussayn, was under the control and direction of the Foreign Office, while the Najd, ruled by 'Abd al-'Azīz Āl Sa'ūd, founder of the third Saudi State, was under control of the India Office. Given the escalating conflict between the two sides, the newspaper came to the conclusion that as long as the Foreign Office aids the former with arms and ammunition and the India Office supplies the latter with the same, the British taxpayer will continue to bear the fiscal burden of this faulty policy.[1]

The following day, Colonel T. E. Lawrence, better known as 'Lawrence of Arabia', and sometimes as the Uncrowned King of the Arabs, wrote an article for the same newspaper entitled 'Secrets of the War in Mecca'. The article, which took on considerable importance since its author was among those who took part in Sharif Ḥussayn's revolt against the Turks, that is, the Great Arab Revolt, endorsed the newspaper's position and recommended that the Government unify its stance vis-à-vis the conflict raging in the Arabian Peninsula. Colonel Lawrence also advised that instructions be issued to Lord Allenby, the British High Commissioner in Cairo and the man responsible for contacts with both parties in his capacity as representative of the Foreign and India Offices, to support King Ḥussayn in his conflict with Ibn Saʿūd.[2]

In the same issue, the newspaper referred to a letter to Prime Minister Lloyd George by some members of the House of Commons, asking him to take control of the situation in the Middle East and to put an end to the chaos. The letter states:

> It is our opinion that the present arrangement which places Mesopotamia, Central and Southern Arabia, and Aden under the control and direction of the India office; Egypt, Palestine and the Sudan and the territory of the King of the Ḥijāz under the Foreign Office, and Cyprus and Somalia under the Colonial Office, has resulted in a serious conflict of policy which has all the seeds of permanence. None of the three existing departments has the qualification, the special organisation and personnel to cope successfully with the new situation.

The signatories ended their appeal with a request to the Prime Minister to put supervision of these territories into the hands of a single new ministry.[3]

Although the *Daily Express*' campaign seemed quite reasonable, and despite the apparent sincere concern of the appeal's signatories, the authorities did not comply with these demands and the situation remained unchanged. Rather to the contrary, all decisions taken after the appeal highlight the old divisions in administrative responsibilities, especially when Palestine and the Emirate of Trans-Jordan were added to the territories under the control of the Colonial Office.

In our opinion, this is partly due to the historical conditions under which British control of the region of the Arab Mashreq (lit. 'Arab East') had expanded, and fostered divisions on the ground, as well. In fact, the conflict was not, as Lawrence understood it, a struggle between different British administrations, as much as it was the embodiment of a *wilfully divisive policy*. Based on that, we can classify Arab countries under British rule into three categories:

1 The Eastern Arabian Peninsula, which included the Emirates and Sultanates of the Arabian Gulf, territories lying further to the South, and Iraq, especially the southern regions. These territories were under

the control of the Government in Bombay, and therefore part of the economic, administrative and social 'Indianisation' policy that gave these territories a distinctly different character than the rest of the Arab world, further to the North and West. In short, they were made to face Eastwards, and turn their backs to the world in the West, i.e., the Arab World, a world they were once a part of under the Ottoman Empire.

2 Given the international complexities associated with the Egyptian Question, since the launch of the French campaign in 1798, authorities in charge of British policy in London handed responsibility for Egypt over to the Foreign Office, very early on in the late eighteenth century.[4] The ensuing close relationship between Egypt and the Sudan – which made it impossible to separate the two countries – resulted in placing the latter under the administration of the Foreign Office.

Thus, Egyptian affairs, and by extension, Sudanese affairs, became dependent on inter-European relations. This fact not only manifested itself in conflicts among European powers – mainly between Great Britain and France – but also in the flow of Europeans to the region, especially to Egypt. To quite an extent, this affected political thought as much as it did economic and social conditions, and created a special Egyptian world oriented towards the North, resulting in Egypt's isolation from the rest of the Arab world.

3 The British presence in Palestine and Trans-Jordan was a result of the post-World War I settlements, and the ensuing British Mandate over these two countries, based on the resolutions of the Saint Remo Conference, in 1920. The special status these two countries enjoyed, as a result, especially in the case of Palestine, automatically placed them under the administration of the Colonial Office.

The Colonial Office had to manage these regions according to the deals struck between the colonial powers during the war, including the famous declaration regarding the establishment of a national home for the Jews in Palestine. Although this declaration was one of the most important foci of Arab consensus later on, it conferred on the region a different reality, a reality that, in turn, fostered more Arab division. The transformation of Palestine into a Jewish state turned this country, and its particular situation, into a cause for more division rather than unity, within the Arab order.

The above situation presents us with an opportunity to trace the role of these policies in fermenting division in Arab territories under British control. However, before we do that, a few remarks are well in order:

First: Though these divisions may be acceptable, they reflect a sense of 'arbitrariness'; one way or another, there was a conspicuous overlap between the responsibilities of different British departments. In Iraq, there was an overlap between the responsibilities of the India and Colonial Offices since Britain's presence in Mesopotamia was legally based on resolutions by the League of Nations granting it a mandatory role. Moreover, despite Sudan's dependence on the Foreign Office, by virtue of its close relationship to Egypt, the fact that its southern and south-eastern borders abutted on countries under the Colonial Office's control (Uganda and British East Africa, including Kenya and Zanzibar), gave this office considerable influence in that country's affairs. This, for instance, was particularly important in Sudan's southern regions, especially with regard to border issues.

Second: It was not simply a matter of conflicting dependencies; it went well beyond that to drawing administrative division lines that eventually became permanent political borders, an issue that would lay in wait and erupt every now and then like buried landmines in the field of inter-Arab relations. The Egyptian-Sudanese border case is a typical example of those British policies that sought to spread a spirit of divisiveness in the Arab World.

Third: Because British Colonial policies revolved round the need to secure the Eastern trade route, especially after the opening of the Suez Canal in 1869, one of the basic tenets of British colonial policy in the Arab world was to establish control over the region's Eastern areas, paying hardly any attention to its Western ones. This could very well be what lay behind the unwritten agreement between the two largest imperial powers of the nineteenth and early twentieth centuries, that allowed France to expand its colonial power towards the West (the Maghreb), in return for British expansion towards the East. In April 1903 this unwritten agreement eventually became an official written document known as the 'Entente Cordiale'. The text of the pact stipulates that France would not hinder British activities in Egypt (its focal point in the East), in return for the London Government giving Paris a free hand in the West (the pearl of the Maghreb).

The only exception, and a deliberate one at that, was when the British encouraged the Italian Government to occupy Libya in 1911, and to expel the Ottomans from the country. The Italian presence in Libya acted as a buffer between Arab areas under the control of the two powerful colonial powers.

By comparing the outcome of this policy to the situation that prevailed prior to the imperialist onslaught of the nineteenth century, we find that the unity the Arabs enjoyed under the Ottomans, despite its Pan-Islamic character, had completely vanished in the wake of the British-led assault. Trade caravans travelling back and forth between the Arab Mashreq and the West came to a standstill when Imperialism reconfigured Arab economies to serve its interests. *Ḥajj* caravans that came from all corners of the Muslim and Arab worlds, and which represented a factor of continuous interaction between the Arab countries, gradually decreased in number, especially after the opening of the Suez Canal and the growing dependence on maritime transport. Furthermore, cultural interaction among Arab universities, especially between al-Azhar and al-Qarawīyīn, grew steadily weaker due to the new generation of Arab intellectuals that inclined towards Western academic institutions, especially towards British and French universities.[5]

Indianisation of the Gulf

Egypt's experiment bore within it the seeds of Arab unity until the British intervened to abort it, regardless of the motives behind Muḥammad 'Alī's project in the Mashreq, which began by sending troops to the Arabian Peninsula in 1811, and ended with a retreat from almost the entire Mashreq Region in 1841.

As is well known, this British intervention went as far as undertaking a military operation in the Levant during the famous crisis that culminated in the London Treaty of 1840. On the other hand, despite being less famous, the British intervention in the Gulf proved even more effective. For while the motives behind the British intervention to abort Egypt's aspirations in the Levant emanated from the need to maintain the unity of Ottoman territory, at least at that particular point in time, its motives in the Gulf were an outcome of its imperial interests. The motive was to prevent any power, be it local or international, from gaining control over this vital eastern route.

Egyptian documents of the period[6] are replete with the warnings the British Government had sent to the Pāshā of Egypt, in an attempt to prevent him from extending his influence in the Gulf. At times, these warnings went so far as to hint at the possibility of using military force, and at others, even did in fact employ it, as transpired in the British occupation of Aden, in 1839.[7]

One of these warnings was sent to Muḥammad 'Alī when Khurshīd Pāshā, Commander of the Egyptian Armed Forces in the region, tried to extend his control to Bahrain. This prompted Samuel Hennell, the British Resident in the Gulf, to issue a complaint and remind Khurshīd that Muḥammad 'Alī had previously insisted to the British representative in Cairo that his forces would not trespass on the Arab countries in the Persian Gulf.[8] Another warning was the result of Egypt's attempt to extend its control over a number of regions belonging to the Sultanate of Oman, especially the Oasis of al-Buraymī. Also on this occasion, Hennell warned Khurshīd Pāshā that any dispatch of troops to al-Buraymī, be it by land or sea, would be taken as clear evidence that Egypt was not interested in pursuing friendly and equal relations between the two countries.[9] He sent a British officer to the Oasis to distribute weapons, ammunition and food to help the locals resist the Egyptian advance.[10]

The Egyptian withdrawal from the area afforded the Government of India the opportunity to begin implementing its plan to politically, economically and socially Indianise the Gulf.

Politically, the Gulf region was placed under the control of His Majesty's Resident High Commissioner in Bombay, and the latter sent a Resident into the region with Bushehr (Iran) as his headquarters. In addition, the British sent agents to the emirates and sheikhdoms in which Britain had considerable interests, and those linked to the Indian Government by special treaties. The first of these agents was appointed to Sharjah in 1823.[11]

Similar to other British departments, the Foreign and Colonial Offices used 'gunboat diplomacy' to spread their power to the four corners of the Empire, which is what the Indian Government also did by forging a special relationship with the Admiralty, and seeking, at times, the assistance of the Foreign Office in matters of international relations. The Gulf was the scene of international rivalry between Great Britain, France, Russia and Germany, as well as the Ottoman Empire, which maintained nominal control over certain areas of the region, especially the northern areas.

The Indian Government demonstrated its responsibility for Britain's presence in the Gulf on many occasions. The most famous such demonstration was the statement delivered in Sharjah in November 1903 by Lord Curzon, the King's High Commissioner in India, while on a trip to the region. He said in the statement that sometimes he thinks that the record of the past is doomed to be forgotten since there are those who wonder why Britain continues to wield such authority. He told his audience that the answer to that is in the history of their emirates and families, as well as in the current status quo in the Gulf. We were in these waters, he said, before any other state in modern history, and brought order out of chaos. Our trade and your safety were under threat, and needed your protection. We saved you from extinction at your neighbours' hands and opened these waters to ships from all nations, and enabled their flags to fly safely.[12]

Additionally, on many occasions the India Government occasioned the assistance of the Royal Navy, the most important such event being the destruction of Rās al-Khaymah by the Navy in 1809 at the Indian Government's behest.[13]

British representatives in the Gulf assumed a number of the local rulers' prerogatives, especially those having to do with British subjects living in the region – most of whom were Indian Muslims and Hindus. The British Commissioner in Muscat had legal authority over these subjects, based on two treaties signed in 1822, and the Order in Council issued by the British Crown, in 1867, is an apt example of this.

The Order in Council granted the Consul in Muscat and the Supreme Court in Bombay legal prerogatives, and the right to issue rules and regulations to maintain security among British subjects, and the same applied to British representatives in the other Gulf countries. The Order in Council designated the Court of Bombay as the place where appeals in criminal cases would be lodged, while civil cases were left for the representatives to deal with as they saw fit, through conciliation, swearing an oath or calling upon witnesses to testify.[14]

The organic relationship between the Indian presence in the Gulf and the British policy that sought to Indianise it is evident in the India Office's extensive use of Indian subjects as basic tools for control. The British used them to run government departments, such as customs and financial affairs, and as key elements in maintaining security in various regions, organised under different names like the Indian Guard, the Indian Police Force and the Indian Military Combat Force.[15]

The Indian presence in the Gulf played an important role in defining the nature of political life in the sheikhdoms and emirates, by orienting the locals more towards the East, as previously mentioned. The success achieved by Indians in the commercial domain made them a considerable economic force, prompting rulers to turn to them for loans in times of crises. This allowed the Indians to play a political role in the conflicts that often arose between different ruling families, even in those between members of the same family.

On 1 December 1920, at a conference he presided over to discuss Middle East affairs, the British Foreign Secretary, Lord Curzon, admitted the extent of the Gulf region's dependence on the Indian Government. He said verbatim:

> The Persian Gulf has always been regarded as Indian interest. The ships sailing on the Persian Gulf were almost entirely Indian ships. The Sultan of Muscat practically is an Indian chieftain. The arrangements for the political control of the Gulf have been made by India. Moreover, before the War, the Indian Government was the one that used to appoint the British Resident in Baghdad.[16]

Economically, the rise of a powerful class of Indian merchants helped develop very close ties between the Gulf and India and was reflected in the large Indian presence in the region, particularly in Oman and Bahrain. Indians also played an important role in Dubai, turning it into the main commercial transit hub in the area.

At first, these merchants monopolised the date trade – especially varieties that were in high demand in India, in particular the '*mbasali*' type as well as dried dates, the latter being a traditional offering at Indian wedding celebrations.[17]

The role of the Arabs in this important commercial field was limited to bringing in the date harvest from remote areas of the country, on behalf of the large Indian commercial corporations that had set up shop in coastal regions. The gum trade, the best quality of which was found in Ḍifār, was also in the hands of Indian merchants, as was trade in tanned leather, glue and beeswax.[18]

In Bahrain, in addition to the coffee trade, Indians monopolised the pearl trade and turned Bombay into the most important centre of pearl manufacture, thanks to regular supplies from the Gulf. The India Office's annual report, for 1876–7, showed that Bahraini exports to India were 74.3 per cent of the overall volume of exports totalling 2.252 million Rupees, followed by Kuwait and Iraq with a total of 483,000 Rupees, and by Persia with 168,000 Rupees. This shows the extent to which Bahrain's trade was oriented towards India.[19]

Since Indian merchants succeeded in turning Dubai, where they settled after leaving Lingah, into one of the most important transit hubs, its rulers, the Āl Maktoum family, encouraged them to settle in their sheikhdom.

Thanks to Indian activities in the Gulf, the Indian Rupee became the most widely-used currency in the region. Its strength was bolstered by the British presence in the Gulf, which was in fact an Indian presence, and because none of the countries in the Gulf had its own official currency.

The use of the Indian Rupee gradually spread to other regions, starting with African areas under the control of Muscat. Thanks to the commercial ties between India and Zanzibar and India and Muscat, these two countries' currencies were tied unofficially to the Rupee, as of 1835, and the entire Gulf region soon followed suit.[20]

It was only natural, therefore, for the number of Indian nationals in the Gulf to increase in tandem with the expansion of their activities in various regions. The resulting strong friction between the latter and the local Arabs had quite a significant impact, reflected mainly in the accelerated pace of Indianisation, and in a more forceful orientation of the region towards the East.

On the social front, Nūrā al-Qāsimī[21] succeeded in tracing the impact that Indian social habits have had on life in the Gulf, relying mainly on field research. These social habits are amply in evidence in the local language, food, clothing, embroidery, jewellery and music, to name just a few categories. Below are examples of the researcher's findings:

- The use of Hindi terminology prevailed in commercial areas where there was a strong Indian presence. One such area was the pearl trade where many Hindi terms, like *danna*, meaning a kind of large and valuable pearl, *jiiwam*, meaning the round white pearl, and *buuka*, the small inexpensive pearl, were used. In the art of navigation, sailors made use of the words: *balam*, meaning a small boat; *hory,* a type of well-known small vessel; *kotiyah,* another type of wooden boat; *brawna*, meaning the boat's propeller; *cooley*, a worker or porter; *noker,* a person who works in the house; and *tandeel*, a foreman.
- Even more important are those Indian words which, based on the researcher's findings, have made their way into Gulf households. Among these are: *punkah*, a fan; *tawah*, a receptacle for making bread; *mouri,* a basin for washing the hands; *batat,* door hinges; *batta,* playing cards; *astra*, clothes iron; *kumchah*, a spoon (the Indian original word being '*chumcha*', meaning skull); *saman*, meaning furniture; and finally, *kugrah*, meaning garbage.[22]

In the culinary domain, the researcher says that the heavy use of spices in Gulf recipes unmistakably reflects the influence of Indian taste, and gives many examples to prove her point, such as dishes like *briyani* and *salona*, among others. The first is a dish made with rice, meat and saffron, and the second is a meat and vegetable stew. There are also *mash*, meaning lentils; *agar*, pickles; and the *gabrah*, the tin-roofed fruit and vegetables market, to name just a few instances.

The clothing industry boasts its own words of Indian origin, like *zangafrah*, meaning flannel; *remal*, handkerchief; *lass*, soft silk; and *ghuttrah*, the white headdress worn by men in the Gulf.

As far as jewellery is concerned, Gulf Arabs were clearly affected by the Indian penchant for gold and silver jewellery, especially as worn by women. Children in Oman's inner regions wear a flat type of anklet with a ring dangling from it called *hawageel*, originally an Indian word. Jewellers have copied the Indian ring style bearing an etching of three cows, and another type of common jewellery is the *banjari*, reflecting a word of Urdu origin that is widely used in the Gulf.

In the field of music, Indian influence manifests itself clearly in both melody and instrument. At the beginning of the last century, some of the most prominent musicians in the Gulf learned and composed their music based on Indian rhythms. Moreover, the heavy metal ring normally worn by drummers in the Gulf is inspired by the Indian art, as are a number of other instruments of Indian origin such as the *merwas*, a small double-face cylinder-shaped drum covered on the side by animal skin, once imported from India.[23]

There is no doubt that the deep impact that the Indian presence has had on the Gulf has helped weaken the region's ties to the rest of the Arab world. Whether deliberate or not, it is one of the consequences of British imperialist policies, though not the only one, by any means.

The Isolation of Egypt

Under the Ottoman umbrella, Egypt continued to have close relations with the rest of the Arab world, and many historians believe that these relations started to deteriorate when the modern state, with its diverse and its multifaceted relationships, first developed. This requires a second look at the first half of the nineteenth century, at least, in particular at Muḥammad ʿAlī's project in the 1830s, given the wide disparity of views regarding this particular period.

One school of historians, led by Muḥammad Shafīq Ghorbāl, saw this project within the context of the overall Ottoman experience. They believe that the veteran Pāshā was simply trying to launch an internal reform movement in an Empire that had already begun to weaken. As proof, they point to his dispute with the leader of the conservatives in Istanbul, a group once led by Khurshīd Pāshā, and to his close relationship with those who mounted a revolt in his support in the Turkish capital. Added to that was that a member of the latter group, Fawzī Pāshā, Admiral of the Ottoman fleet, the *donanma*, had sought refuge – with most of his ships – with the Pāshā of Egypt as a gesture of support for him in the conflict over state reforms.[24]

Another school of historians viewed the experiment within the context of Egypt's history and, as such, considered it a repeat of old attempts at empire-building by various Cairo governments; attempts that usually began by dispatching Egyptian troops to the East. This school of thought had wide support among writers of nationalist history, and for those able to read between the lines, its theories are all too evident in al-Rāfiʿī's writings: the latter having described Egypt's wars under Muḥammad ʿAlī as attempts to 'achieve national independence'.[25]

A third school yet believes that 'Arabism' was the main driving force behind the experiment, a view with which foreign observers and politicians tend to agree.

Baron Bwalkent, who met Ibrāhīm Pāshā near Tarsus in 1833, said in one of his books that Ibrāhīm Pāshā had openly stated his intention to revive Arab Nationalism, grant the Arabs their rights, and appoint them to positions in the administration and army. He also said that he intended to secure their independence, give them a stake in financial affairs, and get them accustomed to being in authority and bearing its cost.[26]

In that same year Baron Sturmer, the Austrian Ambassador in the Ottoman capital, submitted a report to Austrian Chancellor Metternich, which said at the outset that the establishment of an Arab Empire under the banner of Muḥammad ʿAlī was inevitable. He went on to say he could envision a very well-trained Arab army crowned with victory; a mighty fleet with enough resources to treble its size and the size of its army; and that the Arabs were infused with the spirit of nationalism. He finally admitted sensing a growing esteem for Muḥammad ʿAlī throughout the Arabic-speaking world.[27]

More than any other major power, and because of its own vested interests, Britain was concerned about the fallout from the possibility of a powerful Arab Kingdom under the leadership of Egypt. This concern was expressed by Consul Farin, one of its representatives in the region, in a long report he sent to London. The report explained that the establishment of this Kingdom 'gives the Pāshā Baghdad and Basra through northern Syria ... which will extend his growing power to the heart of Asia, from Shīrāz to Muscat, and up to the Red Sea, via the Arabian Peninsula'. He went on to say that, 'the new political power being formed by Muḥammad 'Alī is prejudicial to Britain's interests in the Near East, especially if embodied in a harmonious Kingdom based primarily on Arabism'.[28]

It seems that the target of the London Government was the concept of Arabism at the core of Muḥammad 'Alī's project. It was clear that Palmerston and his ministers had arrived at the conclusion that Egypt should be allowed to play a role further to the south, in Africa, but *not* in Asia where the Arab world lies. Britain did not accept Muḥammad 'Alī's right to extend his power into Asia, though it did not object to its extension into Africa where, they asserted, it would be seen in a positive light, and where he would receive guarantees as to his safety from attack.[29]

This, perhaps, helps explain two relevant points. The first is that British naval attacks to destroy Muḥammad 'Alī's Empire and end its Arab role had perhaps begun, and were concentrated on the Arab side whether by provoking elements in Syria, or bombarding a number of Greater Syrian ports, particularly Beirut. The second point is that while the settlement of 1840–1 aimed mainly at ending the Egyptian presence in Asia, namely in the Arab world, it allowed this presence to continue in the Sudan, Egypt's gateway to Africa.

While the British military intervention did indeed bring to an end Egypt's presence in the Arab Mashreq, the policies of the London Government were doing their part to completely isolate Cairo from the rest of the Arab World, and completely reorient its attention, not to mention the developments Egypt had witnessed at the end of the nineteenth century and up to 1919. The main objective was for Egypt not to have an *Arab* identity, a fact which may be ascertained by closely scrutinising Egypt's history in the period that follows.

The first thing that catches the eye is the stark separation which the settlement of 1840–1 imposed between Egypt and the Arab Mashreq. While it allowed the Ottoman Empire only nominal control over Egypt, it did not allow the Cairo Government to look beyond its eastern borders, regardless of whoever was at the helm.

The second thing we notice is the methodical linking of Egypt's economy to Europe by strongly supporting Muḥammad 'Alī's plan to cultivate income-generating crops, mainly cotton. It was necessary, as a second step, to connect Egypt to the European markets, especially British markets with the most advanced textile industry, and transform it into a channel that connected the East to the West. The endeavour started during the reign of 'Abbās I with the construction of the first railroad network outside America and England, linking Alexandria to Cairo, and then a land route to Suez. This was followed by the construction of the Suez Canal, the famous strategic waterway connecting the East to Europe, which served to bring Egypt even closer to Europe.

Moreover, the reorientation of Egypt towards Europe, and away from the Arab world, effectively transferred the main commercial centre from Damietta to Alexandria.

The port city of Damietta flourished prior to the French Campaign in Egypt, thanks to its links to Arab regions to the East, a fact confirmed by M. Gerard, who wrote the economic section in 'A Description of Egypt', a large volume written by scholars accompanying the French Campaign.

In this section, Gerard writes that in Damietta people manufacture linen, cotton and silk, and that the city is particularly famous for a kind of linen cloth bordered with coloured silk, which they exported to Syria for the manufacture of shawls and turbans. In Damietta, as well as the nearby village of Minyah, there were some 300 looms for the manufacture of linen shawls.

In another section, he speaks about a type of silk textile manufacturing exclusive to Damietta, namely women's veils that were usually black or crimson in colour. He also describes the manufacture of sails for ships, given the high demand for these by ships on laying anchor in the port city.

M. Gerard points to the presence in Damietta of a powerful merchant class whose role was not confined to the export and import of goods, but went well beyond it to the manufacturing of textiles in al-Maḥallah. He said that merchants from Damietta traded between al-Maḥallah al-Kubrā and Greater Syria, by bringing silk over from Syria and returning part of it as Egyptian manufactured goods.[30] It is known that the rise of capitalism in Europe in the modern era began at the hands of this type of merchant middleman, known then as 'free merchants' because they broke rules established and observed by their ancestors, the merchants of [various] sects.

This difference between these two large port cities, Alexandria, the connection between Europe and Egypt, and Damietta, the main bridge between Egypt and the Arab Mashreq, lay at the basis of each of the two cities' social character, a fact that became all too obvious at the end of the nineteenth century. Thus, while Alexandria became Europeanised, Damietta retained its Arab Islamic character. In the same vein, while Europeans flowed in large numbers to Alexandria, giving rise to the famous saying, 'You will hardly find a single nation in Europe that is not represented in Alexandria', there was no place for them in Damietta.

The triumph of Alexandria over Damietta meant a radical change in Egypt's economic orientation, away from the Arab Mashreq, and towards Europe, especially towards Great Britain further to the west, augmenting Egypt's isolation from the Arab world. However, although no one can say if the London Government had planned this shift, we can argue, however, that it was quite satisfied with the way things transpired, and pushed for more.

Another indication of this economic shift is the large European migration to Egypt in the second half of the nineteenth century. This migration, which began on a limited scale during the reign of Saʿīd Pāshā (1854–63), became a large influx of migrants under Ismāʿīl Pāshā (1863–79), before attaining a level of stability during the period of occupation, after 1882.

This European migration also helped spread Western consumer values to Egypt, ushering in an increase in socio-economic ties with the West at the time when Egypt had hardly any ties to the Arab world.

Lord Cromer, the British High Commissioner in Cairo, admitted as much in one of his reports. The first thing the report mentions is the rapid increase in the number of Europeans in Egypt and, consequently, the impact that this had on local customs and mores, especially in terms of imitating Western customs, clothes and style, leading to a rise in demand for European goods. The report goes on to say, however, that one would be at pains to find a single cobbler able to mend a European shoe well, despite them being commonly used. The repair and manufacture of shoes is in the hands of Greeks and Armenians; almost the entire grocery business is in the hands of Greeks; the textile trade is in the hands of the Jews, Syrians and Europeans; and tailoring is in the hands of the Jews.

The report noted, on the other hand, the rapid deterioration of traditional crafts. For example, people no longer rode on donkeys, and the newly-built tramway network caused the saddle industry to become extinct. A decrease in the use of locally manufactured tiles in homes led to a severe deterioration in the manufacturing of straw mats, while for its part, 'the textile industry is rapidly declining as European textiles replace local ones. Indigo dyeing is on the verge of extinction because the cotton textiles used in making clothes for peasants are imported from abroad, and dyed with artificial indigo.' The report says that there is a clear difference between the Egypt of today and the Egypt of ten or 15 years ago. The streets that used to be crowded with craftsmen, such as spinners, tailors, cord makers, dyers, tentmakers, shoemakers, jewellery makers, spice dealers, braziers, water distributors, saddle makers, makers of sieves and locks, among others, are now few in number. It goes on to say cafes and small stores, filled with European goods, have now replaced these old manufacturing stalls.[31]

In turn, Egyptian relations with the Arab Maghreb suffered stagnation very similar to that in its relations with the Mashreq. Traditionally, Egyptian relations with the Arab Maghreb were the result of two factors: the first was the large caravan of Moroccan pilgrims that arrived in Egypt, usually a month prior to the pilgrimage to Mecca (the *ḥajj*); and the second was the caravan itself. The latter started from Fez and was joined *en route* by caravans from Tunisia, Algeria and Tripoli, before continuing its journey from Cairo under the protection of the Egyptian official in charge of the *ḥajj*, who, in turn, enjoyed the protection of a military force led by ïthe Emir of the *ḥajj*', considered quite a lofty position to hold at the time.[32]

Trade lost its importance for the same reason, namely changes in both modes of consumption and the overland trek to Mecca, known at the time as the '*ḥajj* route'. These changes were due, on the one hand, to the opening of the Suez Canal and, on the other, to the invention of steam ships, which meant that by the end of the nineteenth century, things appeared completely different. For while a majority of *ḥajj* pilgrims had opted for the overland route, and only a few crossed the Mediterranean to Alexandria, before continuing overland to Suez and from there across the Red Sea to Mecca – a risky endeavour given the abundant coral reef – now, few did so as the maritime option came to provide a 'door-to-door' service!

What is quite interesting is that the policies of the Ottoman Empire itself helped further increase Egypt's isolation from the Arab Mashreq. The policy of the government in Istanbul aimed at making the journey of Syrian and Iraqi pilgrims to the holy sites through Egypt a difficult proposition, by making the overland trip from Aleppo, Tripoli, Beirut and Damascus rather easy in comparison to the sea route. Thus, to reduce the importance of the Egyptian route, the Ottomans' sultans promoted, among other things, the 'religious' significance of certain Syrian ports by placing a few hairs from the Prophet's beard at the Great Mosque of Beirut, and a few at the Mosque in Tripoli.[33]

Perhaps it was this development, known as the 'Faraman Crisis' of 1892, which put the final nail in the coffin of Egyptian relations with the Arab world. This crisis erupted when the Ottoman State seized the opportunity afforded by Khedive Tawfīq's death and the appointment of his son

'Abbās to attempt to wrest a major part of the Sinai Peninsula away from Egypt. The move led to a British intervention to abort the attempt and culminated in Egypt handing over a number of regions under its control to secure the '*ḥajj* route', including Aqaba, al-Wajh, Mweleh and Daba, all located at the tip or eastern shores of the Gulf of Aqaba.[34] Although this effectively sounded the route's official 'death knell', it marked the very first attempt in modern history to draw borders between Egypt and the Arab world to the East. This sealed Egypt's isolation from the Mashreq.

Once the crisis was over, it was decided to extend the borderline separating Egypt from territories to its East; the decision was based on a telegram Jawād Pāshā, the Grand Vizier, had sent to the new Khedive 'Abbās Ḥilmī II. The border in question, stretching from east of al-'Arīsh to the west of Aqaba,[35] represented a delimitation of sorts between Egypt and the Arab Mashreq. With the exception of the Crusader invasion of the Levant, the events of 1892 marked the very first separation between Egypt and the Levant since the Arab invasion of the region in the seventh century CE, that is, about 12 centuries earlier.

This borderline was consolidated further, in 1906, in the wake of another crisis known as the Ṭābā crisis. The crisis ended when the British issued a warning to the Istanbul Government, in May of that same year, forcing it to accept a separating line between Egypt and each of the provinces of the Ḥijāz and the Governorate of Jerusalem. The agreement was embodied in a document signed by the Egyptian Government's representative Ibrāhīm Fatḥī Pāshā, and the Sublime Porte's representative Muẓaffar Fahmī.

Although this 'dividing line', as both parties called it, did not define Egypt's real boundaries since the country was nominally still part of the Ottoman State, it was, for all practical purposes, a real borderline, as evident in the agreement's provisions. Article 3 of the said agreement calls for poles to be placed along the dividing line, from a point on the Mediterranean coast (Tal al-Kharā'ib near Rafaḥ) to a point on the Aqaba Gulf coast (and Ra's Ṭābā). In the presence of representatives of the two parties, the poles were to be placed in a manner that allowed each to be seen from the one adjacent to it. Article 4 of the same agreement stipulates that the poles marking the dividing line 'should be preserved by both the State of Sublime Porte and the Egyptian Elevated State of Khedive'.[36]

Despite precautions by the Ottoman State, at the end of 1914 and the announcement of the British protectorate over Egypt, the line had become the international boundary of eastern Egypt, thanks to several measures the British occupation authorities had taken to consolidate it. What confirms this is that as soon as the post-war settlements were in place, and the British Mandate over Palestine announced, movements across this line became subject to the same rules governing travel between states, despite the fact that the concerned countries were under the same power's control. This became more evident after the 28 February 1922 declaration granting Egypt some form of nominal independence.

Furthermore, the British occupation of Egypt and its isolation from the rest of the Arab world, both in the Mashreq and the Maghreb, gave rise to two distinct trends within the national movement, both of which became points of departure for the country's relationship with the Pan-Arabist current.

The first trend believed that the tilt towards Pan-Islamism, calls for which had escalated during the reign of Sultan ʻAbd al-Ḥamīd II (1876–1909), would strengthen its ability to resist foreign occupation. The trend gained the upper hand when its orientation was adopted by the National Party, under the leadership of Muṣṭafā Kāmil, a very popular party among the Egyptian masses at the time.

There is reason to believe that Egypt was different from other countries of the Mashreq in that frequent European interventions, beginning with the French Campaign, and the weak Ottoman hold on it with all that this entailed, had greatly weakened the impact of the Ottoman presence in the country, if not expunged it entirely, which was not the case elsewhere in the Mashreq. What remained was the aspect of this presence that touched the hearts of most Egyptians, that is, the *religious* aspect.

The trend's popularity prompted a number of Egyptian intellectuals to reject the Pan-Arabism on the rise in the Levant and Iraq, as a movement, on the premise that it opposed the concept of the caliphate. Their rejection was bolstered by the fact that a number of newspapers that supported the British occupation, and primarily al-Muqaṭṭam, were publishing articles extolling the virtues of Arab Nationalism. In 1906, that same newspaper had published a number of chapters from Najīb ʻĀzūrī's book on the 'Awakening' of the Arab Nation, in which he dreamt of an Arab Empire stretching from the Tigris and Euphrates Rivers to the Isthmus of Suez, and from the Mediterranean to the Sea of Oman.[37] The latter group believed that this empire would be founded on the ruins of the Ottoman Empire.

Other newspapers, mainly *al-Ahram*, gave equal importance to Pan-Arabism, though the notion they supported was closer to a form of Ottoman decentralisation than to 'Jamiʻah al-ʻArabīyah al-Fatāh' (the Young Arab Society). This became clear in a long article the newspaper published under the title 'The Turks and the Arabs – is disagreement possible?'[38]

Al-Ahram was of the opinion that the dispute between the unionists and the growing pan-Arab Movement was like

> a disagreement among members of the same family about the best way to run the household; and all the Arabs want is to be one of the important and respected elements in the country. The Arabs are not saying that they want to secede, but rather to be active members of the state. They also ask that their language be honoured since it is the mother of the Turkish language, and their religion is also that of the Turks; all they want therefore is for the Turks to respect their wishes!

This conciliatory vision, which underestimated the value of the burgeoning Pan-Arab Movement in the Levant, is a good demonstration of the impact of the British occupation of Egypt, seen through public opinion's concern for the welfare of the Ottoman State. This helped *al-Ahram* reach the conclusion that those it calls the 'enemies of the State and the bitter enemies of the Ottoman Nation' are the greatest beneficiaries of the disagreements between the Arabs and the Turks. The newspaper ends its article by stating: 'Let free men build a competent state and a fair reform government for us. Once this happens, each one of us will ask for his rights, and it will, at that point, be able to respond.'

The second trend within the national movement adopted Egyptian nationalism in isolation from any Pan-Arab affiliation. The latter current, as formed by a group of Sheikh Muḥammad 'Abdūh's students, began taking shape in the wake of an incident that took the conflict between the British occupation authorities and the Ottoman State to a climax, namely the above-mentioned Ṭābā incident.

The National Movement, led by Muṣṭafā Kāmil, strongly supported the Ottoman State despite attempts by the latter to carve out part of Egypt's national territory and Britain's intervention to stop this from happening. This prompted a number of Egyptian leading personalities and intellectuals to establish a daily newspaper under the name '*al-Jarīdah*', and one year later (March 1907) to found the *Ummah* Party.

The paper revealed its true colours when it published in its very first issue a series of articles under the heading 'Nationalism in Egypt'. Although the articles were unsigned, everyone knew that the writer was none other than the newspaper's editor, Aḥmad Luṭfī al-Sayyid. The articles focussed on Egyptian nationalism as the other facet of Egypt's relationship with the state – in other words, the relationship between national affiliations as opposed to Islamic affiliation. British documents reveal open sympathy with the *Ummah* Party whose moderate policies, in their opinion, would eventually weaken the ideology of Islamic affiliation,[39] and indirectly sever ties between Egypt and regions to its East.

The Egyptian identity of the *Ummah* Party, as opposed to its Arab identity, was further confirmed by *al-Jarīdah*'s attitude vis-à-vis the Ottoman constitutional coup. As is well known, after the coup a shift took place away from affiliation on the basis of Islam (Pan-Islamism) towards affiliation on the basis of Touranism (pan-Touranism) with all the concomitant reactions to the events in Syria and Iraq. This reaction included the proliferation of secret and public societies that sought secession, such as the Literary Salon, the Qaḥṭānī Society, al-'Ahd, al-'Arabīyah, the Young Turks, and others.[40] However, instead of viewing the revival of Arab Nationalism in the face of Pan-Islamism and Pan-Touranism as a good reason to embrace it, leaders of the *Ummah* Party saw it as an excuse to advocate Egyptian nationalism.

One of the most important battles between *al-Jarīdah* and supporters of Pan-Islamism unfolded during the War of Tripoli between the Ottoman State and Italy (1911–12), when a significant number of Egyptians enthusiastically volunteered to fight on the side of the State. This compelled Aḥmad Luṭfī al-Sayyid to publish a series of articles criticising the phenomenon, under the heading of 'A Policy of Benefits not Emotions'.[41]

Two years before the end of this war, and a few months after the start of the 'Great War' – subsequently known as World War I, in which Turkey allied itself with the Central Powers, Britain unilaterally declared Egypt a protectorate, thus bringing its isolation from the Arab Mashreq – considered at the time as enemy territory – full circle.

Another point linked to the outcome of British efforts to isolate Egypt is worth mentioning here; it concerns what actually transpired during the Turkish advance towards the Egyptian borders, in 1915–16, as part of a military campaign that reached the eastern banks of the Suez Canal. For, while the Egyptian people's sympathy was with the Turks whom they saw as representatives of the Islamic caliphate fighting an occupying country, Pan-Arabism was in the midst of waging a war of resistance, against the Turks, in Syria and Iraq. This war of resistance culminated in what we currently know as the massacre of Jamāl Pāshā, known to the Arabs as 'the Butcher'. Also raging at the time in the Ḥijāz was the Arab revolt against the Ottoman Turks, better known as 'the Great Arab Revolt', under the leadership of Sharif Ḥussayn.

Not long after the end of the war, in November 1918, Egypt witnessed the largest popular revolt of its modern history, the Revolution of 1919. It was within this context that researcher Dhawqān Qarqūt, who wrote about the development of the concept of Arabism in Egypt, made a very feeble attempt to find a relationship between it and the Arab world.

The researcher emphasises the isolationist nature of Sa'ad Zaghlūl's policies, and blames them for the failure of the 1919 Revolution. He tried, later, however, to exonerate the Egyptian leader by recalling the position he took at the start of the Great Syrian Revolt, namely his call to the nation to come to Syria's aid. He said Syria is a 'country to which we are linked by the bonds of language, history, religion, custom and proximity', and urged the public to take active part in a fundraising campaign.[42]

This example is a sign that the walls of isolation that the British had erected around Egypt, throughout the nineteenth century, had begun to crumble, and this much was confirmed in a report written in the early 1930s by Sir Percy Loraine, the British High Commissioner in Cairo. The report states that, 'Egypt is so isolated from the Arab world that it is not easily drawn into movements such as that indicated in the enclosed report'. It goes on to say that no doubt, the Arab countries had a strong desire to unite and that there was a movement in these countries calling for cultural unity. It reported that the movement was being encouraged by the Cairo-based Eastern League, led by 'Abd al-Ḥamīd al-Bakrī, Aḥmad Zakī Pāshā and Aḥmad Shafīq, as well as the Young Muslim Youth Association, led by 'Abd al-Ḥamīd Sa'īd Bey, a prominent National Party member.[43]

The Judaisation of Palestine

Needless to say, in historical terms, the ethnographic change that took place in Palestine as a result of the open door policy to Jewish immigration, and the ensuing obliteration of the country's Arab identity, constituted one of the most significant coups directed towards Arab aspirations for unity. Britain was not that ever far removed from these developments, as far back as the late 1830s and up to the Versailles Conference in 1919.

There is no better description of that fact than A. M. Hyamson's research project, published in 1926 under the title 'British Projects for the Restoration of Jews to Palestine'. However, since this story is oft-repeated and much too lengthy to quote in full, only the most salient points of Hyamson's effort will be outlined here, and these include the following:

1 The instructions that the British Foreign Office sent to the British Vice-Consul in Jerusalem, on 31 January 1839, requesting him to consider the protection of the Jews in Palestine as one of his responsibilities, in his capacity as representative of the British Empire, and to send London regular updates on the condition of these Jews. The Vice-Consul took this responsibility very seriously and began sending piles of reports to his superiors in London, regarding the situation of the Jews in Jerusalem and other population centres in the Province of Acre. He was so enthusiastic about his mission that he described the Jews in one of his reports as 'those to whom God has originally given ownership of this land'.[44]

2 The project launched in the Spring of that same year, by Sir Moses Montefiore, a prominent businessman who became socially active in Jewish circles after 1821. From that point onward, Montefiore became one of the most enthusiastic promoters of Jewish settlement in Palestine, a country he visited a number of times from 1827.

One of his most important trips was in the spring of 1839 while Palestine was under Egyptian rule, when he decided then to submit a project in this regard to Muḥammad 'Alī. The project included the establishment of a company in England that would exploit a large area of Palestine, comprising around 200 villages, and then encourage European Jews to settle in Palestine. The Pāshā of Egypt, however, who at the time was eager to avoid provoking the British, avoided responding to the said proposal, submitted to him on 13 July of that year. His pretext was that he had no right to decide on an issue of concern to a country that was not his in the first place.[45]

3 Once British efforts had succeeded in bolstering the Ottoman State after thwarting Muḥammad 'Alī's project, Lord Palmerston believed that the time had come to make new appeals regarding the Jewish question. One such appeal came from the British Ambassador to the Sublime Porte's Government, proposing that England provide protection to the Jews in Palestine, and act as mediator in conveying their complaints to the Sublime Porte. The Ottoman response was that granting the Jews the right to channel their complaints through official British intermediaries meant placing them under the protection of Great Britain, a development that would be harmful to the Sublime Porte's sovereignty. It added that the Ottoman agreement with France gave the latter the right to safeguard the spiritual interests of the empire's Catholic subjects, and if England's appeal were accepted, France's protection of the Catholics would expand to

> include their temporal affairs, as well, and Russia, in turn, would soon make similar claims, and so forth.[46]

In the years that followed, a number of new considerations affected Britain's policies towards Palestine, the most important of which was the construction and inauguration of the Suez Canal, in 1869. These policies, which culminated in the British occupation of Egypt in 1882, were not enough to guarantee the security of the empire's main communications artery, the empire upon which the sun never set.

There was no threat to the canal from the west, that is, from Egypt through which territory the canal ran. There was also no threat to it from the north or south, where the Mediterranean and Red Seas lie, an area where Britain reigned supreme at the time and faced no rival over the control of those waterways. Therefore, any potential threat could only come from the east, a possibility that prompted Britain to erect two different lines of defence.

The first strategy was to keep the Ottoman State away from Sinai, a policy that precipitated two major crises. The first occurred in 1892, following the death of the Khedive Tawfīq, when the Istanbul Government tried to expand its presence along a line stretching from al-ʿArīsh to Rās Muḥammad. The second was in 1906 when Egypt tried to repeat the attempt by occupying Ṭābā, located at the western tip of the Gulf of Aqaba, and imposing a *fait accompli*. The British repelled both attempts, even issuing a warning to the Ottoman Government after the second attempt, and to back their warning, they mobilised their fleet in the Mediterranean, threatening to use force if necessary. This second crisis ended with the construction of the above-mentioned dividing line, which eventually became the main border between Egypt and the rest of the Ottoman State.

The second crisis was to alter the identity of Palestine in a manner that would dilute the Ottoman presence in the country. The Judaisation policy had moreover established a buffer zone between the Ottomans and the Suez Canal, presenting the British with an ideal opportunity to implement their policies. In his book *Modern Egypt*, Lord Cromer admitted, albeit with obvious brevity, that he gave permission to a German Jew by the name of Paul Freedman to settle with a number of German Jews in Mwayliḥ, an area on the northern shores of the Aqaba Gulf, just south of the famous port of Aqaba.[47] A contemporary Egyptian writer, Mikhāʾīl Sharūbīm, offers a more detailed account of the incident, in which the British role appears to encourage the proposition. Sharubim says in this context:

> The actual incident involves a man (whom he called Friedon) who came to Cairo, met there with the General Consul of Germany, explained to him why he had come to Egypt, and told him that he wanted to occupy Sharmah on the Red Sea coast. The Consul did not encourage him to do that and warned him of the potential consequences. He suggested that he talk to Sir Baring Cromer and then helped facilitate the meeting. His intention was go against the Sultan's wishes and deter him from giving the group a hard time. Friedon went to Sharmah with members of his group, said at the time to be fortification engineers though others claimed they were Jewish rabbis, intent on colonising and exploiting the area.[48]

If this story has any significance, it is that, while the Germans had refused to help early Jewish immigration – despite the fact that the would-be immigrants were German nationals – the British representative in Cairo had actually encouraged it, proving Britain's unwavering intention to turn Palestine into a Jewish entity.

It is obvious that the man, encouraged by British support for his plans, refused to accept the Ottoman State's decision to expel him and his followers from the area, and lodged an appeal against the Egyptian Government at the Mixed Court of Appeal. The tribunal heard the case for over four years and in March 1896 ruled against the appellants and demanded that they cover all court expenses.[49]

It was quite probably that very incident, as well as the policies of Sultan 'Abd al-Ḥamīd II against Jewish immigration to Palestine, that finally succeeded in hindering efforts to turn Palestine into a Jewish entity, despite the pressure from London. Among the obstacles were a number of regulations relevant to the travel of Jews to Palestine, including a pass that every Jew wishing to travel to Jerusalem had to carry, indicating both his nationality and profession. Once in Beirut, or any other Syrian port, the traveller had to show the official in charge his ticket, and in return, would obtain a pass for a limited stay of no more than three months. Anyone exceeding the three-month limit was deemed to be 'in violation of the country's laws'. In effect, the policy succeeded in restricting the flow of Jewish migrants to such an extent that between 1881 and 1903, the number of Jews arriving in Palestine did not exceed 3000.[50]

Later on, however, matters took an entirely different turn. The first Zionist Conference had taken place in Basle, Switzerland, in 1897, and the very well managed and abundantly funded activities of the Jewish Agency, established by the Conference to deal with the issue of Jewish immigration to Palestine, only added to the negative impact of the bloated and corrupt Ottoman bureaucracy. These developments led to a considerable increase in immigration to Palestine, and helped accelerate its Judaisation.

More ominous was the coup against the Ottoman State by the Unity and Progress Party, in 1908, which severely clipped the wings of Sultan 'Abd al-Ḥamīd II, as a prelude to his deposition the following year. The new generation of officials were keen on forging very close relations with Britain in the imagined belief that it would both protect parts of the Empire and pay off the accumulated debts of the country. They thought that the best token of their friendship would be a positive response to London's desire to open up Palestine in the face of Jewish immigration, a subject that became fodder for a number of Egyptian newspapers.

In June 1909, under the heading of 'The Israelites in Search of a Homeland', *al-Ahram* newspaper warned that the Sultan's fall had breathed new life in activist Zionist circles, and explained that their aim was to settle either in Palestine or Iraq, and that they 'have their eyes on areas under Ottoman control. We would like to draw the rulers' attention to that in order for them to wake up and take heed of the situation.'[51]

The article's author was mainly inspired by what Aḥmād Bey Riḍā, Speaker of the Turkish Parliament, had said to the Hakhambashi during a four-and-a-half hour meeting between the two men. Riḍā had asserted, among other things, that:

> The Government is very eager to welcome Russian and Romanian Jews, and Jews from every country where they are oppressed, to Turkey where there is enough land for cultivation, and for industry and trade. The Government is well aware of the Jews' loyalty, and welcomes the settlement of the Jews in Turkey with an open heart!

The author was equally inspired by various speeches delivered by members of Parliament on the Jewish colonisation of Palestine, or other Turkish territories, at official and unofficial occasions. Similarly, he was influenced by the news that Jews had volunteered to join the Unionists Army that marched all the way from Salonika to overthrow Sultan 'Abd al-Ḥamīd and foil his plot against the constitutional regime.

This is perhaps what compelled Egyptian newspapers opposed to British polices to draw attention to the various consequences of Jewish immigration to Palestine. One of them went so far as to write:

> The population of the Ottoman territory, which is six times the area of France, is only half that of France. It is therefore well able to absorb five

> million Israelites. However, settling all of them in one area, their Promised Land, that is Palestine, poses a great danger to them, to the people, and to the State. If the Israelites seek property, then not a single Ottoman would help them in their quest, except after his death. If they, however, are looking to settle in territories where they can find comfort, happiness, prosperity and goodness, then the Ottomans would be glad to receive them.[52]

Under the umbrella of British support, support that officials of the Union and Progress Government were glad to accept, the Judaisation of Palestine continued unabated after the overthrow of Sultan 'Abd al-Ḥamīd II in 1909. This was evident by the large space Egyptian newspapers, and mainly *al-Ahram*, devoted to the subject.

Yūsuf Jrays Farrūjī, a Palestinian from Jerusalem, started the debate when he carried out a comprehensive study on the onset and development of the Zionist Movement, and the dual objectives it sought to fulfil. The first of these objectives was to support any activity that led to the purchase of land in Palestine by different strata of Jews, and the second was to convince various states to accede to the Zionist Society's demands. His conclusion, based on these was that, 'it is clear that the objective of the Jewish immigration to Palestine, and the choice of the Promised Land as their final destination, is not just for cultivation or pure disinterested settlement; their actions have hidden objectives as well'.

Yūsuf Farrūjī, the Jerusalemite, gives as proof the high number of Jewish immigrants to his city, a number that reached the 60,000 mark. He also quotes as evidence the agriculture- and climate-related studies in a weekly journal called '*Palestina*', and the considerable number of industrial and agricultural companies, which, 'regardless of their nature and form, they all have a single ultimate lofty aim, namely to entrench themselves in Palestine until the end of time'.[53]

Aaron Bergman, scion of a settler family, joined the ongoing debate by confirming rather than denying Yūsuf Farrūjī's findings. He first protested against what *al-Ahram* had published to the effect that Jewish-owned farms in Palestine were turning into wasteland because those sent to colonise them hated working the land. He then testified as resident of one of these colonies, and said that the settlements, all 75 of them at the time, were established by Baron Rothschild and the Jewish Federation, and that the young men who left the colonies did so due to the old government's despotic policies. He went on to say, 'but now that there is a stable government and an inclusive constitution, most of those who left Palestine have come back'. He gave as evidence the fact that the ten colonies established in the first five years by the Jews who came to Palestine from Russia and Romania in 1882 had by then increased to 70.[54]

Another Palestinian, by the name of Ḥabīb Jirjis Ḥawwā, produced a very interesting study about land in his country. The study was published on Monday 12 July 1909 in the form of a long article, entitled 'The Colonisation of Palestine', that appeared on the front page of *al-Ahram*. It began by underlining the fact that Palestine was already over-populated, and that not a single inch of land was wasted or neglected except for a few forests whose owners take good care of them, and would never give them up.

According to the author, what had happened previously was that

> our Zionist brethren took advantage of the despotic era to forcibly take lands away from their owners in the Provinces of Safad and Tiberias. They did this by bribing officials in charge at the time, which then put the poor peasants in jail to force them to sign the document of surrender.

Ḥabīb Ḥawwā warns, however, against the financial enticements that Zionists dangle in front of Palestinian peasants to compel them to sell their property. He believes that such tactics 'could produce positive results if the peasants see the sale as a means of getting rid of their heavy taxes', which, he considers, would be a catastrophe if it ever occurred. He suggests that the state amend its policies towards the Palestinian peasants who should not be deprived of the soil of their homeland 'in favour of foreign, Ottomanised colonisers who would then deprive them of their fathers' and grandfathers' land'.

Ḥawwā drew attention to yet a third method by which the Zionists could obtain Palestinian land, namely through the purchase of government-owned plots between Lake Tiberias and Lot's Sea (the Dead Sea). In his opinion, these were lands forcibly taken from their local owners, and

> if the Government intends to sell them now, the Palestinian peasant has more right to them than any others. The locals are ready to buy them based on the same system applied in Egypt, regarding property that belong to the domeyeen and Sunnis. Can anyone deny the locals' right to lands taken from them by the hand of injustice and despotism?[55]

At the beginning of World War I in 1914, the Jews seemed to have, at first, aligned themselves with the Central powers, given their traditional enmity towards Tsarist Russia, a country in which they were badly persecuted. The policies of the London Government did not dwell long on this fact due partly to the strong influence of the Jews in the United States and its desire to avoid any conflict with them. The British also factored into account the deal it struck with France during the war, especially the Sykes Picot Agreement that required the London Government to cede Syria, including Lebanon, to French control. The British were not ready, at the time, to accept the idea of a French presence proximal to the Suez Canal, given the possible threat to the India route.

The outbreak of the Bolshevist Revolution in 1917 helped forge a rapprochement between the Zionist Movement and officials of the London Government, and there were widespread rumours regarding the strong role that the Jews had played in making it possible. This prompted British Jews, under the leadership of Chaim Wiseman, to insinuate the possibility of aiding the Allies in their cause, an initiative that ended with the famous Balfour Declaration.

The Declaration came in the form of a letter addressed by the British Foreign Secretary, Lord Balfour, to Lord Rothschild, the well-known Jewish businessman who enthusiastically sponsored the construction of settlements in Palestine. The text reads as follows:

> Dear Lord Rothschild,
>
> I have much pleasure in conveying to you, on behalf of his Majesty's Government, the following declaration of sympathy with Jewish Zionist aspirations, which has been submitted to, and approved by, the Cabinet.
>
> His Majesty's Government views with interest the establishment in Palestine of a national home for the Jewish people, and will use their best endeavours to facilitate the achievement of this object, it being clearly understood that nothing shall be done which may prejudice the civil and religious rights of the existing non-Jewish communities in Palestine, or the rights and political status enjoyed by Jews in any other country.
>
> I should be grateful if you would bring this declaration to the knowledge of the Zionist Federation.[56]

The declaration was actually not the beginning of efforts by Britain to Judaise Palestine. The aforementioned developments had all taken place before the Declaration was made, as part of an overall British effort to foster division among the Arabs, prior to 1919.

Notes

1. Copies of the newspaper can be found among the Foreign Office's documents: file no. F.O. 371/5062-029744.

2. T.H. Lawrence [Colonel], 'Secrets of the War on Mecca', *The Daily Express*, 28 May 1920.

3. 'MPs Appeal to the Premier to Bring Order out of Chaos', in: ibid.

4. Shafic Ghorbal, *The Beginning of the Egyptian Question and the Rise of Mehmet Ali: A Study in the Diplomacy of the Napoleonic Era Based on Researches in the British and French Archives*, with a Preface by Arnold J. Toynbee (London: Routledge, 1928).

5. Younan L. Rizk and Moḥammad Muzayn, *Tārīkh al-'Ilāqāt al-Miṣrīyah-al-Maghribīyah mundhu Maṭla' al-'Uṣūr al-Ḥadīthah ḥattā 'Ām 1912* (Cairo: [n.pb.], 1990).

6. See documents published in:

'Abd al-Raḥīm, 'Abd al-Raḥmān 'Abd al-Rahmān, *al-Dawlah al-Sa'ūdīyah al-Ūlā 1745–1818 A.D/1158–1233 Hijri* (Cairo: al-Maṭba'ah al-'Ālamīyah, 1969), and *Min Wathā'iq al-Dawlah al-Sa'ūdīyah al-Ūlā fī 'Aṣr Muḥammad 'Alī*, Min Wathā'iq Shibh al-Jazīrah al-'Arabīyah fī al-'Aṣr al-Ḥadīth (series); vol. 2 (Cairo: Dār al-Kitāb al-Jāmi'ī, 1983).

7. Fārūq 'Uthmān Abāẓah, *'Adan wa al-Sīyāsah al-Baritānīyah fī al-Baḥr al-Aḥmar 1839–1918* (Cairo: al-Hay'ah al-Miṣrīyah al-'Āmmah li-l-Kitāb, 1976).

8. Cairo Documents, 27 June 1839 (Document no. 147, File no. 267).

9. File no. 267, 17 Jamādī al-Ākhir 1255.

10. Jamāl Zakariyah Qāsim, *Tārīkh al-Khalīj al-'Arabī al-Ḥadīth wa al-Mu'āṣir*, vol. 1 (Cairo: Dār al-Fikr al-'Arabī, 1996), p. 414.

11. J. G. Lorimer, *Guide to the Gulf: History*, translated by the office of translation in the Dīwān of the governor of Qatar, vol. 1 (Qatar: Maṭābi' al-'Urūbah, 1967), pp. 322–3.

12. Qāsim, *Tārīkh al-Khalīj al-'Arabī*, vol. 2, p. 175.

13. Dr Sultan Mohammed al-Qasimi addresses this incident in his book and states that he gleaned most of his information from the Bombay archives, see:

Sultan Muhammad Al-Qasimi, *The Myth of Arab Piracy in the Gulf*, 2nd ed. (London; New York: Routledge, 1988), pp. 84–150.

14. Nūrah Muḥammad al-Qāsimī, *Al-Wujūd al-Hindī fī al-Khalīj al-'Arabī, 1820–1947* (unpublished thesis, Master's degree), Kullyat al-Banāt, 'Ayn Shams University, 1984.

15. Ibid., p. 246.

16. F.O. 371/5065 Inter-Departmental Conference on Middle Eastern Affairs, 7 December 1920.

17. Lorimer, *A Guide to the Gulf: Geography*, vol. 2 ([n.p]: [n.pb], 1978]), p. 570.

18. Al-Qāsimī, 'Al-Wujūd al-Hindī', p. 100.

19. Jamāl Zakariyah Qāsim, *Dawlat al-Bū S'īd fī 'Umān wa Sharq Afrīqiyā 1741–1861*. p. 212.

20. Al-Qāsimī, 'Al-Wujūd al-Hindī'.

21. Ibid., p. 199.

22. Ibid., pp. 196–206.

23. Ibid., pp. 196–206.

24. Shafic Ghorbal, *Muḥammad 'Alī al-Kabīr* (Cairo: [n.pb.], 1944), and Ṣubḥī Waḥīdah, *fī Uṣūl al-Mas'alah al-Miṣrīyah* (Cairo: Maṭba'at Miṣr, 1950).

25. 'Abd al-Raḥmān al-Rāfi'ī, *'Aṣr Muḥammad 'Alī*, 2nd ed. (Cairo: Maktabat al-Nahḍah al-'Arabīyah, 1947).
26. Ibid., p. 190.
27. Joseph Ḥajjār, *Urūppā wa Maṣīr al-Sharq al-'Arabī: Ḥarb al-Isti'mār 'alā Muḥammad 'Alī wa al-Nahḍah al-'Arabīyah*, translated by Buṭrus al-Ḥallāq and Mājid Ni'mah (Beirut: al-Mu'asasah al-'Arabīyah li-l-Dirāsāt wa al-Nashr, 1976), p. 85.
28. Ibid., p. 93.
29. Ibid., p. 184.
30. B.S. Gerard, *The Encyclopaedia of Economic Life in Egypt in the Eighteenth Century: A Description of Egypt*, translated by Zuheir al-Shayeb: (Cairo: [n.pb.], 1978), p. 195 onwards.
31. F.O. 407/165 no. 142, Annual Report, 1905.
32. Rizk and Muzayn, *Tārīkh al-'Ilāqāt al-Miṣrīyah-al-Maghribīyah mundhu Maṭla' al-'Uṣūr al-Ḥadīthah ḥattā 'Ām 1912*.
33. Anīs Ṣāyyigh, *Al-Hāshimyūn wa al-Thawrah al-'Arabīyah al-Kubrā*. (Beirut: [n.pb.], 1976), p. 47.
34. Rizk. *Azmat al-'Aqabah al-Ma'rūfah bi-Ḥadīthah Ṭābā*, chapter 1 (Cairo: [n.pb.], 1983).
35. Ibid.
36. The text of the agreement can be found in Dār al-Wathā'iq al-Qawmīyah al-Miṣrīyah.
37. Salaḥ Al-'Aqqād, 'Najīb 'Azūrī wa Ārā'uh al-Siyāsīyah', *Majalat al-iqtiṣād wa al-sīysah wa al-tijārah* (Cairo: [n.pb.], 1960).
38. *Al Ahram*, 22 April 1910.
39. F.O. 407/167 no. 82. Finally, to Gray, 5 July 1906, formation of a company for the establishment of 'El-Jaridah', whose principles were daring and original compared with other Egyptian newspapers.
40. Ernest Edmondson Ramsauer, *The Young Turks: Prelude to the Revolution of 1908*, translated by Ṣāliḥ Aḥmad al-'Alī, foreword and editing by Nicola Zīyādah (Beirut: Dār Maktabat al-Ḥayāt, 1960), pp. 26–9.
41. Aḥmad Zakarīyah al-Shalaq, *Ḥizb al-Ummah wa Dawruh fī al-Sīyāsah al-Miṣrīyah*, Dirāsāt fī Tārīkh al-Aḥzāb al-Miṣrīyah (series) (Cairo: Dār al-Ma'ārif, 1979).
42. Dhūqān Qarqūt, *Taṭawwur al-Fikrah al-'Arabīyah fī Miṣr 1805–1936* (Beirut: al-Mu'asasah al-'Arabīyah li-l-Dirāsāt wa al-Nashr, 1972), p. 258.
43. F.O. 371/5282, Sir Percy Loraine to F.O. 27 February 1931.
44. Ḥajjār, *Urūppā wa Maṣīr al-Sharq*, pp. 231–2.
45. Moses Montefiore (Sir), 'Diaries of Sir Moses and Lady Montefoire', vol. II (London, 1891), quoted in: Ibid., pp. 233–4.
46. Ibid., pp. 240–1.
47. Evelyn Baring Cromer, *Modern Egypt* (New York: Macmillan, 1908), pp. 268–9.
48. Mikhā'īl Shārubīm, *Al-Kāfī fī Tārīkh Miṣr al-Qadīm wa al-Ḥadīth*, vol. 5, unpublished.
49. *Al Ahram*, 13 March 1896.
50. William Fahmī, *Al-Hijrah al-Yahūdīyah ilā Filisṭīn al-Muḥtalah* (Cairo: al-Hay'ah al-Miṣrīyah al-'Āmmah li-l-Kitāb, 1971), p. 46.
51. *Al Ahram*, 9 June 1909.
52. *Al Ahram*, 20 June 1909.
53. *Al Ahram*, 6 July 1909.

54. *Al Ahram*, 8 July 1909.

55. *Al Ahram*, 12 July 1909.

56. Maxime Rodinson, *Israel and the Arabs*, translated from French by Michael Perl, Penguin Special Series, 263 (Harmondsworth: Penguin; New York: Pantheon Books, 1968), pp. 10–11.

Walter Zéev Laqueur, ed., *The Israel-Arab Leader: A Documentary History of the Middle-East Conflict*, A Pelican Book, rev. ed. (Harmondsworth: Penguin, 1970), p. 36.

Chapter 2

The Arab Kingdom 1919–23

At the Paris Peace Conference in early 1919, an exchange of three letters took place between Emir Fayṣal Bin al-Ḥussayn, then Sharif of Mecca and King of Ḥijāz, and the British delegation to the Conference, detailing the position of the two parties on Arab unity after the war.

The first of these letters was from Emir Fayṣal; and he initially talks about the way in which he perceives Arab unity [and a territorial entity] at that time, saying:

> The country from a line [from] Alexendretta-Persia southwards to the Indian Ocean, is inhabited by 'Arabs', by which we mean people of closely related Semitic stocks, all speaking the one language, Arabic. The non-Arabic-speaking elements in this area do not, I believe, exceed one per cent of the whole.[1]

He then moves on to the goals of the Arab Nationalist Movement 'of which my father assumed the leadership after several requests by those engaged in it among those Syria and the land between the two rivers [i.e., the Tigris and Euphrates/Mesopotamia]'. He defines these goals as the unification of the Arabs in one nation, and announces that as an old member of the Syrian Committee, he had assumed the leadership of the Syrians, the residents of the land between the two rivers[2] and people of the Arabian Peninsula.

The Emir was more precise when he said in the letter that he was not referring to all the Arabs, but to the 'Arabs in Asia' whose unity 'no one could dispute'. To illustrate his point he refers to the principles cited by the United States of America when it entered the war on the side of the Allies.

He argues in this respect that the Arabs would rely on their glorious past, and 600 years of resistance against Turkish attempts to swallow them up, not to mention their efforts during the war in favour of the Allies.[3]

He then confirms the leadership of his father Sharif Ḥussayn of the new Arab Union, saying, 'he holds a distinguished position among the Arabs as head of one of their biggest families and as Sharif of Mecca'. Fayṣal adds that he is confident that the idea of a union will succeed, unless there are artificial attempts to impose it, or hinder it, by dividing the region among the great powers as spoils of war! Finally, he concludes that: 'Unity among the Arabs of Asia has become much easier in recent years thanks to the development of railway and telegraph lines, and widespread air transport.'[4]

Although the response of the British delegation at the Peace Conference in Paris was disappointing to Fayṣal and to supporters of the Arab Kingdom, which included the Arabian Peninsula, Syria and Iraq, under the crown of Sharif Ḥussayn, it nevertheless reflected the policies of the London Government and its understanding of Arab unity after World War I.

If it is said that a book is often known by its title, then this was exactly the case if judging by the opening paragraph of the British delegation's response, which stated: 'The various provinces in Arab Asia-Syria, Iraq, the Peninsula, the Ḥijāz, Najd and Yemen, are markedly different economically and socially, and it is impossible to constrain them into one frame of government.'[5]

The British memorandum then moved from the general to the specific:

Syria: An agricultural-industrial region densely populated in settled communities. Its political level allows it to manage its internal affairs, and foreign technical assistance would considerably accelerate its national growth rate.

Al-Jazīrah [the Arabian Peninsula] and Iraq: These are two vast provinces dependent on three main cities separated by barren regions inhabited by semi-nomadic tribes. The world is looking forward to exploiting the region between the Tigris and the Euphrates as soon as possible, after which it will be necessary to establish a form of government that relies on manpower and resources provided by the big powers:

> We essentially seek to establish an Arab Government in these regions chosen on a selective basis, especially in long-neglected areas. The Government's

> main task shall revolve around an education process that will raise the standard of the tribes to a level that allows them to adapt to city life.

The Ḥijāz: An essentially tribal region the government of which should be formed, as it was in the past, on a patriarchal basis, with conditions remaining much the same as they have been.

Palestine: The absolute majority is Arabs; the Jews are very close to the Arabs in blood. There is no cause for conflict between them.[6]

This prompted Emir Fayṣal to write his final response in a more direct form, saying:

> I came to Europe representing my father and the Arabs of Asia to say that the hope is that countries at the Conference will not focus on the artificial differences between the Arab countries, and place Europe's material benefits, and the division of the region into zones of power, as a secondary concern. They expect these countries to look upon the Arabs as one nation that is proud of its language and independence. I also came to ask that these states take no step that goes against the immediate unity of these regions under one sovereign government.[7]

In fact, what took place in Paris was not actually the beginning of calls for Arab unity after World War I, in the form of a Kingdom headed by Sharif Ḥussayn; there were many precedents and antecedents.

Arab Unity during World War I

Although most of those 'precedents' are well known, their context, as well as the facts that British secret documents reveal, demand a second look!

What became known in history as the Ḥussayn-McMahon correspondences has acquired great significance since this exchange of letters formed the basis of Sharif Ḥussayn's calls for unity among Asian Arab countries. Moreover, some of the contents of these letters provided the British Government with the excuses it needed to renege on any promises it might have already given.

The circumstances under which the exchange of correspondence took place were conducive to strengthening the Arab position. Among these are the Sanūsī revolt in Libya; the possibility of 'Alī Dīnār, the Sultan of Darfur, joining the Sanūsīyah; Turkish troops approaching the Suez

Canal; the withdrawal of Allied forces from Gallipoli; and, finally, the attacks by Ottoman troops in Yemen on the colony of Aden.[8]

Ten letters were exchanged in all, starting with one from Sharif Ḥussayn, dated 14 July 1915, and ending with one from Sir Henry McMahon, the British High Commissioner in Cairo, on 10 March 1916.

In his first letter, Sharif Ḥussayn listed six demands, the first being the main aspiration of the Arab Movement that had asked Sharif Ḥussayn to represent it. It was the request that England recognise the independence of the Arab Asian countries the borders of which he defined, with the proviso that Britain agree to the proclamation of an Arab Caliphate.[9]

The five remaining requests covered the need for an alliance with Britain, granting the latter preferential treatment in all economic transactions, and the exchange of military and naval assistance. They also covered the position of the parties in the event one of them be attacked by a third party; the agreement of Britain to the abolition of foreign privileges in the Arab countries; and, finally, to limiting the duration of the proposed treaty to a 15-year period.[10]

McMahon's response, dated 30 August of that same year, marked the beginning of British equivocation. What is noticeable is that the response took one-and-a-half months to come, during which time there was an exchange of letters between Cairo and London before the British Government settled on a final response. When it did arrive, it was brief and basically dealt with the main issue raised by Sharif Ḥussayn, namely the Arab Kingdom, or Caliphate, as the latter defined it. The response read as follows:

> With regard to the questions of limits and boundaries, it would appear to be premature to consume our time in discussing such details in the heat of war, and while, in many portions of them, the Turk is up to now in effective occupation; especially as we have learned, with surprise and regret, that some of the Arabs in those very parts, far from assisting us, are neglecting this their supreme opportunity and are lending their arms to the German and the Turk, to the new despoiler and the old oppressor.[11]

A Foreign Office memorandum says that this response did not please Sharif Ḥussayn, as was obvious from his following letter, dated 9 September, in which he criticises what he described as the 'cold and hesitant' attitude regarding the question of boundaries. He said that the issue of boundaries was not like the needs of a single individual that could be placated, 'our peoples... now have their confidence and trust as a final appeal, viz., the illustrious British Empire'.[12]

While Sharif Ḥussayn's response to McMahon's letter arrived just nine days later, McMahon's second letter dated 25 October arrived one-and-a-half months after Sharif Ḥussayn's response. He began by expressing his apologies for the impression that the Sharif drew from his letter, and said that for this very reason, he had contacted his Government and was authorised to inform him what he believed would meet with his approval. The letter says:

> The two districts of Mersina and Alexandretta and portions of Syria lying to the west of the districts of Damascus, Homs, Hama and Aleppo cannot be said to be purely Arab, and should be excluded from the limits demanded. Subject to the above modifications, Great Britain is prepared to recognise and support the independence of the Arabs in all the regions within the limits demanded by the Sharif of Mecca. Great Britain will guarantee the Holy Places against all external aggression and will recognise their inviolability.[13]

The letter goes on to say that with regard to the vilayets [protectorates] of Baghdad and Basra, the Arabs will recognise that the established position and interests of Great Britain necessitate special administrative arrangements to secure these territories against foreign aggression, promote the welfare of the local populations and safeguard mutual economic interests.

In his third letter, dated 5 November of that same year, Sharif Ḥussayn establishes an important principle, as he appears to adopt the secular ideas of the Syrian proponents of the Arab Nationalist Movement. For example, in describing the provinces of Aleppo and Beirut, and their coastlines, he says, word for word,

> the two vilayets of Aleppo and Beirut and their sea coasts are purely Arab vilayets, there is no difference between a Muslim and a Christian Arab: they are both descendants of one forefather. ʿUmar bin al-Khaṭṭāb said that 'the Christians will enjoy the same privileges and shoulder the same responsibility as ourselves'.

In his third letter, dated 14 December, McMahon states that save for areas of interest to France, including Aleppo and Beirut, and the desire to establish a stable administration in the province of Baghdad to guarantee British interests, 'The Government of Great Britain, as I have already informed you, are ready to give all guarantees of assistance and support within their power to the Arab Kingdom.'

Over and above Ḥussayn's efforts to placate British demands, the following four exchanges delineated the nature of British assistance that would enable Sharif Ḥussayn to launch his famous revolt. As this was going on, however, and according to the logic of the spoils of war that Emir Fayṣal forewarned against, the Government of London was concluding treaties with its allies, in total disregard of what it had undertaken in this correspondence. The most important of these treaties was the Sykes-Picot Agreement, signed by British envoy Mark Sykes and French envoy George Picot, during the first half of May 1916, that is only a few weeks after the agreement with the Sharif of Mecca.

In brief, the said Anglo-French Agreement anticipated the division of the Arab Asian region into several areas of control, with each being designated by a different colour: a black region that included Palestine, to be placed under international administration; a red region that included Basra, Baghdad and Khānaqīn, under British rule; and a blue region that includes the Syrian coastline, to be placed under French control. Within these coloured regions an Arab country, or countries, would be established, and divided into two areas of control. Region (a) would include Damascus, Hama, Allepo, Deir Ez-Zor, al-Raqqa and Mosul, and extend all the way to the Iraqi-Iranian borders, and be under French control. Region (b) would be under British control, and would include the Syrian desert area, Tikrīt, Sāmarrā', Kirkūk and Trans-Jordan.[14]

Just over a year later, on 2 November 1917, there would come the third British plot against Arab unity in the form of the Balfour Declaration.[15] Sharif Ḥussayn got wind of what was going on, as is indicated in his long letter of 28 August 1918 to Sir Reginald Wingate, the British High Commissioner in Cairo who replaced McMahon. This was less than three months before the end of the war, the imminent collapse of the Central powers was all too evident, and the date of the peace conference that would draw the map of the world in the post-World War I period was drawing near.

Sharif Ḥussayn attached to his letter the main points that the two parties had agreed on.[16] After stating that the intention behind the agreement was to guarantee the interests of Muslims in general, and the Arabs in particular, and thanking the British for honouring most of the agreement's provisions, he noted that the most important among these – the proviso that delineated the territories agreed upon – had been violated. This was the crux of what the King of Ḥijāz protested against.

The Arab Kingdom

What happened next was, in effect, the embodiment of these violations in international agreements, upon the orders of the London Government. Article 22 of the League of Nations' Charter, which was guaranteed by the Treaty of Versailles, stipulates that:

> Certain communities formerly belonging to the Turkish Empire have reached a stage of development where their existence as independent nations can be provisionally recognised, subject to the rendering of administrative advice and assistance by a mandatory until such time they are able to stand alone. The wishes of these communities must be a principal consideration in the selection of the mandatory.[17]

There were also the articles of the Treaty of Sèvres that devoted four articles to Syria, Mesopotamia and Palestine (94–7), and three to the Ḥijāz (98–100). While Article 94 stipulated the application of Article 22 of the Charter for Syria and Mesopotamia, the next article stipulated its application also in Palestine, although the details of the two cases are somewhat different.

In the first case, these were 'provisionally recognised as independent states subject to rendering of administrative advice and assistance by a mandatory until such time, as they are able to stand alone'.[18] In the second case (Article 95), an addendum stipulates that the mandatory power would be responsible for the implementation of the British Government's Declaration of 2 November 1917, which other states had also adopted. The Declaration in question was the one calling for the establishment of a national home for the Jews in Palestine 'providing that it should be understood that no action should be taken that violates the civil and religious rights of the non-Jews in Palestine or the rights and political status enjoyed by the Jews in any other country'.[19]

As for the three articles relevant to the Ḥijāz (98–100), the first involved Turkey's recognition of the Ḥijāz as an independent state, and its acceptance to abandon any rights and claims it previously had over territories of the former empire, outside Turkey, as stipulated in the treaty under implementation. The second article, which dealt with the sacred status of the two holy sanctuaries, Mecca and Medina, stipulated that the King of the Ḥijāz undertakes to keep the sites open to Muslims from all over the world, coming to perform the *ḥajj*, or any other religious ritual. The last article stipulates that the King of the Ḥijāz undertakes to treat equally all people, ships and goods belonging to the Allied countries, the new countries arising from the ruins of the Turkish Empire, or any of the League of Nations member states.[20]

Subsequent British documents reveal details of the meeting held at the Foreign Office in London, on Thursday 23 December 1920, between Emir Fayṣal, representing the King of the Ḥijāz, and Sir John Tilley, representing the British Foreign Secretary, in which the parties discussed the issue of the 'Arab Kingdom' following the war.[21]

The importance of this meeting lay in the fact that the British Government had begun to tie the details together, now that its policy towards the 'Arab Kingdom' had begun to crystallise. Sir John Tilley initiated the conversation by saying that there was a misunderstanding on the part of King Ḥussayn regarding the British Government's policy, and that the time had come to dispel it. He went on to reassure Fayṣal that any misunderstanding was due to difficult communications in times of war and, as usual, reiterated that his Government's friendly feelings towards the Arabs had not changed!

After a similar reciprocal statement by Fayṣal, Tilley brought up a number of points that the Foreign Secretary, Marquis Curzon of Kedleston, believed were worth discussing. These included the ties between King Ḥussayn and other Arab rulers, the status of British subjects in the Ḥijāz and, finally, the conclusion of a bilateral agreement between the British Government and the Ḥijāz, regarding those measures that were once the subject of treaties and agreements between the London and the Turkish governments.

Fayṣal agreed to discuss these points, and even said that raising them was proof of the British Government's sincerity. However, he asked for the chance to restate his position before going into the relevant details. He started by referring to the cooperation between King Ḥussayn and Lord Allenby during the war, and affirmed that he was neither asking for the impossible nor exerting pressure on the British Government by making demands he knows could not be fulfilled. All he wanted was to remind Lord Curzon of King Ḥussayn's status in the eyes of the Muslim world. He also desired to stress that although the Sultan, as Caliph of the Muslims, had declared *jihad* when Turkey joined the war, Sharif Ḥussayn elected to go to war against the Sultan based on promises made by the British High Commissioner in Cairo. He iterated that he had told the Muslims, at that time, that such a move would have positive results, and that he had taken the decision based on the belief that Arab and British interests were one and the same. He concluded by saying that now that the war was over, he was obliged to demonstrate to the Muslim world that the promises made to him had been kept.

Sir John Tilley's reply was that the British Government was fully aware of this situation, and had kept its promises. Today, he said, there was an Arab government in Mesopotamia and the Arabs were free from Turkish control, which meant that King Ḥussayn could tell the Muslim world that its independence has been guaranteed. Fayṣal replied that the Arabs were asking for more, and that King Ḥussayn did not know the British Government's real intentions towards certain Arab countries.

Tilley rejoined that it should be made clear that the Allied countries had already agreed on the future of liberated Turkish territories, and that the relevant arrangements had been included in the terms of the Peace Agreement. He added that King Ḥussayn had been invited to be part of the agreement whose articles he knew well and would soon sign.

Fayṣal answered that his father would not agree to sign the agreement before officially ensuring that the British Government intended to fulfil the promises that prompted him to enter the war on the side of the Allies. He said that he had in his possession Arab documents, signed by the British High Commissioner in Cairo on behalf of his government, recognising the 'Arab Kingdom'. He added that Lord Curzon had told him in 1919 that British commitments to King Ḥussayn were on an equal footing with those made to other states. He ended by speculating about the real intentions of the British Government regarding the establishment of the Arab Kingdom.

This time, Tilley's answer was unambiguous; the promises made by the British Government, with certain reservations, were to recognise and support the Arabs' independence, not to establish an Arab Kingdom.

Fayṣal stuck to the term 'Arab Kingdom', insisting that McMahon had used it. Still, he expressed his readiness to accept what he termed Britain's friendly spirit, and asked for time to get hold of the letters about which he had spoken to Tilley. To eliminate any doubt as to the content of this correspondence, Fayṣal promised to bring with him the next day copies of letters in question, in order to compare them with those in the possession of the Foreign Office.

A thorough review of these texts shows that Fayṣal was correct about the use of the term 'Arab Kingdom'. It appeared in Ḥussayn's fifth letter, sent on 5 November 1915, and in McMahon's response to the letter, on 14 December of that same year.

The former states: 'We renounce our insistence on the inclusion of the vilayets of Messina and Adana in the Arab Kingdom.' In the latter it is stated:

> In stating that the Arabs are ready to recognise and respect all our treaties with the Arab chiefs, it is of course understood that this will apply to all the territories included in the 'Arab Kingdom', as the Government of Great Britain cannot repudiate engagements which already exist.

The Arab Confederation

British documents reveal a secret that remained hidden for many years, with no one picking up on it even after the 1922 documents became available to researchers. The secret came in an exchange of two letters between Sir Herbert Samuel, the High Commissioner in Palestine, and the Minister for Colonies that succeeded him, and the Marquis Curzon of Kedleston, the Foreign Secretary.

Before divulging the secret and delving into the said correspondence, it is important to know the circumstances under which Sir Herbert Samuel, the most famous High Commissioner in the history of the British Mandate in Palestine who was appointed to the post in 1920 and held it for five consecutive years, got involved in the case.

In the two intervening years between the declaration of the civil administration in Palestine, in July 1920, and the ratification of the Mandate, in July 1922, it appeared as if matters were not going as the Government of London had imagined they would, or according to the plans of the Jewish High Commissioner, who had strong Zionist inclinations.

In May 1921, before the Fourth Palestine Conference was convened, bloody incidents that lasted for 15 days took place in Jaffa between the Arabs and Zionists. The situation in the city and the surrounding areas remained extremely tense despite the intervention of British troops; an intervention that the Arabs believed was aimed at defending the Jews and protecting their colonies, the main object of Arab anger.[22] Official reports regarding these incidents show the very high casualty figures of 48 killed and 73 wounded among the Arabs, and 47 killed and 100 wounded among the Jews.[23]

The Palestine National Movement intensified in the months following the Jaffa incidents. In September 1921, the Palestinian delegation at the League of Nations lodged a protest regarding the failure to hold a referendum to determine the Palestinians' choice of mandatory authority. The delegation then went to London for talks with British officials, where an exchange of letters took place with Winston Churchill, Secretary for the Colonies at the time.[24]

What is noticeable in this correspondence is that the Palestinian delegation's demands centred around the rejection of the mandate instrument on which British Government policy to establish a national home for the Jews depended, and on the fact that nothing would guarantee Arab rights except a national government. It was, however, clear from the Colonial Office's response, in April 1922, that the British Government was determined to continue its declared policy, without giving due consideration to the interests of Palestine's Arabs.[25]

In July of that same year, His Majesty's Government issued the White Paper that comprised the above correspondence, and, at the same time, the League of Nations adopted the resolution placing Palestine under British Mandate. The Palestinian delegation lodged a complaint against the resolution and, in protest, a general strike was declared, and all activities were suspended in most Palestinian cities. The delegation received instructions from the Arab Executive Committee in Jerusalem to cease all negotiations with the Colonial Office and return home, after informing both the British Government and the League of Nations of the Arab Nation's rejection of the mandate.[26]

It was under these circumstances that Herbert Samuel, the British High Commissioner who governed Palestine, first proposed the idea of an Arab union, a proposal which, at first glance, seems strange, since the man was known for his bias in favour of policies aimed at establishing a national home for the Jews in Palestine.

The proposal came in the form of a long memorandum written by the First Secretary of the Mandate Government, Sir W. H. Deedes, upon the request of Herbert Samuel. The importance of this six-page memorandum lies in the fact that it clarifies British policy towards Arab unity[27] at that particular juncture in time. Here, below, is an analysis of this memorandum.

At the beginning of this very signficant memorandum, Deedes refers to its subject: 'The establishment of a Confederation of States in those portions of the late Ottoman Empire south of Anatolia separated from the Empire as a result of the Great War.'[28] Deedes admits that the current political situation in Palestine was the main motive behind the notion, an admission that gives cause for concern. The Arab delegation that was supposed to head for Lausanne, where final status negotiations were under way with Turkey to determine the fate of former territories of the Ottoman Empire, was expected to emerge almost empty handed. At the same time, not much was expected from Mustafa Kemal's Government, whose main concern was to ensure the unity of Anatolia.

Deedes added that the Palestinian delegation was expected to travel to London afterwards, where the hope was that the new government would change its policy towards Palestine. It was an unachievable hope that would have serious consequences on the security situation in Palestine after the delegation's return home, and negatively impact the country's economic development and general stability.

After addressing conditions in Palestine, Deedes goes on to address conditions in other Asian Arab countries, to promote the idea of creating a confederation of Arab Asian states:

Iraq: There is reason to believe that the political situation in that country is less than satisfactory, especially in light of the Turkish threat hanging over the heads of both Arab Nationalism and British interests.

Syria: The situation in that country gives cause for anxiety, a fact that will soon cause problems for the French and indirectly raise problems for the British in Palestine.

Trans-Jordan: An attempt is under way to reach a solution that will satisfy both the British Government and Emir ʿAbdullah; however, factors of potential unrest and insecurity still exist.

The Ḥijāz: King Ḥussayn appears at the same time unhappy with His Majesty's Government, and incapable of pleasing it.

The Central Arabian Peninsula: An independent Arab kingdom is emerging (meaning Saudi Arabia) based on domestic imperatives. It appears to be in a position to wield influence over surrounding states.

Deedes then tries to examine the impact of, in his words, 'this unsatisfactory condition of affairs' on other concerned parties:

The Arabs: Iraq and Trans-Jordan enjoy almost completely autonomous status. However, the prevailing feeling is that divisions are far greater than they were under Turkish rule, for while Syria was under French mandate, Palestine was under British mandate. In general, mandates are unpopular for different reasons. What further exacerbates this feeling is the fact that Trans-Jordan and Palestine are under separate administrations, and that Iraq is now a completely separate state with its own separate administration. Furthermore, the Arabs view the boundaries between different Arab countries as deliberately created obstacles to thwart Arab unity.

The Jews: At last, their hopes for a mandate have finally been realised. However, Arab resistance, not to mention large sections of the British press and a number of influential British political leaders, have hindered their attempts to use the mandate to advance their interests. Added to that is the escalating emnity towards them in neighbouring and far-off Arab countries whose citizens view the Jews with hatred and loathing. Trans-Jordan is virtually closed to them, and we understand that in Syria and Iraq the Jews are afraid to express their Zionist feelings lest they incur the displeasure of the local authorities.

Great Britain: The Jews are grateful for what the British Government has done for them, yet they, like the Arabs, are not fully satisfied. British prestige throughout the region has suffered considerably, and anger at the British has even reached India and other areas where Muslim British subjects live. What has made things worse was to see so many states artificially divided, with what this entails in terms of customs barriers, passport regulations and troops to defend borders. No doubt, Arab satisfaction with the role that Britain played in securing their freedom from Turkish rule is rapidly evaporating. Finally, relations between Great Britain and France have become more difficult due to the policies of the former in the Middle East.

The solution to this complex situation, according to Deedes, is to be found in a three-step plan entailing the following:

1 The establishment of a Council made up of representatives from the above-mentioned countries – namely Syria, Iraq, Palestine, Trans-Jordan, the Ḥijāz, and states in the central region of the Arabian Peninsula that care to join. The Council will attend to issues brought to its attention by any member-states, and to initiate debates on any issue it considers important, in order to attract the attention of member states to it.
2 Council members will cooperate in the legislative and administrative fields on issues that have been referred to it, including the economic domain, such as the removal of customs barriers and passport restrictions; the implementation of various public works projects, like the development of the hydroelectric project in Trans-Jordan, and the unification of postal and telegraph communications. It will also

attend to cultural matters, such as the unification of primary and secondary school curricula in Arab countries, the establishment of technical higher education colleges and, finally, the establishment of a university for Arab students.

3 In the legal domain, legislation relevant to the civil status of Muslim Arabs could be unified through the foundation of a Supreme Islamic Council for all the Arab countries. The Council would replace the Sheikh al-Islam in Istanbul, who, during the Turkish era, was charged with the administration of religious courts.

The author of the memorandum believed that these arrangements could serve as a point of departure for an eventual political confederation between the Arab countries, similar in some respect to the Confederation of German States in the nineteenth century. Deedes expressed the belief that arrangements such as these would increase the Arab people's confidence in the mandate countries and, at the same time, build better relations between the Arabs and the Jews. If the establishment of a Jewish national home was construed as part of an eastern cultural revival process, the hope was that the two sides would arrive at some sort of understanding and cooperation. If the Arabs were assured that Jewish funds would be forthcoming to assist in their economic development, they might be amenable to the presence of a Jewish representative in the Council.

Sir Herbert Samuel appended his personal support for the scheme and submitted it to the Secretary of the Colonies, saying that the First Secretary of the Mandate Government had written it based on that support. His justification was that reviving the idea of a confederacy of Arab states, at this particular time, would be of great help to this Government when the Arab Palestinian delegation returns home from Lausanne empty-handed.[29]

After pouring diligently over the memorandum at the Colonial Office, the Duke of Devonshire, who replaced Churchill as Secretary for the Colonies, sent it to the Foreign Secretary on 10 January 1923, together with the negative opinion of his department's officials. He gave many reasons for the bases of the negative response, which he listed as follows:

1 The scheme might annoy the French who could refuse to have anything to do with the proposed Federate Council, or might use it to conspire with Arabs living in British mandated areas.

2 It would raise the suspicions of Ibn Sa'ūd who might see it as some form of cooperation with his enemies, the Sharifs, a cooperation that would be detrimental to his interests.

3 It will not grant the Palestinian Arabs, the scheme's primary targets, what they want such as Britain abandoning its current policy towards Zionism. Rather to the contrary, it might give them additional cause for more protests and trouble.
4 Any attempt to encourage cooperation among people who do not share enough common characteristics and who are jealous of one another would, undoubtedly, not succeed.

Once the Foreign Office had found the objections of the Colonial Office to be quite reasonable, it had no choice but to agree, and to take steps to abort the entire scheme. What worried Foreign Office officials most, and mainly the Duke of Devonshire himself, was that the scheme might be tantamount to a sort of adventure in the complex world of the post-war period.[30]

British documents reveal, however, that the matter did not end at that; news of the memorandum leaked to circles outside the Mandate Government departments in Palestine, and outside the Colonial and Foreign Offices. This fact became clear from the letter that the British Consul in Aleppo addressed to the Foreign Office, at the end of May 1923.[31]

The letter in question refers to a number of reports that say that negotiations were under way between King Ḥussayn and other Arab kings, on the one hand, and the British Government, on the other, in view of establishing an Arab Federation under British sponsorship. The letter also says that this had, at the same time, aroused French fears and revived the hopes of the Arabs in Aleppo, many of whom asked the Consul whether or not the proposed federation would include Syria.

At the same time, publication of reports in the press regarding a British-Turkish rapprochement prompted Arab Nationalists, sympathetic to Turkey, to envisage the possibility of ousting the French from Syria with British and Turkish support. The Arab Nationalist's main objective at the time was to get rid of the French and release Syria from the French mandate.

Consul Smart commented on this by saying that this way of thinking confirmed the belief that Easterners are always led by their emotions, rather than their intellects, and that the Arabs, in their great desire to get rid of the French, do not fully realise the obvious consequences of a Turkish intervention in Syrian affairs.

Syrian reaction to the Arab confederation plan (1922–3) marked the end of an era, as far as Britain's policy towards Arab unity is concerned.

Soon, the issue disappeared from the British press for approximately eight years, a phenomenon that certainly had its good reasons.

Between the Conference of Lausanne (1923), which finally settled the issue of the Ottoman Empire's former Arab provinces – this time with Turkey's approval – and 1930, which witnessed the signature of the Anglo-Iraqi Treaty and its international fallout, events accelerated unexpectedly, drawing the attention of the London Government away from the issue of Arab unity.

The year 1924 saw the end of the Ottoman Caliphate and the concomitant reaction to it in the Arab world, including the revival of the idea of an Arab Caliph of Islam, and the ensuing rivalry among various Arab kings for the privilege of holding that title. The main rivals were King Fu'ād of Egypt and Sharif Ḥussayn, the King of the Ḥijāz. The following year witnessed the Great Syrian Revolt, and although the Syrians were always at the forefront of Arab Nationalism, the more pressing issue for them, at that time, was to offset French policies of previous years that sought to dismember Syria and effect its atomisation into several small states. The revolt escalated to such an extent that the French had to use extreme violence to suppress it, going as far as shelling Damascus for two consecutive days, causing 6000 Syrian casualties, not to mention the losses among their own ranks.[32]

Once the revolt was over, the Paris Government had no choice but to find a solution to the problem. This is known thanks to British documents containing the minutes of a meeting between the French Minister for Foreign Affairs, M. Berthelot, and King Fayṣal, at the Quai d'Orsay in Paris, in November 1925. During the meeting, the French Minister had asked the King's advice about the best means of handling the Syrian issue.[33]

King Fayṣal replied that there was a difference between quiet peaceful Iraq, where there were only 2000 British troops, and unstable Syria, where there were as many as 30,000 French troops. The reason was that Iraq enjoyed total independence, as far as the management of its internal affairs was concerned, and if the French Government really sought good advice, it should do what the British had done in Iraq and allow Syria a similar constitution.

M. Berthelot rejected the King's advice and said that the two cases were dissimilar in two respects. First, while Iraq was a single state, Syria was a composite of several small states; he seemed to have forgotten, here, that this particular situation was the outcome of French policies in the first place. Second, Syria did not have a prominent leadership personality, like King Fayṣal, at the helm. Here also, he seems to have forgotten that his country had caused Fayṣal's overthrow in Damascus, in 1920, after the battle of Maysalūn.

The meeting ended with Fayṣal pointing out the grave mistake France made by dividing Syria into several small states, and underlining the need to quickly unify the country and adopt measures liable to enhance the autonomy of these smaller states.[34] The French, however, did not heed Fayṣal's advice, and waited for more than five years before acting on it.[35]

In 1926, the struggle between the Saudis and the Hashemites in the Ḥijāz came to an end with the defeat of the latter and with the Sultan of the Najd, 'Abd al-'Azīz Āl-Sa'ūd, taking control of the holy Muslim sites.

The importance of this development, as far as Britain's policy towards Arab unity is concerned, lies in the fact that it relieved the London Government from having to listen to Sharif Ḥussayn's repeated entreaties to London to keep the promises made to him during the war. It also brought the 'Arab Kingdom' project to an end, a project that had kept British Government departments busy throughout the preceding period.

Moreover, Britain was quite at ease with the new ruler, 'Abd al-'Azīz Āl Sa'ūd, especially after sending one of its agents, Munshī Iḥsānullah, to see him in Mecca. After listening to the King's long discourse on the evening of 8 April 1926, Iḥsānullah sent details of what the King had said to the British Consulate in Jeddah, and the latter, in turn, forwarded the report to London.[36]

It is obvious that certain proponents of Arabism saw 'Abd al-'Azīz's capture and annexation of the Ḥijāz to his kingdom as a step towards Arab unity. This is evident from the letter King 'Abd al-'Azīz sent to Prince Shakīb Arsalān, thanking him for his message of congratulations on the unification of the Najd and the Ḥijāz, and on his efforts to forge a united Arab nation in the Arabian Peninsula, a letter which *Fatāt al-'Arab* newspaper published on 15 March 1926.[37]

In the meeting with the British agent, King 'Abd al-'Azīz said that several people had advised him to be wary of the British Government, because it sought to dismember the Islamic world in general and the Arab world in particular. He swore that he never received anything from the said Government, whether oral or written, indicating their desire to divide the Arabs; rather to the contrary: it always tried to spread peace and prosperity among them. He added that Britain had done its best to bring about reconciliation between himself and King Ḥussayn, but that hesitation by the latter made him opt for war to resolve their differences, and, further, that Britain had maintained neutrality during the conflict and 'respected my religion, honour and independence'.[38]

British officials seemed to be so comfortable with their policies in the Arab Mashreq and with conditions in that part of the world after 1923 that they took time to turn their attention to the western wing of the Arab world, the Maghreb. This was clearly based on a Foreign Office memorandum, dated 21 June 1921, entitled 'The political situation in North Africa'.[39]

The author of the memorandum notes the considerable growth of the Nationalist Movement in the Arab Maghreb, and the possibility for some sort of cooperation between it and the Nationalist Movements in the Mashreq, if a leader capable of unifying the two wings were ever to appear. The situation needed close monitoring even if the risk of this happening was not entirely imminent.[40]

However, by the end of the 1920s the situation had begun to clear up. The Arab countries had witnessed important developments, especially Palestine and Iraq, allowing the British to turn a new page in their policy towards Arab unity. In Palestine, the crisis dramatically intensified during the three following years, reaching its climax in 1929 with the Palestinian uprising against British Mandate policies intent on implementing the Balfour Declaration. The uprising was ignited by the conflict around the famous wall adjacent to al-Aqṣā Mosque, known to the Arabs as the 'Burāq Wall' (*ḥā'iṭ al-burāq*)[41] and to the Jews as the 'Wailing Wall'.

The events of that particular year were the worst that Britain had yet faced as the result of the Palestinian issue. The British formed a committee to investigate the situation under the leadership of Sir John H. Simpson, and the following year its findings were published in the form of a White Paper. The Arabs accepted the Committee's findings because they spelt out the real situation in the country and admitted that Palestine had no room for more immigrants. The Committee also recommended that the transfer of property from the Arabs to the Jews be halted, given the severe harm the practice was causing to Arab farmers.[42]

Despite the fact that the Arabs had very reluctantly accepted the White Paper, the Zionist movement succeeded, once it mobilised its forces and put pressure on the British Government, in forcing the latter to renege on their commitments. The British change of heart came in a statement by the Government, issued in the form of a letter addressed by the Prime Minister to Dr Wiseman, explaining the contents of the White Paper in a manner compatible with Zionist aspirations. This prompted the Arabs to term the document 'the Black Paper'.[43]

Although these developments diverted the attention of the British Government away from the issue of Arab unity, they were the very developments that ultimately forced London to turn its attention back to the issue. It was this confusion besetting British policies vis-à-vis the Palestinian issue, and the religious character of the 1929 revolt, that transformed the issue from a purely Palestinian into a generally Islamic one. This was a source of great concern for the British Government, especially considering its potential impact on Muslims in India who were subjects of the British Empire, and who, over and above their large numbers, were the most enthusiastic defenders of Islam.

This same period also witnessed significant developments in the Fertile Crescent region. Iraq gained international stature after concluding the Treaty with Britain, in 1930, and this new stature renewed the hopes of the local educated elite, active in the Nationalist Movement, of seeing their country play an active role in the Movement. What further raised their hopes was that the French mandate authorities in Syria were, at the time, reviewing the fate of areas under their control, and Syrian Nationalists did not see in the situation anything that would prevent their country's union with Iraq.

The above developments forced the issue once again onto the attention of various British Government departments. It forced it upon the attention of the India Office in view of the impact on Indian Muslims, and Arab regions of the Gulf under its control; on the Colonial Office that oversaw the Mandate in Arab countries, mainly Palestine; and, finally, on the Foreign Office, overwhelmed by these developments and their impact on regions under its jurisdiction. Documents from each of these departments provide us with insight into the second phase of Great Britain's policy towards Arab unity.

Notes

1. F.O. 371/9007, Peace Conference: Paris Memorandum by the Emir Fayṣal.
2. We notice here that in his letter, Fayṣal did not use the term 'Iraqis' but rather he uses the term 'those living between the two rivers' (i.e. the Tigris and Euphrates); the reason is perhaps due to the fact that under Ottoman rule, Iraq was not a single province.
3. F.O. 371/9007.
4. Ibid.
5. Ibid.
6. Ibid.
7. Ibid.
8. Anīs Ṣāyigh, *al-Hashimiyūn wa al-Thawrah al-ʿArabīyah al-Kubrā* (Beirut: [n.pb.], 1976), p. 67.
9. Firstly: England to acknowledge the independence of the Arab countries bounded on the north by Mersina-Adana up to the 37th degree of latitude, in which

degree full Birijik, Urfa, Mardin, Midiat, Amadia Island, up to the border of Persia; on the east, by the border of Persia up to the Gulf of Basra; on the south, by the Indian Ocean, with the exception of the position of Aden, to remain as it is; on the west, by the Red Sea, the Mediterranean Sea up to Mersina. England to approve the proclamation of an Arab caliphate of Islam.

F.O. 371/5066, Foreign Office Memorandum on possible negotiations with the Hedjaz, Appendix B.

10. Ibid.

11. Ibid.

12. The British memorandum included two excerpts from Sharif Ḥussayn's letter, one in good English and the other a literal translation of the passage.

13. F.O. 371/5066.

14. See Annex 1, Arrangement of May 1916, commonly known as the Sykes-Picot Agreement (English Text in: ibid., Appendix D).

15. See Chapter 1 of this book.

16. Translation of the Agreement to the British Government, regarding the Rising and its Foundation:

'1. Great Britain agrees to the formation of an independent Arab Government in every meaning of the word "independence", internally and externally, the boundaries of the said government, being on the east, the Persian Gulf; on the west the Red Sea, the Egyptian frontier, and the Mediterranean; on the north, the northern boundaries of the valley of Aleppo and Mosul up to the River Euphrates and its junction with Tigris as far as their mouths in the Persian Gulf, but with the exception of Aden colony, which is excluded from the boundaries.

The Arab Government will undertake to respect the agreements and contracts which the British Government makes with any Arab or individual Emir who happens to be within these boundaries namely; that she will replace the British Government in seeing the rights involved in those agreements and contracts are maintained for the benefit of those who are entitled to them.

2. Great Britain undertakes to shield the said government and protect it against any interference or encroachment of any kind or form whatever affecting her internally or her boundaries by land or sea; and even, in the case of an internal rising caused by enemy intrigues or the jealousy of Emirs. The British Government will give the Arab Government normal and material help in putting down the rising; this help in internal disorders and risings shall be limited to the time when the Arab Government shall have completed its material formation.

3. Basra shall be in the occupation of the British Government until the said new Arab Government shall have completed its material formation as above mentioned. A sum of money shall be allotted by the British Government in assessing which of the requirements of the Arab Government will be taken in consideration, seeing that the said Government is like a minor in the keeping of the British Government, and the sum referred to will be a gift made in respect of the said occupation.

4. Great Britain undertakes to supply her foster daughter, the Arab Government, with all its requisitions of arms, ammunition, war materials and money, in the way of subsidies, for the duration of war.

Great Britain undertakes to cut the railway line at Marsin or any other convenient spot in that area.'

F.O. 371/5066, Appendix A.

17. Ibid., Appendix C.

18. Ibid.

19. Excerpt from the famous Balfour Declaration.
20. F.O. 371/5066, Appendix C.
21. F.O. 371/5067, Report of a conversation between Sir J. Tilley, KCMG, CB, reporting the Secretary of State for Foreign Affairs, and His Highness Emir Fayṣal representing the King of the Hejaz (held at the Foreign Office on Thursday 23 December 1920).
22. 'Ādil Ḥasan Ghonaim. *Al-Ḥarakah al-Waṭaniyah al-Filisṭīnīyah 1917–1936.* Cairo: al-Hay'ah al-Miṣrīyah al-'Ammah li-l-Kitāb, 1974.
23. Ibid., p. 93.
24. The text of this correspondence is in White Paper no. 700.
25. Ibid.
26. Ghonaim, *Al-Ḥarakah al-Waṭaniyah al-Filisṭīnīyah 1917–36*, pp. 103–6.
27. See Appendix 2 of this book.
28. F.O. 371/9001/3997, Secretariat - Government House - Jerusalem, 22 December 1922.
29. F.O. 371/9001, from Herbert Samuel to the Duke of Devonshire.
30. F.O. 371/9001, from the Duke of Devonshire to Marquis Curzon of Kedleston, 16 January 1923.
31. F.O. 371/9053–39804, Consul Smart to Marquis Curzon of Kedleston, Aleppo, 31 May 1923.
32. Elizabeth P. MacCallum, *The Arab Nationalist Movement* (New York: Foreign Policy Association, [n. d.]), vol. 11, no. 5, p. 55.
33. F.O. 371/10851, Telegram from Lord Crewe to Mr Chamberlain, Paris, 4 November 1925.
34. Ibid.
35. See Chapter 3 of this book.
36. F.O. 371/11436, Vice Consul Jordan to Sir Austen Chamberlain, Jeddah, 17 April, 1926.
37. F.O. 371/11445, Consul Smart-Damascus to Foreign Office, 16 March 1926.
38. F.O. 371/11436, Enclosure in no. 1, Precis of Munshi Ihsanuallah's Report.
39. F.O. 371/40064, Memorandum on the political situation in North Africa by F. R. Rodd, 21 June, 1924.
40. Ibid.
41. The reference is to Muslim belief in the so-called 'night journey' (*al-mi'rāj* or *al-isrā'*) of the Prophet Muḥammad to the 'Far Mosque' (al-Masjid al-Aqṣā) in Jerusalem, mentioned in the opening verse of *surat al-isrā'* of the Qur'ān. While the Qur'ānic reference is brief, the *ḥadīth* and apocryphal literature assert that the Prophet was borne on a beast (of burden) known as *al-burāq* (depicted later in Muslim art – especially in Ottoman paintings – as a human headed horse, often with wings). It is from the temple mount – the current site of the Dome of the Rock and al-Masjid al-Aqṣā, that the Prophet is understood to have ascended to heaven. – Editor.
42. Emille, Al-Ghūrī, *al-Mu'āmarah al-Kubrā, Ightīyāl Filisṭīn wa Ḥaqq al-'Arab* (Cairo: Dār al-Nīl, 1955), p. 69.
43. Najīb Ṣadaqah, *Qaḍīyat Filisṭīn,* introduction by 'Abd al-Raḥmān 'Azzām and Sayyid Jamāl al-Ḥusaynī (Beirut: Dār al-Kitāb, 1946), p. 150.

Chapter 3

The Arab Conference 1931–3

One of the traditional mainstays of British imperialism relied, in the Arab world, on keeping a close eye on all that was happening in each and every country, and observing, monitoring, analysing and evaluating whatever transpired. Reports submitted by its agents in the region were vital for decision makers in London, when planning future policies.

In Cairo, this watchful British eye was in the form of the European Department, a subsidiary of the Home Office long associated with the name of its founder, Ken Boyd, and in Khartoum, it came in the form of the Sudan Intelligence Bureau, associated with Sir Francis R. Wingate, one of the most prominent personalities to govern the country. In Palestine, it was under the aegis of the Criminal Investigation Department, the function of which was to write political reports, a role that might seem incongruous with its name.

One of the main tasks of each of these departments was to submit weekly reports, in the form of surveys, dealing with security-related matters or issues that could potentially affect British presence in a given country. The latter involved the movements of public personalities and activities of local political groups, including the attitudes of their newspapers and the international activities of their members.

One of the reports by the Criminal Investigation Department in Palestine marked the onset of a new phase in British policies towards Arab unity. The report in question, dated 18 February 1931, examines and assesses various events that took place during the week ending on 14 February. It addressed five different events, four of which were of utmost importance to officials in London, mainly to the Colonial and Foreign Offices.[1]

The first of these was entitled 'Shawkat 'Alī's tour of Palestine'. The latter was an Indian Muslim leader whose interest in the Palestinian issue had increased after the incidents of 1929, which were markedly religious in character. The report states that during his tour of the Arab areas of Palestine, Shawkat mounted an anti-European attack, which, at the same time, endorsed Pan-Islamism and Arab Nationalism. It revolved around two distinct issues, namely a call to boycott European goods and the revival of Pan-Islamism.

The report says that Shawkat 'Alī raised this case, every now and then, and although the Arabs seemed to favour the idea, it was doubtful that they would be able to take any concrete steps towards its implementation, except perhaps on a very limited scale.

The opposite was true regarding the second topic. According to the report's writer, Pan-Islamist activities seemed very serious indeed, and the fact that steps to promote Pan-Islamism ran parallel to the concept of Arab Nationalism serves only to increase its appeal in the Arab countries. Shawkat 'Alī and Ḥajj Amīn al-Ḥusaynī, Mufti of Palestine, have together developed an intensive plan according to which the former, after visiting Egypt, will undertake a tour of Syria and Iraq, and designating Palestine as the headquarters of Pan-Islamism.

Mawlāya Shawkat 'Alī, as Egyptian newspapers referred to him, explained these ideas in an interview with one of the newspapers. Among other details, he said that his call for a conference stemmed from the disagreements and conflicts he had witnessed, disagreements and disputes that 'killed us'; he added: 'My aim is to put an end to them, and forge unity in the service of Islam.'[2]

Here another report of the European Department in Cairo regarding Shawkat 'Alī's visit to Egypt commends inspection. The document states that the latter received a cheque for the amount of LE 10,000, in support of the Muslims of India, from Tawfīq Nasīm, head of the Royal Court, in return for promoting the interests of King Fu'ād in his country, and countering propaganda in favour of Ibn Sa'ūd. The report goes on to belittle the importance of the Egyptian King's ambition to play a significant role in the Islamic world, since he can barely preserve the very throne on which he sits.[3]

The report also includes an evaluation of Egyptian ties to Arabism. Its author believes that these ties are quite weak, and that the strong nationalist tendency in the Arab countries towards some sort of cultural union has only limited support in Egypt among groups like al-Sharq Association, led by 'Abd al-Ḥamīd al-Bakry, Aḥmad Zakī Pāshā, and Aḥmad Shafīq

Pāshā. It also has the support of the Muslim Youth Association, headed by 'Abd al-Ḥamīd Sa'īd Bey, one of the National Party's prominent leaders.

The report then reveals Nūrī al-Sa'īd's intention to embark on a tour that includes Trans-Jordan, Palestine, the Ḥijāz, Levant and Egypt, and says that he will receive no encouragement worth mentioning, in the latter country, from King Fu'ād. The King sees the Arab nation from the perspective of his ancestors' conquest of it, which refers specifically to the Egyptian forces having reached Greater Syria and the Arabian Peninsula, under Muḥammad 'Alī's reign. His view is based, therefore, on the notion of extending his hegemony over these territories, a view that would not be well received by Arab Nationalists.

The European Administration's report ends by minimising the level of alarm over the issue of Pan-Islamism, brought up by the Criminal Investigation Department report, and suggests that attention be focussed instead on the future of Arab Nationalism. It adds that resistance activities in Palestine could easily spread to Egypt, even if the latter appears far removed from Arab influences.

The report by the British officials in Cairo aside, that of their peers in Jerusalem attaches importance to the second stage of Shawkat 'Alī's visit, in particular the issue of Pan-Islamism to which the said report dedicates its fourth and fifth paragraphs. Under this very title, the report states:

> Pan-Islamism is beginning to be felt in a concrete form. Forces are gathering from various quarters and point to its approach. The past discussions and activity respecting the Arab Confederated States, the present activity towards cultural unity as instanced by the step taken in Egypt for the compilation of an Arab Encyclopaedia, the rumoured intention of the Iraqi Prime Minister to visit Ḥijāz for discussing the question of Arab unity, the meeting of Shawkat 'Alī with ex-King Ḥussayn and his subsequent declaration in favour of the latter and against Ibn Sa'ūd, are some of the factors at work towards the unity of the East against Europe.

The report names Palestine as the potential arena of conflict between the East and Europe. The reason is that the Criminal Investigation Department that authored the report believed that the political movement in Palestine was on the verge of a major shift. It was about to break out of its confines, in moves that would involve activism against Zionism and a struggle for national independence in order to become part of a wider movement within the Arab Islamic World. If the Mufti, Ḥājj Amīn al-Ḥusaynī, were to succeed in getting the funds he yet lacked, he would be able to overcome major obstacles that impeded his movement.

However, less than four months after reporting on the impact of Shawkat 'Alī's visit, some of the fears of a Pan-Islamic revival began to come true for the Colonial Administration in Palestine, and the British High Commissioner's Residency in Cairo, which previously had belittled these concerns, admitted as much. Officials at the Residency had received a report from the European Administration to the effect that those spreading propaganda in Muslim countries were unhappy with the situation at al-Azhar University, the curricula and student body of which, in their view, did not rise to the level of their aspirations.[4]

According to them, al-Azhar lacked the religious enthusiasm that could prove effective in various Muslim countries. The report believes that the alternative, sought by Shawkat 'Alī, was the establishment of an Islamic University in Jerusalem to counter-balance the Hebrew University, on condition that Ḥājj Amīn al-Ḥusaynī be appointed its first Sheikh. Officials of the European Administration in Cairo feared that the new institution would be a centre for spreading Soviet propaganda in the Muslim countries.

Reasons behind this fear are not very clear, except if seen in light of the constant and seemingly endless British fear of the potential spread of Bolshevism in the Arab world. It is a fear that would rear its head whenever a national movement against imperialism ratcheted up its activities in the Arab world, a fact which was well known to students of the 1919 Revolution in Egypt, for example.

Concerning the issue, Ken Boyd and his colleagues went so far as to say that Shawkat 'Alī had launched an extensive fund-raising effort in India in favour of the establishment of the said university. They asserted that many of al-Azhar's scholars had contacted Sheikh Rashīd Riḍā, owner of *al-Manār* newspaper, to express their readiness to join the new university as soon as it was established.

After studying its content, officials at the High Commissioner's Residency in Cairo gave their own assessment of the report. They admitted at the outset that the previous four months had been a significant landmark as far as support for the university and for Arab Nationalism in the Middle East was concerned, especially in Syria and Palestine and, to a lesser degree, in Egypt. They believed that this support had begun when Shawkat 'Alī visited the Middle East, on his way back to India. The officials note that the latter's visit to Palestine was so successful, that clashes between the followers and opponents of the Mufti had ceased. The religious spirit that Shawkat 'Alī had aroused succeeded in uniting the Arab Muslims.

The Residency of the High Commissioner in Cairo then turned its attention to Shawkat 'Alī's plans, which it perceived to be in two phases. The first involved his call for the establishment of an Islamic University in Jerusalem and, the second, his call for holding an Islamic Conference the following summer. Prominent Muslim personalities from each Muslim country would be invited to attend, and talks would focus on issues of concern to the Muslim world, notably the establishment of a federation of Arab states.

British officials admitted that the Palestinians and Syrians received the Indian preacher's plans with obvious enthusiasm, and that a fund-raising drive was under way to collect the necessary revenue for the establishment of the Muslim University in Jerusalem, with those in charge receiving promises of large financial contributions from all the Muslim countries. On the other hand, Residency officials denied what the European Administration's report had said concerning a link between Shawkat 'Alī and Soviet Russia. They insisted that, on the one hand, there was not a single shred of evidence that such a relationship existed, and, on the other, that they did not agree with what the report had said regarding the readiness of al-Azhar scholars to work at the new university. They said that their sources confirmed that Sheikh Rashīd Riḍā had actually contacted some of these scholars expressly for that purpose, but they had not welcomed the establishment of a new university in the region that would compete with their own esteemed establishment.

What they could not deny, however, were certain facts regarding the other focus of Shawkat 'Alī's attention, namely the efforts to hold an Islamic Conference in Jerusalem. This conference did in fact take place, and had considerable impact on British policy towards Arab unity.

The Islamic Conference in Jerusalem

All the indicators show that towards the end of 1931, as advocates of the Islamic Conference in Jerusalem forged ahead with their plans, and their work was nearing fruition, British Mandate officials in Palestine could find no excuse to prevent the Conference from taking place. They knew that a move of active suppression on their part would have a negative effect in Palestine, and in other areas of the Muslim world under their control, especially among Indian Muslims. Therefore, all they could do was attempt to minimise its impact. This was clear from the long telegram sent by the British Secretary of State to the Indian Government, on 18 November 1931.[5]

The first part of the telegram details the British Government's position on the Conference and states that as long as it does not violate public order, it would be difficult to separate between its religious significance and political objectives. The telegram adds: 'There are obvious objections to taking any action which might be represented as interference in Muslim religious matters.'

The telegram also states that the British Government has received protest notes and enquiries from a number of foreign governments, including Turkey, Italy and the Ḥijāz, Egypt, Yugoslavia and Spain, all very worried that the Conference might cause international difficulties. Italy is worried that its policy in Tripoli will come under severe criticism, while the Government of the Ḥijāz sees the Conference as an anti-Saudi endeavour.

For its part, Turkey is concerned that the Conference might raise the issue of the caliphate, and its foreign secretary declared that his country would not be attending. The latter said that he has received assurances that Iran, Afghanistan and the Ḥijāz will also not attend, and that Egypt and Iraq will only send unofficial delegations.[6]

The second part of the telegram notes that the British Secretary of State has considered these protests carefully, and has decided to reassure those governments that all precautions will be taken to eliminate their fears, including:

- Obtaining a promise from the Mufti, despite the doubts attaching to this, that the issues of the caliphate, Tripoli or any other matters liable to raise the concerns of foreign governments will not be raised.
- Attempting to prevent the Conference from convening on British Mandate territory, under the pretext that this might cause international complications. To do that, however, the British would need either a resolution from the League of Nations that mandated them over these territories in the first place, or a formal request from one of the protesting countries, none of which had yet made any for fear of the potential reaction to such a move.

British officials in London, Jerusalem and Cairo looked on anxiously as the ten-day Conference convened in the holy city, between 10 and 17 December 1931.

* * *

The Arab press abounded with news about the Conference prior to its convening. Prominent personalities, known for their long history of service to

Pan-Arabism, penned their opinions, and chief among them was Aḥmad Zakī Pāshā (Sheikh al-'Urūbah), who wrote a long article in *al-Ahram* entitled 'To the Men of the Islamic Conference – A Supplication and a Plea'. He requested that the Conference be practical, that its resolutions be limited in number so as to be easily applicable and that the participants avoid raising the issue of the caliphate to eliminate the risk of division.

Most worthy of note in Sheikh al-'Urūbah's article is his plea to

> safeguard the land of Palestine for the Arabs of Palestine, so that it is no longer forcibly taken away from them and placed into someone else's hands, lest they lose all reason to stay, or have any say, in their own country.

The only way to do this, in Aḥmad Zakī Pāshā's opinion, was for Muslims to raise a sum of at least 1 million pounds and use it to purchase land from the debt-ridden Palestinians. Once purchased, the land would become an endowment of al-Aqṣā Mosque, and used to build a Muslim college, as well as orphanages, hospitals and schools.[7]

As the sessions of the Islamic Conference started in Jerusalem, so did the problems of the British Government. The Italian Government was the first to submit a protest regarding events that took place before the Conference had ended. Reuter's News Agency sent a telegram stating that the head of the Egyptian delegation, 'Abd al-Raḥmān Bey 'Azzām, had mentioned in his address to the Conference the terrible acts committed by Italy in Barqah. Senior Mameli, the Chargé d'Affaires at the Italian Embassy in London, hurriedly met with Mr Rendel, Director of the Eastern Department at the Foreign Office, and handed him a note of protest concerning 'Azzām's speech and the fact that he had suspended the session for a minute of silence in memory of 'Umar al-Mukhtār, the well-known Libyan leader. In his note, to which he appended the Reuters telegram, Mameli asked that the High Commissioner in Palestine be instructed to condemn these moves and to issue a statement to that effect in a manner that would satisfy the Italian Government.[8]

However, that was not strange coming from a man with 'Azzām Bey's history who, during World War I, had joined the Sanūsī resistance movement against the Italian occupation of Libya, and was sentenced to death by the Italians for doing so. Although he later ended his military involvement and became active on the political scene, especially after joining the al-Wafd Party and becoming a member of the parliament representing the 'Ayyāṭ constituency in the Governorate of Giza, he had continued to be known for his interest in pan-Arab issues.[9]

Acting on the Italian Government's request, the Colonial Office instructed its High Commissioner in Palestine to expel 'Azzām Bey from the country, with the shortest possible delay, and these instructions were carried out in quite a dramatic way. A police officer arrived at 'Azzām's hotel and asked him to leave the country immediately, upon which the latter

> travelled by car to Gaza, followed by a cortege of his friends in their cars. Upon his arrival in Gaza, masses of people came out to greet him and many became angry and agitated when the police tried to prevent them from doing so. People came in demonstration-like processions and their numbers kept increasing until they were allowed to see 'Azzām, though the police officer in charge asked 'Azzām to meet with his visitors at the hotel, and not to leave its confines. This incident had a deep impact on all of Palestine,[10]

The same could be said for its impact on various British Government departments.

While the Palestinians were demonstrating in honour of 'Abd al-Raḥmān 'Azzām, the Mufti was explaining to the British High Commissioner, Sir A. Wauchope, why he could not fulfil his promise to prevent the delivery of such speeches, saying that he could not stop a speaker so eager that he was almost shouting. As for the minute of mourning for 'Umar al-Mukhtār, it had come as a suggestion by some of the members, and he therefore could not object to it.[11] Wauchope did not accept the Mufti's excuses and expressed his dissatisfaction with all that had transpired; the result was a decision to expel 'Abd al-Raḥmān 'Azzām from the country.[12]

In light of these incidents, the Colonial Office asked the Research Department to carry out a detailed study of the Islamic movement in Palestine. From that study, it is known that the movement had begun in 1924, when Mawlāy Muḥammad 'Alī, the brother of Shawkat 'Alī, first met with Ḥājj Amīn al-Ḥusaynī at the Islamic Conference in the Ḥijāz. The two men had agreed that Indian Muslims would lend their assistance to the Palestinians, and help save the holy sites from Jewish aggression.[13]

Based on the terms of the said agreement, Mawlāy Muḥammad 'Alī arrived in Palestine on 21 November 1928, and on his way to Jerusalem, stopped in Nāblus and met Ḥājj Amīn al-Ḥusaynī in al-Bīreh. During the meeting, he delivered an important speech in which he introduced Islam as a social as well as religious tenet. His aim was to prove that the true faith was entirely capable of dealing with whatever modern culture brought in its wake, and he insisted on the Muslims' need for unity and solidarity.

Among the main results of Mawlāy Muḥammad 'Alī's visit was the strengthening of different Muslim Youth Association branches, which were all linked one way or another to the main Association in Egypt. Although these Associations seemed to be predominantly cultural in nature, there was nothing which would prevent them turning, in due course, towards political activism.[14]

The Islamic Movement in Palestine gained political strength after the Burāq Wall (the Wailing Wall) incident, in 1929, particularly in the wake of the Conference that convened in early November of that same year, bringing together some 500 personalities. The British report that covered that particular event focussed on the widespread participation of Arab Nationalists in the Conference, chief among whom were Shukrī al-Qūwatlī from Syria, and other participants from Lebanon and Trans-Jordan, which gave it a distinct Arab character.

The Conference took a number of decisions most important among which, over and above protecting the holy sites in Palestine, was assisting the Syrian delegation in submitting the issue to the League of Nations. The relevant report commented on the Arab character of the Movement, stating:

> What is well known is that the ideology of this group, led by Ḥājj Amīn al-Ḥusaynī, agrees with the Syrian Istiqlālists' (independents) aim of linking Palestine to an Arab Confederation. By this, they hope to be in a better position to fight both the (alleged) Zionist peril, and foreign rule.

Once again, the report addresses the issue of the Arab confederation as far as the Palestinians are concerned, this time after 1929. It states: 'the nationalist leaders, having subsequently become absorbed in local affairs, the Movement fell into a state of dormancy and was soon superseded by discussions of arrangements for the Arab Confederation.'

While research departments of relevant British ministries were busy studying the Conference, contacts were under way in the Egyptian capital between the London and Paris Governments on its potential impact. M. Laforge, Secretary of the French Agency in Cairo, met with the Eastern Secretary at the Residency of the High Commissioner, and asked his opinion on the Conference, particularly since many Arab Nationalists had come from Egypt to Palestine to attend it. He predicted that work would resume on the Ḥijāz Railway, the main symbol of Pan-Islamism prior to World War I, and expressed the hope that the Conference would not have any significant impact on Syria, despite the fact that many Syrians attended it.[15]

The Conference's participants asked the Executive Committee to do all it could to restore stolen parts of the Ḥijāz Railway, repair it, and re-launch its operations under the management of an Islamic organisation.[16] However, since the French diplomat saw this as a worrisome development, the Oriental Secretary reassured him that King Ibn Saʿūd was not sympathetic to the Conference, and that no decision would be implemented regarding the railroad without the Saudi King's approval.

The final report, written in March 1932 by Wauchope a few months after the conclusion of the Jerusalem Conference, established the broad lines of a future British Government policy towards this type of gathering.[17]

The British were concerned mainly that the resolutions that the Conference had adopted gave it an institutional character. For, in addition to the decision to convene once every two years, an Executive Committee[18] which had been formed to follow up on the adopted resolutions was given the prerogative of overruling the two-year restriction by calling upon the Conference to convene whenever it deemed necessary. In turn, the Executive Committee set up a special bureau to deal with urgent matters.

In his report, the British High Commissioner in Palestine said that the said Committee had not met even once during the past months and that the special bureau had not yet been established. He added that the Secretary General, Ḍīyā' al-Dīn al-Ṭabaṭabā'ī, an Iranian national who had great organisational skills, was still in Switzerland and doubted that he would ever come to Palestine to take up the duties entrusted to him.[19] Wauchope expressed his doubts as to whether the Executive Committee or its special bureau would ever convene, a fact that went a long way in mitigating the fear of officials at the Colonial Office of the Conference's institutional character.

The report also minimised the impact of the Conference on the situation in Palestine, stating that while religious and racial disturbances in that country had taken place while the Conference was in progress, the level of their intensity had remained the same, as if the Conference had never taken place. Wauchope added that the conflict between the Mufti and his local political enemies, who believed that he used the Conference to advance his own interests, had remained as it had been and not escalated in intensity.

Yet, Wauchope added that this did not mean that such a Conference would be allowed to convene in Jerusalem ever again, since the conditions under which the Mandate authorities had permitted it to happen might not present again. He concluded by saying:

> [What] I can undertake to do is to watch carefully the development of the situation arising out of the last Conference and, if I think necessary, advise you at a latter date that the holding of another Conference in Palestine will jeopardise the peace, and to act as I think best, in the circumstances existing at the time, to minimise or prevent those evil consequences which I foresee will arise from the holding of a Muslim Conference in Jerusalem.

Based on the above report, two different conclusions can be drawn. First, as usual in the Arab world, events of this sort often start with considerable strength only to fade away once they are over, or soon afterwards. In my opinion, the main difference between this world, that is, the underdeveloped world in general, and the developed world, is that the latter has the ability to follow-up on the issue at hand, and see it through to its conclusion. Second, the Government in London would have subsequently refused to allow the holding of another such Conference at the same location. We can thus say that with this, the 'the Islamic Conference' phase had come to an end and another was just about to begin.

The Arab Conference in Baghdad

Coterminous with the Islamic Conference in Jerusalem, both Syria and Iraq witnessed important developments in the early 1930s that caused a major shift in the efforts to hold the Conference. The political situation in Syria was quite fluid in the aftermath of the 1925 Revolution. It was time to consider drawing up a constitution for the country, and Monsieur Ponsot, the French High Commissioner, was pursuing manipulative policies. After the Foundation Council had drafted a constitution for the country based on the national aspirations of the Syrian people, especially for political unity, the High Commissioner issued an entirely different constitution that was not entirely to the liking of the National Movement.[20] As a result, a wave of disturbances wracked the country, especially in Damascus; a fact that is revealed by different newspaper headlines from that particular period. Among these headlines was one that read: 'Electric Political Atmosphere in Syria – Damascus Shuts Down in Protest.' Under this title came news of what had transpired in the Syrian capital on 14 December 1931, and of student demonstrations in support of the National Movement.[21] Newspapers appearing around the end of 1931, and the beginning of the following year, spoke about clashes between followers of that Bloc and so-called 'agents hanging on France's coat-tails'.

As for Iraq, things were proceeding quite well following the signature of the Anglo-Iraqi Treaty of 1930, which stipulated the end of the Mandate and granted Iraq total independence. As to the motives behind the Agreement, as noted by Great Britain's report to the League of Nations, they included the ability to maintain the country's stability and safeguard its security, and the judiciary's ability to protect foreign interests and minority rights as provided for in the constitution.[22]

Within the context of a fluid political situation in Syria and internal stability in Iraq, there were suggestions regarding a possible union between the two countries under the crown of King Fayṣal. Other suggestions proposed the establishment of an independent kingdom under King 'Alī, the brother of Fayṣal and former King of the Ḥijāz, or, alternatively, under 'Abbās Ḥilmī, former Khedive of Egypt. The subject was of great interest to both Egyptian newspapers and British Government departments.

The above issues were the object of a British document, issued in the form of a long memorandum that the Colonial Office sent to the British Representative in Baghdad.[23] The document unveils the start of a new phase in British policy towards Arab unity, an entirely different phase than the one that preceded it, when Britain was still subject to the effects of World War I.

The memorandum first examines the possibility of establishing a kingdom in Syria, and considers various propositions in this regard. It starts by defining what 'Syria' as a territory involves, especially since for the French the term refers to the particular territory of the same name excluding the 'Alawite and Jabal al-Drūze regions. The memorandum also says that the French intended to keep this territory under their control as long as Britain remained in Trans-Jordan, and intended to stay in Tripoli and Beirut as long as Britain remained in Palestine, meaning that Lebanon was unlikely to be part of the new kingdom.

The Colonial Office then considers various indicators relevant to Paris' attitude towards the establishment of a Syrian Kingdom, based on a speech by the French representative at the Permanent Mandate Committee Meeting, in June 1931, regarding France's policy towards Syria. The representative had voiced his country's readiness to conclude treaties with the Syrian and Lebanese governments to demonstrate the progress achieved by the two countries since the establishment of the Mandate. British officials believed that these treaties would be drawn along the lines of the Anglo-Iraqi Treaty of 1922, and would involve a referendum that allowed the Syrian people to choose whomever they willed to lead them, be he a king or a president. A search was under way for candidates to the throne of

Syria, regardless of whether they were members of the Hashemite family or not.

The British learned that the French had offered the throne of Syria to Fayṣal when the latter told their representative in Baghdad, on 9 October 1931, that it had almost been decided that he would assume the throne of Syria alongside that of Iraq, and that as he understood it, the British Government had no objections to this.

However, there were indications, as the British soon learned, that the throne had also been offered to Khedive ʿAbbās, the former ruler of Egypt, a development with a story all on its own. On 12 December, *al-Ṭān* newspaper published an article regarding the nomination of ʿAbbās to the throne of Syria,[24] and despite doubts about the story's accuracy, the trip of Egypt's former Khedive to the Levant elicited great interest among various parties. On 21 December the former Khedive travelled from Istanbul to Aleppo by train, and arrived two days later in Beirut, whereupon he suddenly left by car for Jerusalem. Although the Khedive had mentioned in an interview with *al-Ahram* that what was being said regarding his ascending the throne of Syria 'is not rooted in fact and I know nothing about it',[25] British official departments believed otherwise, a fact confirmed by the long report that Sir Morgan, an official at the British Embassy in Ankara, sent to his government.

The report follows the Khedive's trip to the Levant, which he began with a visit to Trans-Jordan in response to an invitation from Emir ʿAbdullah. From there, he went on to Beirut where Monsieur Ponsot, the French High Commissioner, gave an official reception in his honour; and from Beirut, the Khedive went on to Jerusalem where he stayed for several days. Morgan concludes that ʿAbbās was looking forward to ascending the throne of Syria, especially since, on 18 December the Anatolian News Agency had published a report to the effect that Monsieur Ponsot and the French Government had agreed to nominate the former Khedive to the throne, and that soon the monarchy would be declared in the country.[26] These developments prompted the Colonial Office in London to look closely at the situation and arrive at a final and precise decision that reflected a new phase of British policy towards Arab unity, a policy that had just begun to crystallise.

The British Government's decision was that:

> So far as the interests of His Majesty's Government are concerned, it would be preferable that Syria should be a republic with a Syrian president. In that case, the Syrians could develop their country in their own way, possibly on

> similar lines to Iraq, and would be free from the inevitable intrigues, which would result from a connection with the Hashemite family, or, for that matter, with the royal families of Najd, the Ḥijāz and Egypt, but both events are undesirable. If the Syrian throne is to be offered to King Fayṣal, he would accept it, because it is difficult for him to resist the temptation of returning, as a king,[27] to Damascus. It will not be clear in this case if the thrones of Syria and Iraq will be united, or if Fayṣal will transfer his throne from Iraq to Syria.

The report concludes by delineating the British Government's policy as stringent opposition to the unification of Iraq and Syria under one crown. If this happens, according to the document, King Fayṣal will most probably choose Syria as his main headquarters due to its fine weather and appoint a deputy-governor in Iraq. However, given that his status in this country is weak, to begin with, and reasons for Iraq's independence have grown, while those for maintaining British control have weakened, these headquarters will also gradually weaken if this happens.

The Colonial Office also objected to Fayṣal becoming King of Syria without Iraq, as this could result in what it called the 'Extreme Nationalist Party' taking over power and declaring a republic. This would only increase the difficulty of the British Ambassador's future mission in Baghdad.[28] Similarly, the same objections applied to the coronation of 'Alī, former King of Ḥijāz and brother of Fayṣal, as King of Syria, due to his weak character, a development that would have the most dire consequences for the Kingdom of Iraq.

It was for all the above reasons that the British Government issued instructions to its representative in Iraq to not encourage Fayṣal to accept either of the two options. This marked the closure of this particular file and the opening of another before the end of 1932.

* * *

Just as a report from the Police Department in Palestine signalled the start of the 'Islamic Conference' issue, another report by the same agency signalled the beginning of the 'Conference' issue. The report in question, dated 2 December 1932, said that negotiations had taken place between Emir 'Ādil Arsalān and his brother, Emir Shakīb, regarding efforts to convene a Conference, and that the latter had gone to Baghdad to discuss the matter. The report added that no agreement had been reached so far on either the date or place of the Conference, due to a number of reasons, some of which had to do with the conflict between Ibn Sa'ūd and Fayṣal's supporters in the Istiqlāl Party, or with personal issues.

While Fayṣal's followers sought to hold the Conference in Baghdad to promote the issue of an Iraqi-Syrian union, a subject of great interest to the Iraqi King, Ibn Saʿūd's followers feared lest the Conference would elevate Faiṣal's status and thus allow him to advance his own personal agenda. The latter therefore proposed Mecca as a convenient alternative site for the Conference, or any other neutral location, such as the border area between Iraq and the Najd. Finally, the report says that another group within the Party suggested holding the Conference in Damascus itself.[29]

Less than 20 days later, King Fayṣal was talking to the British Ambassador in Iraq about convening the Conference in the Iraqi capital. He based his desire to do so on the fact that the Iraqi Government could not afford to ignore the Arab Nationalist Movement; for although it was incumbent on this government to develop the country's resources and raise the people's standards of living and education, it was also obliged to look towards the future. Iraq was surrounded on the north and east by powerful neighbours that could eventually threaten its future.[30]

In Persia, at the same time, there were dreams of reviving the Sassanian Empire; and although relations with Turkey were peaceful following the settlement of the Mosul issue in 1926,[31] still no one knew whether the latter's aspirations regarding the said province would eventually resurface or not. On the other hand, Iraq would continue to face a threat from the West as long as the French remained in their strong position. They, in turn, were eyeing Mosul and its oil, and no one could be certain that they also did not harbour the dream of one day controlling its oil fields.[32]

Fayṣal supported his view by saying that it was not fair for Iraq to stay dependent on British assistance in order to guarantee its future survival, especially since this assistance could not go on forever, which is why he felt it was necessary for his country to seek a new source of power. Therefore, once Iraq was able to rely on the support of Arab countries, and once it had formed a union with the Arabs of Syria, future threats would be drastically reduced.

After this detailed explication of his point of view, Fayṣal concluded by asking the British Ambassador specifically about whether his government was still sympathetic to the Pan-Arab cause, and whether or not it looked favourably on holding a Conference in Baghdad. He might have been unaware, at the time, that he had kept British departments busy with the Pan-Arab cause for quite some time, so much so, that by then quite a large file had already been compiled on the issue.

The very first reaction came from Sir Francis Humphreys who, at that same meeting, tried to alleviate the King's fears. On the one hand, Persia would undoubtedly be worried about the rising tide of Arab Nationalism; it was seeking to extend its power southwards by sea towards the Gulf, a region inhabited essentially by Arabs. France would have similar worries, and would object to any political move liable to lead to Arab unity, a development, which in its view, would threaten Lebanon from the east. He ended by saying that if this were to happen, instead of strengthening Iraq, Arab unity might stoke the hostility of its neighbours, which is exactly what the British Government was afraid of as far as this particular idea was concerned.

The British Ambassador refuted King Fayṣal's reasons to apprehend Turkish and Persian aspirations in Iraq. France had more territories under its control than it could handle, and neither Baghdad nor London should be preoccupied with what was likely to happen ten years down the line. The best way the Iraqi Government could serve the Arab cause was by promoting economic and cultural development, so that the Arabs could regain the status they once enjoyed among the world's nations.[33]

Regarding Fayṣal's final question, Humphreys gave a vague answer to the effect that the King of Iraq should be well aware that Britain's policy towards his country was the best proof of its sympathy for the ambition of the Arab Nation to assume its legitimate place among the world's advanced nations, once again. He said that he could not add anything else in response to this part of the question. As to the other part, namely the convening of a Conference in Baghdad, he believed that the idea was quite natural. The Ambassador expressed his belief that there would be no problem at all, especially if the participants behaviour was based on a proper understanding of the situation at hand.

He, however, then tried to intimidate Fayṣal, in the event that the Conference were to take place in Baghdad, by placing responsibility for what might happen, such as insolent remarks by certain participants against neighbouring governments, squarely on Iraqi shoulders. Humphreys' response was couched in a personal rather than an official tenor. He ended by advising the King that he had to abide by certain conditions if he wished to hold the Conference in Baghdad. These included confining the Conference's agenda to economic and cultural issues and the exclusion of all political matters; doing his best to convince the Syrians not to use methods other than peaceful ones to settle their issues with France and barring the Palestinians from raising the issue of their relations with the Jews. Finally, the Conference should take into consideration King ʿAbd al-ʿAzīz Āl-Saʿūd' fear that the Hashemite family would use the Conference to threaten his position. In brief, the British Ambassador in Baghdad voided the Conference of any nationalist content.

What is strange though, is that Fayṣal accepted Humphreys' remarks, though he expressed some reservation regarding the possibility of certain participants not adhering strictly to the proposed Conference agenda, despite the fact that all the invited guests would be highly-experienced personalities. At the end of the meeting, and in answer to the Ambassador's question about the expected date of the Conference, the Iraqi King said that it would take place in March, some three months later.

British policy in the six months that followed the above meeting revolved around two major objectives. The first was to slow the pace of King Fayṣal's preparations for the Conference, a process that had begun at the meeting the King had with Humphreys, and the second was to wait until June, the date of the King's planned visit to London to hold talks with British officials, mainly with Sir John Simon, the Foreign Secretary.

Meanwhile, officials at the Ministry headed by George Rendel, director of the Eastern Department, were preparing a full report to the Foreign Secretary to guide him during his upcoming meeting with Fayṣal. The report was written at the behest of Humphreys, so that the King would be discouraged from proceeding forward with the Conference.[34]

First on the agenda was minimising the importance of considerations quoted by Fayṣal to justify the holding of the Conference, such as gaining support for Iraq's international position. Then there was the argument that the Conference might produce the opposite results, at least due to the possible French reaction, which could complicate ties between Iraq and Syria. Second on the agenda was the need to warn the King about the Conference being used as an opportunity to raise embarrassing questions about the Hashemite family, such as Emir 'Abdullah's position regarding Jewish settlements in Trans-Jordan, the relationship with King Ibn Sa'ūd, and the position vis-à-vis Arab political parties in Palestine.

It was also decided, according to the British document, that one of the Foreign Secretary's pretexts at the meeting with Fayṣal would be the possibility of the Conference providing troublemakers the opportunity to launch campaigns against foreigners, similar to those that had taken place during the Jerusalem Conference in 1931. This would not only pique European sensitivities, in France and Italy for example, against Islamic interests, it would also give the Hashemites' enemies the opportunity to disseminate their propaganda. Thus, rather than spread the spirit of friendship and cooperation among the Arab people, this might exacerbate conflicts already existing within Arab public opinion. It was also important to make the Iraqi King understand that both the Colonial Office and the British High Commissioner in Palestine would not agree to such a

Conference being held in Jerusalem; it could lead to various comparisons that, in the final analysis, would not be to his advantage.

Finally, it was important to use Fayṣal's hesitations, at the time, regarding whether to hold the Conference, or give up the idea entirely, by giving him the pretexts he needed. To help him make up his mind about abandoning his support for the Conference, he should hear directly from the Foreign Secretary, rather than just from the Ambassador in Baghdad.

Before the expected meeting between the Foreign Secretary and the King, the entire issue of Pan-Arabism was put under the microscope. The entire British bureaucracy, well known for its great accuracy, mobilised its resources at that moment to formulate a comprehensive vision of Britain's position vis-à-vis Arab unity. George Rendel, who had joined the diplomatic service 20 years earlier, and who now occupied the post of Director of the Eastern Department at the Foreign Office,[35] was in charge of coordination among various departments.

Contacts began with concerned departments to know their opinion about the idea, chief among which were, of course, the Colonial and India Offices. To assist them in their task, a long and very comprehensive memorandum, compiled as a working paper by the Eastern Department, was placed at their disposal.[36] The paper began with an unfair and unfavourable assessment of Arab unity, which, it said, was a very ambiguous term with multiple connotations!

The second paragraph confirms this judgement. In Rendel's or his department's view, this ambiguous term surfaces on special occasions, such as Arab or Muslim Conferences, as was the case at the Islamic Conference in Jerusalem, in the Autumn of 1931. It is used on these occasions as a means of public outcry against Western imperialism and Zionism, and is rarely the product of a mature concept of cooperation among peoples in domains other than education and propaganda, though it sometimes appears in issues of a political-religious nature, like the Ḥijāz Railway, the fate of the holy sites, etc. Arab unity in this sense is rather akin to Pan-Arabism, and therefore has no more significance than the Pan-Islamic concept of which one heard so much 20 years ago.

In the third paragraph, Rendel presents what he describes as a political and practical understanding of 'Arab unity', namely a union within a single state or within a confederation of self-governing states, made up of territories south of present-day Turkey, once part of the Ottoman Empire and predominantly inhabited by Arabs. He then moves on to the origins of the concept that was conceived during the war, and eventually became the ultimate objective of the Great Arab Revolt and the ideal to which the

Hashemite family aspired. There was no doubt in his mind that the two sons of Sharif Ḥussayn, Fayṣal and ʻAbdullah, never abandoned this dream despite subsequent developments that made it exceedingly difficult to achieve.

The most important among these 'subsequent developments', in the Eastern Department's opinion, was the rise to power of Ibn Saʻūd and his conquest of the major part of the Arabian Peninsula, including the former Kingdom of Ḥijāz, and the ensuing dynastic rivalry between the Saudis and the Hashemites. This rivalry made union between territories ruled by one or the other of these families almost impossible to imagine. However, although the memorandum expresses certain reservations in this domain, given the improvement in relations between Fayṣal and Saudi Arabia, it still believed that this improvement neither did away with the rivalry, nor strengthened the chance for a form of union between the two sides: 'While the Arabs are themselves divided into these two camps, any talk of Arab political unity in the wider sense must be illusory.'

He then attempts to define the British Government's position regarding the two camps. As far as the Hashemites are concerned, there is something to be said about their support for the Allies' cause, during World War I, not to mention various forms of cooperation with subsequent British policies. He mentions in particular the assistance provided by Emir ʻAbdullah of Trans-Jordan, at least on two separate occasions, namely for the Syrian Revolution in 1925, and the Palestinian Revolution in 1929. This places some responsibility on Britain towards him, a responsibility that also applies to his brother King Fayṣal of Iraq, by virtue of the Treaty of 1930. On the other hand, King ʻAbd al-ʻAzīz was not only content to build friendly relations with Britain, but proved to be one of the few rulers capable of establishing a stable government in the Arabian Peninsula. Furthermore, given Britain's considerable Muslim interests in India and elsewhere, it is important for the British Government to maintain friendly relations with the ruler of the holy sites of Islam. He concludes that the Government has no choice but to maintain a balanced relationship with the two parties.

He then enumerates various factors in the Arabian Peninsula that were not conducive to Arab unity. Among these was the independent Kingdom of the Yemen whose ruler was Imam Yaḥyā, whom he describes as short-sighted and quarrelsome, as well as minor Arab rulers, such as the sheikhs of Kuwait, Bahrain, Qatar and the Trucial Coast, who were extremely jealous of one another and very protective of their independence. He believes, however, that both the Sultanate of Muscat and Oman and the

Protectorate of Aden enjoyed a special position thanks to their particular relationship with Britain.

Although the Eastern Department's memorandum did not exclude the impact that the promoters of Arab unity could have on these countries, if their primary objective were to become a reality, which is what actually happened about a quarter of a century later with the rise of the nationalist tide in the 1950s and 1960s, it shows that British policies did indeed seek to sow division among the Arab countries. This is evident in paragraphs eight and nine of the memorandum, which later attained to great prominence.

In the first of these two paragraphs, the British Government reveals its intentions vis-à-vis the Gulf region, namely its efforts to prevent its small states from being absorbed by their powerful neighbours. It says that they should remain separate units under British control, and details various potential consequences.[37] In the second paragraph, the document admits that the London Government cannot allow the integration of Palestine in any comprehensive Arab union, in which the Arabs form the overwhelming majority, since it would mean Britain reneging on its commitment to establish a national home for the Jews in that country.[38]

As far as its own policies were concerned, the British Foreign Office reached the conclusion that, based on the aforementioned considerations, any eventual Arab unity should be limited to Iraq, Trans-Jordan and Syria. The memorandum then proceeds to undermine the chance of this so-called unity from ever taking place.

As for Trans-Jordan (despite a potential union with Iraq given that the two countries are ruled by the brothers Fayṣal and ʿAbdullah), on the one hand, the country is subject to the same mandate as Palestine, which makes it necessary to reject such a union. On the other, it could encourage the Jewish minority there to establish a settlement on its territory. The situation of Syria was, however, more complicated. Although it was true that France showed signs of moving towards signing a treaty with that country, and that Arab Nationalists in both Iraq and Syria were enthusiastic over unity between their two countries, the fact that a treaty between France and Syria, similar to the Anglo-Iraqi Treaty, would place each of these countries under the aegis of a different power could lead to serious political complications.

The specific conclusions inherent in the last paragraphs of this important memorandum constitute, in fact, the main features of Britain's policy towards Arab unity, at that time, and therefore also towards holding a Conference in Baghdad.

First: The memorandum states that the idea of a political union along European lines is inapplicable, not to mention all the geographical and human impediments, which it proceeds to describe with much pessimism. It states:

> Southern Arabia, although it appears to possess a certain unity from a first glance at the map, is really more accurately described as an archipelago of human settlements in a sea of desert, inhabited by tribes who are driven by the exigencies of desert life into becoming, as it were, land pirates ceaselessly preying on each other.

Second: If the question of the Conference is raised with King Fayṣal, the British Government's position must be the encouragement of peaceful economic cooperation, and development of close cultural ties between the Arab countries, which would void the expected Conference of any political context.[39]

On 22 June the scheduled meeting between His Majesty King Fayṣal, King of Iraq, and Sir John Simon, the British Foreign Secretary, took place at the Foreign Office in London. The two sides discussed a number of issues of interest to both parties, including the Iraqi Railroad Authority, British Judges in Iraq, the palm groves owned by the sheikhs of Kuwait in al-Muḥammarah, contracts of the British Military delegation in Iraq and, finally, the Conference scheduled to take place in Baghdad.[40]

While discussing the subject of the palm groves owned by the sheikhs of Kuwait in Muḥammarah, Fayṣal took the opportunity to bring up the subject of Arab aspirations. He began by saying that he would not go too far back in his recollection of the history of these aspirations, or of Britain's position towards them, but would simply mention the conversation that took place in 1921 between himself and Churchill, then Minister for the Colonies, before he left England as candidate to the throne of Iraq. He said that Churchill had explained to him then what the future king's policy should be, a policy he had approved at the time, and since then one which he had pursued to the letter.[41]

He then went on to say that the phase that made these policies necessary had now ended, and a new phase had begun. The way he saw it, the policies proposed for this phase should reflect the current alliance between Iraq and the British Government. He said that Iraq was considering securing for itself access to the Mediterranean Sea and that the road could go either through Syria or through Palestine, and added that the Iraqi Government was vacillating between the two options. As far as Syria was concerned, the way the French were governing the country did not give the impression that there will be a government eager to fulfil Arab aspirations anytime soon. As for the Palestinian option, and despite his personal appreciation for the British Government's good intentions, the exponential growth of Zionism raised many doubts regarding the future of the Arabs in Palestine, and made it unrealistic for Iraq to choose it as a conduit to the Mediterranean.

According to Fayṣal, these were all solvable problems if the Arabs were to work in tandem with British policies. There was a growing desire among the Iraqi people and among its representatives in Parliament and the Government to assist the Arabs in Syria. He said that one specific proposal in this regard was that Iraq, as a member of the League of Nations, would oppose France by calling for the application of Article 22 of the League's Charter to Syria. As long as this country remained under the French Mandate in its then present form, it would be an obstacle to an eventual Mediterranean point of access.

Since Sir John Simon could not directly respond to all those arguments, he promised to submit the Iraqi proposals to his colleagues at the Foreign Office. His attitude changed completely, however, when it was time to discuss the convening of the Conference in Baghdad as he was quite ready for that.

The British Foreign Secretary was the first to raise the issue; he expounded on the previously agreed British view, and described how the convening of such a Conference would seriously complicate Iraq's relations with its neighbours. Fayṣal's response was that for him working with the British Government to achieve Arab aspirations was more important than convening the Conference, and that if this objective were achieved, he would do his best to scuttle the Conference.[42] After the King's return to Baghdad, the British policy of applying pressure on him to prevent the Conference from convening in the Iraqi capital continued, as evident from the report of Sir Francis Humphreys, Baghdad's British Ambassador, regarding his meeting with the King, on 18 July 1933.

Humphreys had broached the issue and told Fayṣal that he would be making a serious mistake if he agreed to hold the Conference in Baghdad, or anywhere else for that matter, and that convening it would raise his neighbours' suspicions. The King's response was that the idea behind holding the Conference was to express the Arabs' feelings and promote Arab unity, and that in light of the British position, all he could promise was to intervene to prevent the Conference promoters from holding it that autumn.[43] Barely a few weeks after this meeting, Fayṣal died, and the idea of holding the Conference in Baghdad was buried with him; in fact, the present documentary study shows that it was buried well before he was!

Notes

1. F.O. 371/15282, Weekly Appreciation Summary no. 7, 18 February 1931.
2. *Al-Ahram*, 2 December 1931.
3. F.O. 371/15282, the Residency, Cairo, to the Right Honourable Arthur Henderson, 27 February 1931.
4. F.O. 371/15282, the Residency, Cairo, to Sr. L. Oliphant, 12 June 1931.
5. F.O. 371/15282, Cypher Telegram from the Secretary of State to the Government of India, dated 18 November 1931.
6. *Al-Ahram*, 5 December 1931.
7. *Al-Ahram*, 7 December 1931.
8. F.O. 371/15283, Italian Chargé d'Affaires (Conversation), 16 December 1931.
9. F.O. 407/221, enclosure in no. 25 – Egyptian Personalities.
10. *Al-Ahram*, 18 December 1931.
11. F.O. 371/15283, from the High Commissioner in Palestine, to the Secretary of State for Colonies, 17 December 1931.
12. F.O. 371/15283, from Foreign Office to the Italian Embassy, 18 December 1931.
13. F.O. 371/16009, the Pan-Islamic Movement.
14. Ibid.
15. F.O. 371/16009, the Residency, Cairo, to Sir John Simon, 26 November 1931.
16. 'Ādil Ḥasan Ghonaim, *Al-Ḥarakah al-Waṭaniyah al-Filisṭīnīyah 1917–36* (Cairo: The General Egyptian Book Agency, 1974), p. 229.
17. F.O. 371/16009 Colonial Office-Moslem Conference in Jerusalem, 21 May 1932.
18. The committee comprised Ḍīyā' el-Dīn al-Ṭabṭabā'ī, Secretary General, Riyāḍ al-Ṣulḥ, Assistant Secretary General, Muḥammad 'Alī Pāshā, Treasurer, Ḥājj Amīn al-Ḥusaynī, 'Abd al-'Azīz al-Tha'ālibī, Sa'īd Shāmil Bey and Nabīh al-'Aẓmah members. See *Al-Ahram*, 18 December 1931.
19. F.O. 371/16009, the same document.
20. Ṣalāḥ Al-'Aqqād, 'Najīb 'Āzūrī and his Political Views', Economy, Policy and Trade Magazine (Cairo, 1960), pp. 17–19.
21. *Al Ahram*, 18 December 1931.
22. Wamīḍ Jamāl Naẓmī, Ghānim Muḥammad Ṣāliḥ and Shafīq 'Abd al-Rāziq, *al-Taṭawwur al-Siyāsī al-Mu'āṣir fī al-'Irāq* ([Baghdad]: Baghdad University, Faculty of Law and Politics, Political Science Department [198–??]).
23. F.O. 371/15364, Sir P. Gunliffe-Lister to Sir F. Humphreys (Baghdad), 27 November 1931.
24. *Al Ahram*, 18 December 1931.
25. *Al Ahram*, 27 December 1931.
26. F.O. 371/15364, Morgan to Sir John Simon, 23 December 1931.
27. The document refers to the downfall of Fayṣal's monarchy in Damascus, during World War I, when the French attacked the Syrian capital in 1920, and defeated the Arab force defending the city in the famous battle of Maysalūn.
28. Ibid.

29. F.O. 371/16011, Extract from Palestine Police Secret Appreciation Summary, 2 December 1932.

30. F.O. 371/10611, Sir F. Humphreys to Sir John Simon, 21 December 1932.

31. Fāḍil Ḥussayn, *Mushkilat al-Mūṣul: Dirāsah fī al-Diblumāsīyah al-'Irāqīyah-al-Inglīzīyah-al-Turkīyah wa fī al-Ra'y al-'Ām,* 2nd ed. (Baghdad: Maṭba'at As'ad, 1967), pp. 184–7.

32. F.O. 371/16011.

33. Ibid.

34. F.O. 371/16855, Proposed Conference, 13 June 1933.

35. George Rendel (Sir), 'The Sword and the Olive: Recollections of Diplomacy and the Foreign Service, 1913–54' (London: J. Murray, 1957).

36. F.O. 371/16855, Position of His Majesty's Government towards the question of Arab Unity, 13 June 1933.

37. 'It is a basic principle of the policy of His Majesty's Government in the Middle East that these states should not be absorbed by any of their powerful neighbours, but should remain as far as possible separate units under effective British control. The development of inter-imperial air communications, both civil and military, has in the last few years given this well-established principle a new importance. In the case of Kuwait, both King Fayṣal of Iraq and King Ibn Sa'ūd of Saudi Arabia have at various times shown signs of wishing to acquire a hold over the territory, which would be a useful acquisition to either. Both on treaty grounds, however, and on grounds of imperial policy, it is important that Kuwait should not be absorbed by either Saudi Arabia or Iraq. Similarly, as regards Bahrain, apart from our treaty obligations to protect the Sheikh against aggression, it would be definitely against British interests that the islands should be absorbed by either Saudi Arabia or Persia.'

38. 'His Majesty's Government are equally precluded from allowing Palestine to be absorbed in any way in any kind of predominantly Arab union, if only in view of their deep commitment to the policy of the Jewish national home, quite apart from the obligations to the other non-Arab or non-Muslim communities and interests in Palestine proper.'

39. F.O. 371/16855.

40. F.O. 371/16855, Memorandum-Points under discussion with King Fayṣal and his Ministers at present in London.

41. F.O. 371/16855, Conversation between Secretary of State and King Fayṣal, 22 June 1933.

42. Ibid.

43. F.O. 371/16855, From Sir F. Humphreys (Baghdad) to Mr Sterendle Bennett (Colonial Office), 5 October 1933.

CHAPTER 4

Between Arab Unity and Pan-Arabism 1936–41

On 29 May 1941, British Foreign Secretary Anthony Eden delivered an important speech at Mansion House, the residence of the Mayor of London. In it he said:

> The Arab world has made great strides since the settlement reached at the end of the last war, and many Arab thinkers desire for the Arab peoples a greater degree of unity than they now enjoy. In reaching out towards this unity, they hope for our support. No such appeal from our friends should go unanswered. It seems to me both natural and right that the cultural and economic ties between the Arab countries, and political ties too, should be strengthened. His Majesty's Government for their part will give their support to any scheme that commands general approval.[1]

As far as some observers and scholars were concerned, this declaration became necessary due to developments relevant to World War II, which had broken out less than two years earlier, and they tried to interpret it on that basis. However, British documents tell otherwise, and they also constitute an important chapter in Britain's position towards Arab unity, a chapter that had begun five years earlier, in 1936.

Between 1935 and 1936, the Arab world witnessed momentous events especially in Syria and Egypt, not to mention instability in Iraq and disturbances in Palestine, which escalated to such an extent that they had become a fully-fledged revolution.

In Syria, the treaty that France tried to impose on the country at the end of 1934 led to serious disturbances in Damascus due to the many restrictions it contained. The Nationalist members of Parliament succeeded in forming a majority against the treaty, forcing the High Commissioner to suspend Parliament.

The situation became even more complicated when protests against the government that had agreed to sign the treaty increased, forcing it to resign. Instead of withdrawing the offending treaty, the French High Commissioner appointed a new government to suppress the nationalist movement, only to make things worst. The French resorted to violence in reaction to these events, attacking the offices of the National Bloc, arresting its leaders and putting many of them in jail, all of which gave the impression that Syria was on the verge of an all-out revolution.[2]

In Egypt, the winter of 1935–6 witnessed serious student demonstrations, known as the 1935 events. These began as the result of British Government intervention in the country's internal affairs by insisting on nullifying the provisions of the 1923 Constitution, abrogated five years earlier. The British intervention came in support of the Palace and the Government of Tawfīq Nasīm.

Anti-British resistance shifted from simply calling for a boycott of British goods to demonstrations by university and secondary-school students, and eventually to large-scale clashes with police that caused many casualties among the demonstrators. The High Commissioner's Residence in the Egyptian capital was eager to contain this movement and re-establish peace in the country.[3]

In Iraq, the period that followed King Fayṣal's death in 1933 and the ascension of King Ghāzī to the throne was rather unstable, mainly due to the absence of Fayṣal's well-balanced character that had previously served to ensure the country's stability. Among the symptoms of the country's instability was the intense competition over power among prominent political personalities, resulting in successive short government tenures of no more than six months on average. Moreover, and during that same period, sectarian and tribal revolts spread throughout the country, with the Assyrians rebelling in the north, in 1933, and tribes in the middle of the country soon following suit.

The Iraqi central government's frequent use of the army to suppress these revolts provided some of its leaders with the opportunity to interfere in the country's political affairs. They tried to achieve their aims by seizing power, which is precisely what transpired in 1936 with the coup of Bakr Ṣidqī.[4]

In Palestine, a new wave of resistance by the Arabs against British policies began, especially after the exponential increase in Jewish immigration to the country and the transfer of large areas of land from Arab to Jewish hands that had been encouraged by the resolutions of the Zionist Conference held in Prague in 1933. Soon afterwards, a number of Arab political parties were established, most of which soon came together to form what became known as the 'Party's Committee'. The latter Committee's first act was to hold a major strike, which it called for on 26 October 1935, in protest against the Mandate Government's policy of ignoring Zionist attempts to turn Palestine into an arms depot. More important, however, were the activities of the Arab Resistance Movement that had resorted to armed tactics in November of that same year. Typical among these was the movement founded by Sheikh 'Izz al-Dīn al-Qassām, killed a few days after announcing the birth of his movement. News of Qassām's martyrdom spread further afield, causing considerable agitation among the people.[5]

In the last few weeks of 1935 and the beginning of the following year, the crisis reached the threshold of a revolution, as evidenced by the call to reject cooperation via a variety of methods, such as refusal to pay taxes, mass-resignation of Arab employees and the formation of armed resistance groups.[6]

In response to all these developments, British officials turned once again to the issue of Arab unity in the belief that alluding to it would help mitigate the prevailing hostile atmosphere in the country. This British exercise started with two different reports, one issued by the British Embassy's Residence in Baghdad, and the other by the High Commissioner's Residency in Cairo. It is worth noting that both reports bear the same date, 24 February 1936, which is indicative that British officials in the Iraqi and the Egyptian capitals wrote them upon the instructions of the Foreign Office in London.

The first report, entitled 'Arab Unity', was written by Sir A. C. Clark Kerr, the British Ambassador in Baghdad,[7] and begins with an admission regarding the recent revival of Arab Nationalism among the Iraqi public. He attributes this revival to the disturbances that had taken place in Syria, Egypt and Palestine, over the previous months, news of which had occupied large sections of Iraqi newspapers accompanied by comments of the editors. This heightened the Iraqi public's need for cooperation among the Arab people.

The ambassador in Baghdad went on to say that attention to this particular aspect had increased even more thanks to a visit to Iraq by a number of Arab personalities. He cited as an example the visit, during the month of February, by Emille al-Ghūrī from Palestine and 'Abd al-Qādir al-Māzinī from Egypt, who were both very warmly received by Arab and

Islamic clubs and associations, with speeches extolling the virtues of the concept of Pan-Arabism. What further strengthened feelings for the Arab common destiny, in his opinion, was the recent arrival in the Iraqi capital of Dr al-Sanhūrī to assume the position of Dean of the Faculty of Law, as well as a number of Egyptian professors and teachers hired by the Ministry of Education to work in its academic institutions. He remarked that the latter were very warmly received as symbols of growing understanding between the brotherly Egyptian and Iraqi people.

Clark Kerr observed that the arrival of the Egyptian teachers coincided with that of a large number of Yemeni students to study in Iraq, and that of Sheikh Yūsuf Yāsīn from Saudi Arabia. News spread about negotiations between the latter and the Iraqi Government regarding the signature of an Arab Charter. The British Ambassador did not forget to mention the Sultan of Muscat's request that the Baghdad Government send him an expert in planting palm trees, and how such a development increases the public's interest in Arab nationalism.

Just as the British Embassy in Baghdad's report was interested in the presence of Arabs in Iraq, it was also interested in the presence of Iraqi nationals in other Arab countries. In this context, its author follows the trip by 30 Iraqi students from the Faculties of Law and Education, during that same month of February 1936, to a number of Arab countries, including Syria, Palestine and Egypt.

What is noteworthy in this report is the British document's perception of change in the way the Arabs express their understanding of what unity means. For while in the past it mostly meant convening conferences, a notion held by some activists or members of political organisations, like the Muslim Conference, or even by certain rulers, like efforts to hold the Conference, by the mid-1930s it became more of a populist notion.

Clark Kerr notes this change in the sixth and seventh paragraphs of his report. In the sixth he says that it is quite noticeable that talk about organising an Arab Unity Conference, King Fayṣal's preferred option, has considerably decreased. In the seventh, he writes that it seems that the movement's current advocates understand that before considering any kind of real political unity among the Arabs, they should first spread a spirit of common aspirations and ideas. They should therefore seize every opportunity to spread the principles of Arab brotherhood and pride in the Arab race, and raise awareness regarding joint action to achieve national freedom and future prosperity.[8]

A final point about the memorandum of the British Ambassador in Baghdad is that it illustrates where Britain believed the Arab world's centre of power lay at that particular point in time. Clark Kerr sent copies of his memorandum to the British High Commissioners in Cairo and Jerusalem, the Minister Plenipotentiary in Jeddah, the Consul General in Beirut, and to the British Consuls in Damascus and Aleppo.

* * *

Though a brief one, the second memorandum written on the same day by Sir Myles Lampson, the British High Commissioner in Cairo, included a long addendum by the Sudan Agency in Cairo. This Agency had replaced the Sudan Intelligence[9] when the latter ceased its activities as an operation that had lasted from 1898 to 1924, due to the expulsion of the Egyptian Army from the Sudan in the wake of the famous incidents of that particular year: the assassination of the Sirdar Lee Stack, Governor General of the Sudan, and its ensuing repercussions.

The Sudan Agency in Cairo followed the same precedent and system as the Sudan Intelligence before it had done; that is, it did not hire a single Egyptian or Sudanese national, despite what its name might have implied; therefore, all its officials were British, with a few collaborators from the Levant. They also had well-placed sources of information, in various places, to help them prepare their regular weekly or monthly reports that monitored public opinion, including the one Sir Myles Lampson relied on when preparing his own.

The Agency blamed the disturbances, which by then had spread to Damascus, Aleppo, Hama and Homs, not only on poor French administrative skills, but also on the general upheaval in the Muslim Arab World; this required a re-evaluation of the political future of the Near East.

The report then traces the origins of Pan-Arabism and blames it on the spread of education and on Syria's close contact with Europe. This had served to heighten national sentiments severely suppressed by the Ḥamīdī regime, sentiments that had finally and successfully been heard and which seemed on the verge of future prospects under the federal regime.[10]

The authors of the Sudan Agency's memorandum addressed an issue that few others had addressed previously, namely the sense that the British and the French had betrayed the Arabs' trust. It talks of a widespread notion among the Arabs that by establishing a Christian state in Syria – namely greater Lebanon – and a Zionist state in Palestine, the two imperialist powers seek to establish buffer zones separating the Syrians and Iraqis from the Egyptians, Sudanese and other Muslim African nations. The people of the Fertile Crescent in Syria and those in Iraq have begun to look upon the anti-British movement in Egypt with increasing sympathy and interest.

It seems that the British officials who wrote the memorandum in the Sudan had been deeply influenced by conditions under which they were living; that is, conditions where religious affiliation played a major role in determining such matters. What they failed to realise, however, was that the Christians of the Levant were the first promoters of the nascent Pan-Arabism, which explains why they continued to advance their own interpretation of events up until the end of the memorandum.

Next, the writers addressed the changes that had taken place in recent years, and how advances in methods of communication had brought the Arabs closer together. They gave as an example the fact that Cairo newspapers could be read on the day of their publication in Syria and Palestine, and on the following day in Mesopotamia. They then noted that a considerable number of young people from all over the Arab world were getting together in various academic institutions, like the American University in Beirut, where they maintained contact, exercised their freedom of expression and looked forward to achieving their future aspirations.

The report's authors go on to say that, as a consequence, educated elements now lead various political movements in the Arab world, and the only thing lacking is a leader able to coordinate among them, which is exactly what King Fayṣal of Iraq had tried to do. His death had left a large gap as far as such coordination was concerned, and it seemed that the situation would remain unchanged as long as France were to continue its hegemonic policy in Syria, and Britain to continue its suppression of the Pan-Arab Movement in Palestine. The state of instability was also envisioned to continue so long as students remained politically active.

As far as Syria is concerned, the report's authors were of the opinion that French mismanagement only added fuel to the fire, and that the ongoing disturbances were a consequence of the rising despair regarding continuing efforts by the French to quash all attempts by the Damascus Government to gain a measure of independence. They predicted imminent violent and bloody incidents in that country.[11]

Commenting on the memorandum, Sir Myles Lampson, the British High Commissioner in Cairo, arrived at three separate conclusions. The first concerned the influence that Egypt wielded on Syria and Palestine and the cultural status it had attained throughout the Arab world thanks to its press, as evidenced by the impact that tensions in Egypt had had on these two countries during the past several years. The second conclusion concerned the latest press reports regarding widespread disturbances in France's North African territories, which Lampson saw as a natural reaction to what was taking place in the Eastern Mediterranean Arab countries. In his third conclusion, he recommended that the British Government place the establishment of peace in Egypt high on its list of priorities, and that it try to isolate the Egyptians from the anti-European climate that was prevailing in neighbouring countries.[12]

British Foreign Office departments were interested in the contents of the report, especially in light of the month-long strike that gripped various Syrian cities, and asked the High Commissioner's Residency in the Egyptian capital to provide them with additional reports on the issue. The Residency responded by asking the Sudan Agency to prepare a second report on the same subject.[13]

The major part of this new report was devoted to a review of developments in Syria from the early World War I years up to 1936. The High Commissioner in Cairo found nothing new to add and said as much to the Foreign Secretary when he submitted the report to him.

That in which Sir Myles Lampson and his officials at the Sudan Agency were most interested was the apparent dramatic shift in French Government policy towards Syria. This shift was reflected in its agreement to meet with a delegation of Syrian national leaders in Paris, after the 50-day strike was over, marking a 180-degree turn-around in French policies towards the National Movement. On the one hand, the focus of the report in question was an attempt to interpret this shift and, on the other, to foresee its impact on the Arab world.

The High Commissioner attributes the shift in French policy to three factors: French fears of the deteriorating conditions in Europe, given that the policy change occurred only a few days before the Rhine incidents[14]; the Syrian uncharacteristic and unexpected determination to continue the strike for a long time; and the worldwide propaganda campaign launched by the Syrian National Movement. Moreover, the strike had attracted considerable attention all over the Arab world, as was evidenced by the official protest lodged by the Iraqi Parliament and the campaign in Egyptian newspapers, not to mention the heightened sentiments in Palestine.

The report noted various signs of Arab jubilation over France's willingness, after all, to negotiate with the real representatives of the Syrian National Movement. In Iraq, the rejoicing turned into great celebrations coinciding with King Ghāzī's birthday – celebrations that soon spread to most Syrian cities, including Damascus and Beirut.

In Egypt, a campaign of contributions was launched in aid of those aggrieved by the incidents in Syria. The High Commissioner in the Egyptian capital drew attention to Emir ʿUmar Tussun's contribution of

LE 50, not because of its considerable amount, but due to its significance. The Emir had never shown much concern for the Pan-Arab Movement, and had hitherto devoted his political efforts to the service of the Ottoman Caliphate, until its demise in 1924, after which he worked hard to revive it. The Emir and his friends declared that the only way to confront European imperialism was to agree on an Arab charter.

Also in Egypt, an Iraqi parliamentary and student delegation was greeted with warm hospitality and much interest, and speeches and poems were delivered rejoicing in the spirit of unity among the Arab states.

Lampson approved most of the report's contents and sent a copy to the British Ambassador in Baghdad, since it addressed the Arabs' intention to form a united front against European imperialism. He admitted that the new atmosphere in the region would undoubtedly have an impact on the proposed Anglo-Egyptian negotiations.[15]

A review of relevant British documents confirms that the London Government had placed its representatives in Cairo, Baghdad and Damascus on full alert, to keep a close eye on the fast-developing Pan-Arab movement. This material record presents an excellent opportunity to become acquainted with the very interesting British attitude towards Arab unity.

Pan-Islamism-Arabism

From the Egyptian capital came three long reports written in the five months between the beginning of April and the beginning of September 1936. They reveal the main reasons that led the British Government to reconsider its policy towards Arab unity and, more importantly, to rectify its perceptions in this regard.

Sir Myles Lampson, the British High Commissioner in Cairo, sent a letter dated 8 April 1936, to which he attached a report written by the European Department at the Egyptian Ministry of the Interior. The said department was established in the aftermath of the 28 February 1922 declaration accepting Egypt's independence with four reservations, however, including the need to protect 'foreigners and minorities', the intention being to find appropriate means of providing them with necessary protection. The department's prerogatives were expanded later on to cover all political security-related issues, so much so that a 'Special Section' was established and became notorious for pursuing nationalists in Egypt, at the time.

The above department's report, dated 1 April, says that one of its agents attended a tea party, organised by the Muslim Brotherhood Association, in honour of members of the Syrian al-Maqāṣid Charitable Association on a visit to Cairo. According to the report, 200 Muslim Brothers attended the party, most of whom were students at al-Azhar University. Speeches were delivered calling for the revival of past Arab glories, and the expulsion of imperialism from the region. It goes on to say that the speeches were interspersed with quotations from the *Qur'ān* and the *ḥadīth* (transmitted accounts of the sayings and doings of the Prophet Muḥammad), calling on people to choose martyrdom for God and country.

The members of the Syrian Association responded in kind, and delivered fiery speeches calling for cleansing the region of British and French imperialism. They said that the Arabs should be proud of their race, just like the Germans, Italians and British were, and one of them did not forget to even single-out the Italians for attack.

In his speech, the President of the al-Maqāṣid Association promised that, as soon as they returned home, he and members of his delegation would begin spreading the principles of the Muslim Brotherhood, form a united front to confront imperialism and work at reviving past Arab glories. The celebration ended with cheers of 'Arabs above all others'!

When Sir Lampson submitted this report to the British Foreign Office, he appended a personal note to the effect that the fiery and fanatical tone of the speeches attacking imperialism and calling for independence had come from both Egyptians and Syrians alike.[16] In the same context, the Residency of the High Commissioner in Egypt was equally interested in the Muslim Brotherhood Association's activities regarding the Palestinian issue. This was the subject of the letter Lampson sent to London on 28 May of that same year, including a report written, this time around, by the Public Security Department at the Egyptian Ministry of the Interior.

The report states that the Muslim Brotherhood Association has begun establishing branches in Palestine, over and above those already established in a number of major Egyptian cities. It also states that the Association is calling for a return to the purity of Islam, and for cleansing all Islamic countries of all European presence. It added that the Brotherhood's leaders had recently published several articles in the Egyptian newspapers attacking British policy in Palestine. The report goes on to say that, at a secret meeting on 16 May the decision was taken that Ḥasan al-Bannā, the Association's president, would call upon all Egyptians, both Muslims and Coptic Christians, to defend the al-Aqṣā

Mosque and start enlisting persons in a demonstration of support for the Palestinian cause. It said that the participants in the meeting had reached a number of other decisions, including sending telegrams to the High Commissioners in Egypt and Palestine, the British Foreign Office and the League of Nations, stating their support for the Pan-Arab cause. They also decided to publish articles in the local press calling upon 'Alūbah Pāshā, Emir ʿUmar Tussun and Dr 'Abd al-Ḥamīd Saʿīd to form various groups in support of the Palestinians, collect contributions in mosques and schools and send representatives to Palestine to keep an eye on the situation.[17] It is interesting to note that the report's authors chose to term it the 'Pan-Islamic Arab Movement', which shows a certain confusion regarding these two concepts, a confusion which the British Embassy in Baghdad would take care to dispel later on.

While the Residency of the High Commissioner in Cairo was sending successive reports to the British Foreign Office, an event drew everyone's attention further towards the East. A letter had arrived from the British Ambassador in Baghdad stating that 15 members of the Iraqi Senate and Parliament, and a number of Iraqi personalities, had visited Syria, Palestine and Egypt, and had returned to the Iraqi capital on 1 April.

Clark Kerr's letter indicates that members of the delegation were received warmly wherever they went, and that they in turn stated their intention to do whatever was necessary to strengthen religious and social links between Iraq and the rest of the Arab world. The report also said that members of the delegation had delivered a number of speeches in which they underlined the importance of unity among the Arab countries, and that Iraq would provide all forms of assistance to its Arab brethren in their struggle for independence.

The letter also specifically indicates that the speeches of some delegation members, such as that of Saʿīd Thābit – Mosul's representative in Nāblus, had gone over the (acceptable) limit. This prompted the British Ambassador in Baghdad to warn Prime Minister Nūrī Pāshā al-Saʿīd that if anyone else were to do likewise, the Iraqi visitors to Palestine would no longer be able to enjoy the warm welcome or the assistance they had previously received from the authorities.

At the end of the letter, Clark Kerr expresses fear over rumours about the intention of a number of influential groups from Syria, Palestine and Egypt to visit Iraq. He also draws attention to rumours regarding the intention of some Iraqi senators to undertake an unofficial visit to the Gulf region. The level of British apprehension regarding these movements is in abundant evidence, given that the British Ambassador in Baghdad saw it necessary to send copies of the letter also to the High Commissioners in Cairo and Jerusalem, the Minister Plenipotentiary in Jeddah, the Consul General in Beirut and the British Consuls in each of Damascus and Aleppo.[18]

Pouring over the Concepts

After reading the report of his colleague in the Egyptian capital, the British Ambassador in Baghdad quickly acted to dispel any confusion regarding various relevant concepts, a fact quite evident from the long memorandum he sent to his Government, on 28 May 1936. He began by referring to the misunderstanding in question, saying: 'I think it is perhaps a little misleading to use the term Pan-Islamic when discussing the modern movement which springs from Arab Nationalism.'[19] He added that while recent efforts to revive the spirit of Islam have had a religious and universal character, Arab Nationalism has maintained its political and regional character. Moreover, although the two movements share a number of common elements, this does not justify dealing with them as one and the same phenomenon.

He then moves on to a diagnosis of Pan-Islamism after the abolition of the Caliphate in Turkey in 1924, and the latter country's adoption of a secular system, which deprived the Islamic world from the central body about which Muslims used to rally. He said that there had been several subsequent attempts to revive the Caliphate since that time: once, when Ḥussayn the King of Ḥijāz proclaimed himself Caliph in that same year; and another time during the Cairo Conference of 1926 when the issue of the Caliphate was raised. Both attempts had failed. The Islamic World Conference, which convened in Mecca upon the invitation of King 'Abd al-'Azīz, in the summer of 1926, also produced no results worthy of mention.

This important memorandum blames the failure to establish a body representing the entire Islamic world on the suspicions with which Muslim governments viewed such attempts. The Turkish and Persian governments viewed this trend as a reactionary and obscurantist movement, while the Kingdoms of Iraq and Saudi Arabia were unhappy with the fact that they would not have a major influence on it. Moreover, while Egypt stood aside of the issue, Afghanistan was too busy with its own internal strife, meaning ultimately that the Arab countries had no option but to rally round their respective flags.

In the effort to distinguish between the Pan-Islamist and Arab Nationalist Movements, Clark Kerr's memorandum says that the Arab

National Movement, which seeks political unity among all the Arabs, has charted for itself a different path forward. Arab national sentiments, which Emir Fayṣal and Laurence had embodied in the Ḥijāz, did not elicit the appropriate response from other Arab countries. In the heart of the Arabian Peninsula, namely in the Najd and Ḥā'il, people were quite unmoved; in Mesopotamia, the peoples of the desert regions knew nothing about the Arab Revolt, and, in Egypt, the debate centred round whether the country was even Arab at all. In Syria and Palestine, the Revolt elicited a significant reaction, but the tight Turkish grip over the region prevented the populace from giving it effective support.

The British Ambassador in Baghdad believed that the dream of Arab unity under the Hashemite throne had encountered two setbacks. The first was when King 'Abd al-'Azīz conquered the Ḥijāz in 1925, and the second upon the death of King Fayṣal, in 1933. The latter had worked throughout his life to make this dream a reality, though later on, the men who helped him lead his troops, and were later to become his ministers, developed a new Arab unity plan that, at the time, had lent the movement its main characteristics.

Clark Kerr believed that the core of Pan-Arabism had shifted to Iraq, where political leaders were now masters of their country's destiny. Both Palestine and Syria were still under a Mandate, and as long as this continued the attention of the leaders of these two countries was liable to stay focussed on the local struggle for independence. For its part, although it was free of foreign domination, Saudi Arabia was considered too backward and inward-looking to be able to take the lead, which left Egypt, which, like Palestine, was too involved in tending to its own relationship with Britain.

Based on the above conclusions, one can understand the Iraqi leaders' efforts to strengthen national sentiments among the Arab people through incessant propaganda and various attempts to forge close personal relationships between the leaders of major Arab countries. As for Iraq, Egypt, Saudi Arabia and Palestine, their dream seemed more realistic than that; they did not plan for the establishment of an Arab Empire under a single monarch, but rather a federal set-up that would allow, at the same time, each country a wide margin of autonomy. This way, the hope was that there would be a state 'which might perhaps stretch some day from the Persian border to the Atlantic'.[20]

The significance of this important memorandum by the British Embassy in Baghdad lies in the fact that it is the first serious attempt to distinguish between the Pan-Arab and Pan-Islamic Movements, and its revelation of policies that reflect the Iraqi leaders' new understanding of Arabism. It addresses the Iraqi-Saudi negotiations that demonstrate a desire to conclude an Arab defence pact and to forge a joint Arab foreign policy, provided these were to be preceded by efforts to formulate a joint Arab cultural and economic policy.

Clark Kerr ends his unique memorandum on an optimistic note, as far as the Arab Nationalists' attitude towards the British Government is concerned. He believed that the bitterness that the Arabs once felt towards the British Government's failure to honour the promise of the MacMahon-Ḥussayn correspondence was almost on the verge of becoming a thing of the past. He added that British policies in Iraq, the friendship with Ibn Sa'ūd, the position towards the Abyssinian crisis,[21] and increasing hopes for a resolution in Egypt, inspired confidence in the goodwill of the British Government. As proof, he said that he received information to the effect that the Arab Nationalists in Syria were lauding the success of British policy in Iraq. The only issue that still affected relations between Britain and the Arab Nationalists, however, was the Jewish presence in Palestine, although most Iraqi leaders had not yet lost hope in the British Government's desire to reach an equitable solution to the problem.[22]

The British Ambassador in Baghdad arrived at the conclusion that he saw no reason why the Arab Nationalist Movement should harbour enmity towards Britain or attempt to hurt British interests. However, if the situation in Palestine were to continue to deteriorate, only then could there be uncomfortable consequences for British interests in major Arab countries.[23]

Almost at the same time, G. MacKereth, the British Consul in Damascus, wrote a memorandum on the same subject entitled 'Arab Nationalism', also upon the request of the British Foreign Office, offering an entirely different perspective to that of his colleague in Baghdad. Aside from the long historical introduction in which he traces the path of Arabism since 1905, he addresses the meeting convened in 1932 by Arab Nationalists from different countries in Jerusalem, under the leadership of Iraqi President Yāsīn al-Hāshimī. The participants had followed the advice of the late Egyptian leader Sa'ad Zaghlūl and avoided raising religious issues to 'deprive imperialist policies of the main weapon used to subjugate Eastern peoples'. Their agenda included the establishment of an Arab Zollverein,[24] currency unification, the establishment of an Arab Bank and the abolition of entry visas. Once achieved, Iraq, Syria and Trans-Jordan would have one flag and unify their postage stamps.

The outcome of this preparatory meeting was to be discussed at a conference held in Baghdad, but the conference never took place due to conflicts among participating countries. MacKereth omitted to mention the role that Britain had played in precipitating these conflicts in the first place.

He then enumerated the obstacles that hindered Arab Nationalism in a manner that clearly evidences his lack of enthusiasm for it. These include the existence of separate Arab states in Mesopotamia, Syria and Arabia, coupled with growing chauvinism among their respective populations; in his opinion, national sentiments were developing steadily, even if at a slow pace. Eventually, each of these countries would have its own administrative system along European lines, a system over which the officials would be anxious to maintain their authority and protect their personal interests. One should also take into account the significant conflict between the political and legal systems, not to mention the eagerness with which they might safeguard the borders drawn between them during the war.

The British Consul in Damascus does not forget to allude, on this occasion, to local jealousy of Arab national elements who occupy high positions in their countries. He gave Egypt as an example, where elements from the Levant occupied a number of high positions within the British administration, causing the Egyptians to continue to see them as foreigners.

MacKereth pauses here, for he believes that Egypt's attitude towards Arab Nationalism is rather ambiguous, given that it showed no willingness at all to shoulder any collective responsibility for an eventual Arab or Islamic confederation. He also believes that the Egyptians had not yet decided whether they were Arab, Pharaonic or some other identity along Western lines, as yet undefined.

Still, MacKereth could not deny the impact that the spread of modern Arabic literature and the development of journalism had had on strengthening the concept of Arabism, or the essential role Egypt had played in transforming classical Arabic from an almost dead language, like Latin, into a living language read by all Arabs. He recounts a scene he often witnesses in Damascene coffee houses, where one of the customers reads aloud from a newspaper, while others around him discuss what they have just heard.[25]

The role played by Egypt in the domain of Arab unity was never absent from the minds of British policy-makers, a fact readily ascertained by the continuous and diligent monitoring of Egyptian activities in this regard, on various occasions. One such occasion was at the end of 1936 when, in light of the momentous events unfolding in Palestine, some saw the need for a conference and surmised that the Egyptian capital would be the right place to hold it. They based their opinion on the fact that Egypt had signed the famous 1936 Treaty with Britain – a treaty that many saw as putting limits on the latter's ability to interfere in Egyptian internal affairs.

On the other hand, this same group believed that developments in Egypt were conducive to the establishment of an Arab Union Society in Cairo, with an agenda that aimed at strengthening Arab social and economic ties. The report of the British Embassy in Cairo comments on the issue saying that this society was basically an Islamic body and that its members had met in early 1937 under the chairmanship of Maḥmūd Bassyūnī, President of the Senate. It had formed a committee to study the possibility of convening the said Conference in Cairo, to which representatives from Iraq, Syria and Palestine would be invited. During that same period, there were similar efforts by university students to establish an Arab Students Union and to prepare for a students' conference in one of the Arab capitals.[26]

Hopes regarding the possibility of holding the Conference revived after the convening, in Cairo, of the Medical Conference for Near East Countries. This coincided with a visit by a number of educated Arabs and notables to the Egyptian capital to discuss the proposition, though the talks did not produce definite results. Commenting on these developments, Sir Myles Lampson stated that a degree of mistrust between Iraq and Egypt was hindering the Conference. This prompted the Palestinians, who were behind the original idea, to consider holding the Conference in Mecca during the *ḥajj* season. However, Saudi Arabia's Minister Plenipotentiary in London, Ḥāfiẓ Wahbah, told officials at the British Embassy in Cairo, while on a visit to Egypt, that King ʿAbd al-ʿAzīz bin Saʿūd was not in favour of the idea.

Lampson concluded that the Egyptians were leaning towards constraining their relationship with the Arab world merely to the encouragement of social and cultural ties. He said that there were some signs of activity in this respect by the Arab Union, under the leadership of Maḥmūd Bassyūnī, President of the Senate, although the man himself was not inclined, by virtue of the office he held, towards increasing his own activities in this regard. The friction this caused between him and members of the Union affected the organisation's activities, a turn of events much to the liking of the British Embassy.[27]

The issue, however, did not disappear so easily. Towards the end of 1937, an Egyptian newspaper published an article stating that Saudi Arabia had refused to hold the Conference in Mecca, and according to the *Umm al-Qurā* newspaper, the fact that the article was quoted in some Syrian and Iraqi newspapers had enraged King ʿAbd al-ʿAzīz bin Saʿūd.

While all this was unfolding, the British delegation in Jeddah had its ear close to the ground.[28]

The said newspaper published another article, on 3 December 1937, stating that reports published in certain Arabic newspapers regarding this incident were untrue, and that no individual or group had submitted a request to convene such a Conference in Mecca. It was, therefore, wrong to say that Saudi Arabia had refused such a request since none had been made in the first place.

Umm al-Qurā launched an attack against the newspapers that had spread the rumour, as it described the situation, and accused them of seeking to divide the Arabs who were in dire need of harmony and unity. The newspaper went on to say that no one, except the enemies of the Arabs and Islam, benefited from false rumours regarding King Ibn Sa'ūd. It added:

> Everybody knows that King 'Abd al-'Azīz does not behave according to his desires and whims. He is a man for all the Arabs and has devoted himself to spreading truth and the faith, without paying attention to newspaper propaganda against him; he will never shirk from any activity he believes would further the interests of the Arabs and Muslims.[29]

British documents provide a record of contacts between Ḥafiẓ Wahbah, the Saudi Minister in London, and Rendel, Director of the Eastern Department at the Foreign Office, in January 1938. They show that Sheikh Wahbah had spoken to British Officials about the telegrams that Saudi officials had received from a number of al-Azhar students, asking them to support the Palestinian cause. Rendel confirmed that the Foreign Office had received similar telegrams and had decided to ignore them, which is what Sheikh Wahbah also decided to do.[30]

It seems that the British Government was satisfied with this result, a success as far as the issue of holding a Conference in 1937 was concerned, especially since the developments in Palestine were the motive behind it. It was only natural for British Government departments to believe that if held, the Conference would serve as a platform for attacking British policies in the region.

Among the reasons for this belief were the campaigns in the Egyptian press against British policy in Palestine, with one newspaper stating that Egypt would not allow its internal preoccupations to distract it from the Palestinian issue and going as far as to call upon Britain to heed Arab demands.[31] Another newspaper quoted its correspondent in Jerusalem as saying that Saudi clerics had protested the decision to divide Palestine, and that Ibn Sa'ūd had notified the British Government of his disapproval.[32]

Despite this positive conclusion, as far as the London Government was concerned, in the months that followed, officials in charge of Arab affairs at the British Foreign Office did not allow any development regarding Arab issues to escape their attention. This is evident from the instructions Eden sent to Sir Myles Lampson regarding the policy he should pursue vis-à-vis the Egyptian Government, in light of the alliance between the two parties.

Although the above instructions focussed on conditions in Egypt, Eden draws attention to the British Government regulation that allows its Ambassador in Cairo to intervene, in certain specific cases, in the country's internal affairs. The London Government allowed such interventions in only six potential cases: the first three concern Egyptian Government commitment to the Treaty provisions, and two others to violations of public order or the deterioration of the country's financial conditions. The sixth is the only one relevant to Egyptian foreign policy, and it has to do with the country's position vis-à-vis the issue of Arabism. It states, verbatim, that the British Ambassador can intervene in the case of any 'support by the Government or King Fārūq of Arab elements hostile to His Majesty's Government or the launching of some undesirable Pan-Arab or Pan-Islamic scheme'.[33]

Based on these instructions, the British Embassy in Cairo began diligently monitoring all Arab activities in the capital city and sending regular reports about them to the Foreign Office. These secret reports reveal details about the Arab Parliamentary Conference and the Arab Women's Conference, both held in Cairo in October 1938.

The first Conference took place between the 7th and 11th of that month, and 'Alūbah Pāshā,[34] the man behind the idea, addressed an invitation to 'all members of Parliaments and prominent personalities in the Arab countries who do not have a parliament of their own'.[35] Representatives from Egypt, Syria, Lebanon, Iraq and Trans-Jordan attended the Conference, in addition to representatives from Morocco and Yemen. The second Conference was held between 15 and 20 October thanks to the efforts of Mrs Hudā Sha'rāwī, President of the Egyptian Women's Union, who personally sent invitations to attend the Conference, which was attended by a large number of Arab women from Egypt, Syria, Lebanon, Palestine, Trans-Jordan and Iraq.[36]

The exhaustive report that Sir Myles Lampson sent to London included the British Embassy's comments on the two Conferences. He started by expressing his satisfaction at the moderate tone of the Parliamentary Conference, which he said was thanks to the influence of 'Alūbah Pāshā, who had come under pressure from Prime Minister ʿAlī Māhir. He also attributed this moderation to the lack of popular interest in the Conference, since the Wafd Party had decided to boycott it despite Naḥḥās Pāshā's warm reception of the participating delegations to assure them that al-Wafd's absence should not be interpreted as a lack of enthusiasm for the Palestinian cause. On the other hand, the absence of Saudi Arabia, Turkey and Iran had deprived the Conference of its ecumenical character, since most of the delegation members were prominent political personalities in their own countries.[37]

Lampson describes Cairo as having become the nerve centre of the Arab and Islamic worlds, and says that the participants were all prominent personalities from the Near and Middle East, and from the North African countries. He adds that the gathering would undoubtedly disseminate a sense of unity among them, especially with regard to the opposition to His Majesty's Government policies in Palestine, and general Muslim cooperation against Western violations, as stated in the Conference resolutions. These included the annulment of the Balfour Declaration, an end to Jewish immigration to Palestine and rejection of the division of Palestine. The special attention accorded by the Conference to the issue of Palestine was quite natural, to the extent that the participants called it the 'Arab Islamic Parliamentary Conference for the Defence of Palestine'.[38]

The British Ambassador in Egypt believed that the Conference's establishment of a permanent committee, headquartered in Cairo,[39] showed an intention to promote a spirit of cooperation between the participating countries. In this context, he specifically mentions the speech that Sheikh al-Marāghī, the Sheikh of al-Azhar, had delivered when delegation members visited the Grand Mosque. In the speech, he expressed his hope that the Conference would signal the beginning of a series of such conferences to discuss Eastern and Islamic problems.

Since two British newspapers, *The Times* and the *Manchester Guardian*, had given their readers the good news that the Conference had failed to achieve its objectives,[40] it was only natural for the British representative to hope that personal ambitions and the usual machinations of Oriental politicians would undermine cooperation efforts between the two conferences. In his opinion, however, this did not negate the fact that conferences such as these strengthen feelings of cohesiveness between those countries, even if only remaining a purely emotional sentiment 'among peoples who place emotions above reason'.

As to the Women's Conference, what most concerned the British was the fact that it strengthened the emotional bond between the women who attended, from all over the Arab world, and made them focus on the same issue, namely, the Palestinian cause. Otherwise, this Conference was less well organised than the Parliamentary Conference.

Sir Myles Lampson ends this seminal report by warning his Government of the danger that such Conferences pose to Britain's position, especially when coupled with the difficulties it is facing in Europe and the Far East. In view of this

> it is not possible to ignore the risks that the Arab-Islamic Movement, revolving around the Palestinian issue, represents, not only because of the relations between the Jews and Arabs, but more importantly because of its strategic impact on the British interests.

The same international developments that led to the outbreak of World War II also necessitated viewing the issue of Arab unity from a strategic perspective. This development signals entry into an entirely new phase, as revealed by the British documents of the period.

The Impact of the War

Barely a few days after the outbreak of World War II, the Eastern Department at the British Foreign Office drafted a comprehensive, 14-page memorandum on Arab unity. It was in the form of a survey of conditions in the Arab world at this decisive point in time, a fact which makes it, in our opinion, a highly significant document.[41]

The document starts by drawing a map of the Arab World based on existing concepts. The states that make up the Arab world are Egypt, Iraq, Saudi Arabia and Yemen, in addition to Syria, Lebanon and Trans-Jordan, which, though each has its own government, are still under the control of the Mandate Powers (France and Britain). Then, there is the British Colony of Aden, the British protectorates of Kuwait, Bahrain, Qatar, Kalbā, and the six Trucial Coast Sheikhdoms. As for Muscat, although it is legally independent, in practice it is still under British control. Moreover, while some consider Tripoli an Arab country, as they do other North African countries, the memorandum openly excludes them, as it does Sudan, which at the time was subject to an Anglo-Egyptian condominium; 'for although Arabic is spoken there, it cannot be called an Arab country'.[42]

The memorandum then moves on to what it calls 'the Arab Dream', which foresees a union among all Asian Arab countries plus Egypt, and describes it as difficult to achieve. However, both the invention of the wireless and use of the motor car have removed many obstacles hindering contacts and communication, not to mention the discovery of oil that helped resolve many of the region's financial problems. There is thus 'no intrinsic reason why the whole of the Arabian Peninsula as far north as Anatolia and the Iranian plateau should not unite into a single political unit. Egypt will always be likely to remain apart.'

The Eastern Department's memorandum then addresses various Arab unity proposals, and carefully examines each separately:

- The federation of Syria and Iraq, a plan discussed some years ago based on a dual-monarchy under the Iraqi monarchy
- The federation of Syria, possibly Lebanon, Palestine and Trans-Jordan
- The federation of Palestine, Trans-Jordan and Iraq, which is the project advocated by Iraqi Prime Minister Nūrī al-Saʿīd

The memorandum's authors end the above exposé by saying that the situation of Palestine and Trans-Jordan is similar to that of Syria and Lebanon in the sense that they form together a geographic, economic and political union – meaning that any separation between them would be artificial. At the same time, a union between Iraq and Syria, including Lebanon, in addition to Palestine and Trans-Jordan, is a natural one. For the part, the boundaries between these countries are purely political, since all the Arab countries, with the exception of Egypt and Iraq, have no natural geographic boundaries.

The memorandum adds, in the process of enumerating the positive factors of unity, that as the world slides into war, small countries are finding it increasingly difficult to maintain their independence, and must therefore rely, one way or another, on the support of a strong neighbour. In other words, being part of a larger state would guarantee independence in the fullest sense possible.

In other regards, the Eastern Department lists four obstacles that face such a potential union, namely the rulers of different countries, in addition to France, Turkey and Great Britain, and they gave most weight to the projected negative impact of the first.

Individual rulers are plagued by jealousies and rivalries that mar relations between them. The most important and influential among these is Ibn Saʿūd; and while the territory he rules over is the most backward, the imminent discovery of oil and gold would soon turn it into a rich country.

He personally believes that if there is ever to be a single Arab ruler, it should be himself, although, presently, he is embroiled in a traditional conflict with the Hashemite family on the throne in Iraq and Trans-Jordan. However, even the latter two countries are envious and jealous of one another. King ʿAbdullah, who rules in Trans-Jordan, believes that Iraqi attempts to unite with Syria are a threat to his interests. Another aspirant to the leadership of the Muslim world is King Fārūq of Egypt, which automatically makes him the object of Ibn Saʿūd's suspicion. Even the Sheikhs of Aden and the Persian Gulf, although they object to British control, still prefer it to being swallowed up by a powerful neighbour.

The memorandum draws attention to the fact that the jealousies and rivalries among the Arab rulers now afflict their ministers and high administration officials, as well. The Iraqi Government, for example, would be severely criticised if it employs a Syrian, a Palestinian or an Egyptian, revealing a form of heightened nationalistic sentiment, more pronounced in Egypt than in any other Arab country.

As regards France, the Government of Paris has on several occasions voiced its categorical rejection of Arab unity and of any other move that could potentially weaken its position in Syria, and especially in Lebanon. The French insist that it is in their interest, as well as Britain's, to maintain the status quo in the Arab world. The British do not know how to explain French reticence to rid itself of its Syrian burden, be it economic or political, except to blame it on its historic cultural relations with this country, and its jealousy of Britain which it always believed had robbed it of its share of the spoils after World War I!

As for Turkey, although Ankara's Government has repeatedly said that it has no territorial ambitions in the Arab world, many refuse to believe it, especially after it annexed the Sanjak of Alexandretta. The authors of the report maintain that Turkey has designs over Aleppo and Mosul, meaning that it views any Arab unity plan as a threat to its interests, although it is difficult for the Turkish Government to admit this openly.

There is finally Great Britain, and the prevailing belief that the current configuration in the Middle East, that is, one of several small individual states, suits its interests better than any other arrangement. According to British Foreign Office Departments, the interests in question revolve around two main factors: communications and oil.

Regarding communications, the memorandum states that Britain has two main avenues of communication between the Mediterranean and India, Australia and the Far East. The first, which is primarily a sea-route, runs through the Suez Canal and the Red Sea, and onwards to the Indian

Ocean. The second, which is an air corridor, runs from the Mediterranean through Palestine, Trans-Jordan and Iraq, all the way to the Persian Gulf and the Indian Ocean.

As for oil, Iran and Iraq are its principal sources, in addition to Bahrain and Saudi Arabia, which are fast developing their oil fields. The fact that Iraqi oil is shipped to Tripoli and Haifa makes it necessary for Britain to maintain a strong influence in these regions.

In view of all the above factors, the memorandum arrives at a decision regarding the policy that the London Government should pursue vis-à-vis Arab unity. This, in our opinion, is the most important part of the memorandum, especially the texts of paragraphs 20 and 21, which we quote verbatim below:

The first paragraph reads:

> It is sometimes supposed by advocates of the concept of Pan-Arab ideas that Great Britain must necessarily be opposed to these ideas for much the same reasons as France opposes them, and particularly because a single State embracing all the Arab countries would not be amenable to British influence in the same way as a number of small and weaker States ... But, there is some truth in this and it is unlikely that the British Government would, of their own accord, ever wish to promote and encourage Pan-Arab ideas, even if the attitude of the French Government left them free to do so, and even if their relations with the various Arab rulers were of such a kind that they could support a policy which seemed to favour one among them without causing offence to the other.

The second paragraph reads:

> ... Pan-Arabism is a phenomenon in the politics of the Middle East which has come to stay. This being so, any attempt to oppose the idea, which it embodies ... would not only be ineffective, but extremely unwise. His Majesty's Government have therefore taken the line, when the question has been discussed in the past that while they would be unwilling to take any initiative and think that this initiative should and must come from the Arabs themselves. They would if the point were to arise, endeavour to avoid displaying active opposition or open lack of sympathy, and would instead endeavour to guide the movement along lines which should ensure that the ensuing federation or union was friendly to Great Britain.[43]

This important memorandum, sent to the British official in charge of Arab Affairs in London and to British representatives in a number of Arab capitals, elicited a variety of reactions. The first of these was from the British War Office, for which the region was now central to its interests due to the way the war was transpiring. Its response abounded with reasons to cast doubt on the concept of Arabism.

Officials at the War Office identified three objectives for Arabism: a renaissance of Arab culture based on a common language and religion, and on a degree of racial affinity; a commonwealth of Arab states; and an Arab empire. It then proceeded to rebut these one by one.[44]

In regard to the first objective, the memorandum concluded that it was highly exaggerated, since:

> Arab civilisation from the historic point of view is a blend of the Greek and Asian civilisations together with ties of the Islamic faith and racial unity binding them together. Apart from that, differences are apparent; the Egyptian farmers are the descendants of the Ancient Egyptians; the Moroccan blood dominates the people of Libya and Morocco, etc. With the exception of Arabia, the majority of Arabs inhabit Trans-Jordan, Palestine, Syria and Iraq.

As for the second objective, the analysts of the War Office believed that the establishment of an Arab Commonwealth sounded more like a Western notion rather than an Eastern one. Individuality is prevalent in the region, which probably explains the failure of Muḥammad ʿAlī's experiment in the first half of the nineteenth century, since it was a matter of pure personal ambition. The first collective expression of the notion came as part of the Beirut Secret Society's agenda, in 1875, though its recent revival is undoubtedly due to European pressure on many regions of the Arab World.

The third objective, that is, the establishment of an Arab empire, was in the eyes of British War Office officials the most representative of the Arab mentality. The notion is the exclusive domain of Iraq, on one side, and Saudi Arabia, on the other, especially since Ibn Saʿūd is now the leading political figure in the region, and, for many reasons, his attempts at becoming the 'King of the Arab world' seem to make most sense.

The War Office's memorandum recommends charting a middle course between Iraq and Saudi Arabia, a move made necessary by strategic requirements.[45] From among the British representatives in the Arab countries, British documents give only the opinions of Mr Havard, the Consul General in Beirut, and of Mr MacKereth, the British Consul in Damascus.

Though Havard's memorandum was short, it was replete with reasons to reject Arab unity. He primarily based his rejection on the fact that, on the one hand, the Christians of Lebanon would be extremely opposed to the idea and, on the other, that France would do its best to abort it.[46]

The longer response came from Colonel Gilbert MacKereth, the British Consul in Damascus, and it seems that he was highly influenced by the atmosphere of the Syrian capital, constantly abuzz with the promotion of Arabism. MacKereth agreed with the Eastern Department's conclusions, namely that His Majesty's Government should avoid getting involved in Arab domestic policies or in making any positive overtures regarding the issue of Arab unity, as long as possible. He added that instructions must be sent to all British officials in the region not to discuss the issue with anyone in a manner that could give the impression that they are conveying the opinion of His Majesty's Government.

Then he rejects the idea that had begun to circulate among British Foreign Office officials that a cooling off of the situation in Palestine would foster sincerity and goodwill among the Arabs towards Britain. In his opinion, as long as England keeps what is in its power to give, the Arab would want to remain in its good favour, but if it does not 'doors will be slammed in its face'.

Because Colonel MacKereth lived in Damascus and had good knowledge of French policies in Syria and Lebanon, he derided the Eastern Department's interpretation as to why France insisted on remaining in Syria. He gave an entirely different interpretation based on a number of factors. These included fear that the notion of Arab unity might spread to its colonies in North Africa, plus the belief that leaving the region would encourage one or more European powers to take its place, which would be very harmful to French interests. In particular, the Paris Government was fearful of Italian and German ambitions in the region. MacKereth also mentioned the belief, held by a number of French officials, that the Arabs had not yet reached a level of social development that would allow them to establish an independent national government in such a turbulent part of the world.[47]

On the other hand, it seems that Britain was increasingly worried about deteriorating conditions in several regions of the Arab world, especially in Iraq and Palestine. In Iraq, developments accelerated after the outbreak of the war and, in April 1940, culminated in the formation of a government under Prime Minister Rashīd al-Gaylānī, as an outcome of the struggle between various politicians and military officers. The crisis worsened when Britain intervened to force the latter government to resign, and the government of Ṭāhā al-Hāshimī, that replaced it, was not to the liking of the Army which subsequently took over power in April 1941 in an incident known as Gaylānī's coup.[48]

In Palestine, the second phase of the 1936 Revolt began in the summer of 1939, and continued for two years. The revolutionaries were not content with demonstrating, cutting telephone lines and sabotaging roads, but went as far as to attack Lidda Airport and launch guerrilla attacks against British facilities. These attacks were particularly harmful to the British, especially at a time when they needed to concentrate fully on their confrontation with the Axis powers.[49]

Meanwhile, the British Government was moving in more than one direction to crystallise its policy towards Arab unity. Among these moves was the initiation of contacts with the French, in May 1940, to formulate a joint policy in this regard, even though these attempts came to naught.[50] They also attempted to encourage King Ibn Sa'ūd to play a more effective role in bringing about Arab unity, in view of mitigating the influence of the extremist Mufti.[51]

It seemed that reason for worry had made its way across the Atlantic Ocean, when a high official at the Near East Section of the American State Department, Mr Wallace Murray, invited a British Embassy official in Washington for talks on the situation in the Arab region. The American official expressed his apprehension regarding events in Palestine and Iraq, and his fear that these might turn into a fully-fledged revolution throughout the Arab countries. He asked whether it would be possible for Ibn Sa'ūd to place the Jews under his protection, but the British Official told him that this was highly unlikely and that his Government was about to issue a public statement on the region as a whole.[52]

In the meantime, Foreign Office departments were busy preparing this 'public statement', including a long memorandum which Anthony Eden, the Foreign Secretary, had himself written and submitted to the Prime Minister. At the beginning of the memorandum, Eden admits that his country had to make very important decisions regarding its policies in the Arab world and said that the Palestinian problem will occupy a prominent place in it, due to its dangerous impact on Arab public opinion. He highlighted the fact that given the existing situation, he viewed this issue as an integral part of what he called the 'Arab Problem'. Though he acknowledged that with respect to the Palestinian problem, the Germans would always be able to offer more than the British, he hoped that the British Government's White Paper would help mitigate the severity of the problem. Based on that, he made the following specific recommendations:

A. With respect to Palestine: No change.
B. Syria: If the Free French Government proves unable to offer anything there, we should issue a statement supporting its independence.
C. Iraq: Establishing a friendly government and urging it to pursue policies that conform to conditions on the ground.
D. Saudi Arabia: Continue our support.
E. Support the Arab unity plan in a manner that enables the Arabs to implement it.[53]

Two days later, Eden made the famous declaration which was very well received by several Arab parties. It was so welcome that Sir Myles Lampson, the British Ambassador to Cairo, noted that Aḥmad Ḥussayn, leader of the Miṣr al-Fatāh Party, who was in hiding from the Government and known for his animosity towards Britain, issued a statement from hiding praising the Secretary's speech without reservation. Lampson seized the opportunity to advise the British Government to give the declaration full coverage on the Arabic service of the BBC[54] to allow people to say that, as far as British policy towards Arab unity was concerned, it was the end of an era and the beginning of a new one.

Notes

1. Because the Arab Press and some Arab authors quoted this statement freely using their own personal interpretation of some of its aspects, I chose to quote the original in English.

F.O. 371/27044, Arab Federation – Foreign Research and Press Service, Balliol College, Oxford, 9 June, 1941.

2. Maḥmūd Ṣāliḥ Mnassā, *al-Mashriq al-ʿArabī al-Muʿāṣir* (Cairo: [n.pb.], 1995), Section 1: al-Hilāl al-Khaṣīb, pp. 194–5.

3. Younan Labib Rizk, *Ḥawādith 1935 fī Miṣr ʿalā Ḍawʾ al-Wathāʾiq al-Bariṭānīyah: Buḥūth fī al-Tārīkh al-Ḥadīth* (Cairo: [n.pb.], 1976).

4. Wamīḍ Jamāl Naẓmī, Ghānim Muḥammad Ṣāliḥ and Shafīq ʿAbd al-Rāziq, *al-Taṭawwur al-Siyāsī al-Muʿāṣir fī al-ʿIrāq* ([Baghdad]: Baghdad University, Faculty of Law and Politics, Political Science Department, [198?]), pp. 186–7.

5. ʿĀdil Ḥasan Ghoneim, *al-Ḥarakah al-Waṭaniyah al-Filisṭīnīyah min Thawrat 1936 ḥattā al-Ḥarb al-ʿĀlamīyah al-Thānīyah* (Cairo: al-Khānjī, 1981), pp. 14–16.

6. Ibid., pp. 19–20.

7. F.O. 371/19980, Clark Kerr to Eden, 24 February 1936 – Arab Unity.

8. Ibid.

9. See Chapter 3 of this book.

10. F.O. 371/19980, Enc. Movement-Sudan Agency, Cairo, 14 February 1936.

11. Ibid.

12. F.O. 371/19980, Sir M. Lampson to Mr Eden, 24 February 1936.

13. F.O. 371/19980, Enc. Report on the Pan-Islamic Arab Movement, Report on the Pan-Islamic Arab-Sudan Agency, Cairo, 28 March 1936.

14. At the end of May 1935, France signed a joint-cooperation agreement with the Soviet Union, prompting Hitler to declare, on 7 March 1936, that the said agreement nullified the provisions of the Locarno Conference, signed by the European countries in 1925, which foresaw, among other events, the disarmament of the Rhine region, and ordered his troops to occupy it. Available in: Maḥmūd Ṣāliḥ Mnassā, *al-Ḥarb al-'Ālamīyah al-Thānīyah* (Cairo: [n.pb.], 1989), pp. 60–1.

15. F.O. 371/19980, Sir M. Lampson to Mr Eden, 2 April 1936.

16. F.O. 371/19980, Sir M. Lampson to Mr Eden, 8 April 1936, Pan-Islamic Arab Movement.

17. F.O. 371/19980, Sir Lampson to Mr Eden, 28 May 1936, Pan-Islamic Arab Movement.

18. F.O. 371/19980, Sir A. Clark Kerr to Mr Eden, 3 April 1936, Arab Unity. Visit of Iraqi notables to Syria, Palestine and Egypt.

19. Sir A. Clark to Mr Eden, 28 May 1936.

20. We believe that the opinion expressed by the British document in 1936 remained the ultimate objective of the Arab Movement, eventually becoming its motto, in the 1950s and 1960s: 'From the Ocean to the Gulf'.

21. In autumn 1935, Italy attacked Abyssinia, and Britain and France led a group of countries at the League of Nations to table a resolution that describes Italy as an 'aggressor'. The resolution was approved by 50 countries.

22. See Annex 4.

23. F.O. 407/19980, Sir A. Clark Kerr to Mr Eden, 28 May 1936 – Arab Unity.

24. Under Prussia's leadership Germany established a Customs Union, and in 1834, Saxony, Bavaria and 14 other German states joined in, paving the way for the establishment of a Customs Union later on.

25. F.O. 371/19980, Consul MacKereth to Mr Eden, 15 May 1936; Memorandum on Pan-Arabism.

26. F.O. 371/20780, Pan-Arab Conference; note by Samuel Bey Attiya, 13 January 1937.

27. F.O. 371/20786, Sir M. Lampson to Mr Eden, 9 January 1937 – Arab Unity.

28. F.O. 371/20786, Sir R. Bullard (British Legation, Jeddah) to Foreign Office, 7 December 1937.

29. Ibid.

30. F.O. 371/21872, Saudi Minister, Conversation, 7 January 1938.

31. Article by Tawfīq Ḍīyāb in *al-Jihād* (7 November 1937).

32. *Al-Maṣrī*, 17 November 1937.

33. F.O. 371/21945, Eden to Lampson, 10 February 1938.

34. Muḥammad 'Alī 'Alūbah, an Egyptian Jurist, started his political career as a member of the National Party before joining al-Wafd, which he also quit to join al-Aḥrār Constitutionalist Party, though he later became closer to members of the National Party. After 1929, he devoted his efforts to Arab and Islamic issues and became a member of the Executive Committee of the Islamic Conference, which he represented on a tour of India in 1933. He became Minister of Education under Prime Minister 'Alī Māher (January–May 1936), and was appointed later to the Senate.

35. F.O. 371/21883, Lampson to Halifax, 24 October 1938 – Arab Parliamentary Conference and Arab Women's Conference. The Syrian delegation was headed by Parliament President Fāris al-Khourī, the Iraqi delegation by Parliament President Mawlūd Mukhliṣ Pāshā, the Lebanese delegation by Jubrān Twainī, and the Moroccan delegation by Muḥammad al-Makkī al-Naṣirī. *Al Ahram*, 6 October 1938.

36. *Al Ahram*, 12 October 1938.

37. Ibid.

38. F.O. 371/21883, Lampson to Halifax.

39. The Conference's seventh resolution stipulated the 'Election of a Permanent Committee to represent the Conference in adopting any measure it deems necessary to implement these resolutions. It would be located in Cairo, and would have the right to invite or delegate whomever it chooses based on a majority vote of its members.' See the resolutions adopted by the Conference in:

Al Ahram, 12 October 1938.

40. *Al Ahram*, 11 October 1938.

41. See Annex 5.

42. F.O. 371/23239, Memorandum on Arab Federation, 28 September 1939.

43. Ibid.

44. F.O. 371/23195, Major Todd (War Office) to Mr Baggallay, 3 November 1939 – Arab Federation.

45. Ibid.

46. F.O. 371/23195, Havard (Beirut) to Mr Baggallay, 14 November 1939, Arab Federation.

47. F.O. 371/23195, Notes by Gilbert MacKereth, British Consulate, Damascus, 15 November 1939.

48. Naẓmī, Ṣāliḥ and 'Abd al-Rāziq, *al-Taṭawwur al-Siyāsī*, pp. 205–17.

49. Ghonaim, *al-Ḥarakah al-Waṭaniyah al-Filisṭīnīyah min Thawrat 1936 ḥattā al-Ḥarb al-'Ālamīyah al-Thānīyah*, pp. 14–16.

50. F.O. 371/24584, Stonehewer Bird to Baggallay, 8 April 1940.

51. Ibid.

52. F.O. 371/27043, British Embassy, Washington D.C., to Charles Baxter, 9 May 1941.

53. F.O. 371/27043, Arab Policy Memorandum by the Secretary of State on the whole question of our policy in Palestine, Syria, Iraq and Saudi Arabia, 27 May 1941.

54. F.O. 371/27043, From Sir M. Lampson, Cairo, 3 June 1941, Secretary of State's Speech of 29 May on the Middle East, 4 June 1941.

CHAPTER 5

British Policy Towards Arab Unity During World War II 1941–3

In August 1941, less than three months after British Foreign Secretary Anthony Eden made his famous declaration, the Saudi Arabian Minister in London proposed that the London Government take the initiative to draw up an Arab unity scheme without waiting for the end of the war. The British Foreign Office wrote to its ambassadors in Cairo and Saudi Arabia, and the High Commissioner in Palestine, asking them their opinions on the matter.

All British representatives in the region concurred that it would be unwise to promote an Arab unity scheme at that time and recommended that, if any action were to be taken, it should be to encourage closer cooperation between the Arab countries in the economic and cultural domains.[1]

Although it was proven afterwards that the Saudi Minister in London had acted alone without his government's consent, the British Government still took it upon itself to consult others regarding the appropriate means of implementing Eden's proposals. One of these consultations took place during a meeting, on 28 November 1941, between Oliver Lytellton, the Minister of State,[2] and General Catroux, representative of the Free French Government in the Egyptian capital.

At the meeting, General Catroux said that he was not one of those who believed that any form of Arab unity was applicable from the practical point of view, and that the best that one could hope for in the near future were closer economic ties between the Arab countries. The British Minister agreed with his French colleague and said that differences between the rulers, not to mention the geographical, social and other disparities, were too wide to allow any kind of Arab unity at the time. He believed that the only avenue of progress possible was along the lines suggested by General Catroux. At the end of the session, he expressed his pleasure at the meeting of minds between the two parties, and said that it was very important for France and Britain to coordinate their policy in this respect.

The British Government deemed it appropriate, under the circumstances, to form a committee under the War Cabinet[3] charged with drawing the broad lines of the policy that the British Government should pursue vis-à-vis Arab unity, based on the Foreign Secretary's declaration, rather than leave the matter to the Foreign Office and its representatives in the Arab countries to handle.

New Planning

The said Committee held a meeting at the Foreign Office on 26 September 1941, and drafted another report comparing arguments in favour and those against Britain taking the initiative at that point in time. The Committee summarised the arguments in favour of the proposal in three points, the first being that King ʻAbd al-ʻAziz bin Saʻūd, whom it believed was the strongest Arab leader at the time and a reliable friend of Britain, was at the height of his power. The second point in favour was that Britain had the strongest military presence in the region, a force unlikely to be matched in the near future. The third point was that the eventual independence of Syria and Lebanon, coupled with the end of the French mandate, was liable to revive Arab aspirations everywhere, especially in Palestine and Trans-Jordan. Therefore, if Arab unity as a concept were to carry within it any acceptable solution to the Palestinian problem, 'it is then better to act immediately rather than wait for the war to end'.[4]

The Committee summarised the arguments against Britain taking the initiative in implementing Arab unity into three counterpoints as well. First, nothing at the time indicated that Arab public opinion was amenable to political unity among the Arab countries. Second, the implementation of such a scheme would undoubtedly give rise to several politically contentious issues within the Arab World, and probably also among the Jews. Finally, any unity scheme that Britain might adopt would be liable to suspicion and might arouse anti-British sentiment at a time when Britain's enemies in the region are looking for just such an opportunity. The Committee then elaborated each of the above points separately.

In regard to the first argument, the Committee members were of the opinion that Arab unity was never a genuine objective for the Arab countries, or for the Arab people as a whole, and that there was no nascent Arab scheme of the sort, at that time. They explained this by saying that had they really desired unity, nothing would have prevented the three Arab countries that have been independent for a number of years – Iraq, Saudi Arabia and Yemen – from forming a unified country. All they had done, instead, was to conclude the Treaty of Arab Brotherhood and Alliance between Iraq and Saudi Arabia, in 1936, which Yemen joined the following year. The Treaty's objective was to promote brotherly cooperation and understanding on matters of mutual interest for the three kingdoms.

Although in the Committee's opinion the articles of this Treaty included a number of commitments to promote consultation and cooperation among the signatories, there was no attempt to establish a political system, or any other joint political or administrative authority. As such, this Treaty was a good example of the Arabs' conception of unity, namely of the fact that they sought neither unity in a single state, nor in a federation of states.

As to the second argument, any unity scheme liable to raise long-term difficulties was considered best left alone for the moment. Among these difficulties were the elements that provoked jealousy between Ibn Saʿūd and the King of Yemen, and between Ibn Saʿūd and the Hashemite rulers of Iraq and Trans-Jordan. There were also rivalries between the citizens of various Arab countries – namely between Damascus and Baghdad, between the Sunnis and the Shīʿites, the Muslims and the non-Muslims and, finally, between Bedouin and city-dwellers. There were, moreover, strong objections to Arab unity on the part of the French and the Zionists.

The third argument drew on the fact that any Arab unity scheme that Britain supported would be liable to be the object of suspicion. It was therefore better for Britain to adopt measures that encouraged closer cooperation among the Arabs, in a manner that showed sympathy with their cause and its willingness to assist in the removal of barriers between the Arab countries. The Committee submitted five different schemes in this regard, and evaluated the pros and cons of each.

Before attending to the scheme, it divided the Arab countries into four groups:

1 The Kingdom of Egypt.
2 The Kingdoms of Saudi Arabia and Yemen; the Sheikhdoms of

Kuwait, Bahrain, Qatar and the Trucial Coast; the Sultanate of Oman; the Colony of Aden; and the Protectorate of Aden.

3 The Kingdom of Iraq.

4 The Syrian and Lebanese Republics (both independent under French Mandate), and Palestine and Trans-Jordan under British Mandate.

After excluding Egypt from those schemes due to Egyptian fears that joining an Arab union would restrict the country's independence, members of the Committee provided the following details for the different schemes:

Scheme I: Total unity comprising all the countries named in (b), (c) and (d) above, with the proviso that each would retain its independence, have the right to conclude treaties with other nations and maintain diplomatic relations with foreign countries. A Unity Council would be formed in which each country would have a representative, and its presidency would be on a rotational basis or, alternatively, Ibn Sa'ūd would be named president for life. The Council would be responsible for all issues concerning unity, and each of the constituent countries would have a number of votes relative to its size and population.

According to the scheme, each member country would retain responsibility for security on its own territory, and a federal mechanism would be set up for the peaceful resolution of disagreements among member states. If any inter-Arab dispute were to degenerate into an armed conflict, other members would not be bound to become party to it; however, if any member of the Union were attacked by a foreign country, then other members would act as a single bloc. Since this type of confederation cannot stand on its own, it would require military guarantees from the British Government, in return for guaranteeing British interests and strategic needs in the region.

According to the Committee, the plan had three advantages: it would show the Arabs that Britain took their aspirations for unity seriously; it would show the world that the British Government had adopted a comprehensive view of post-war settlements; and, finally, as part of a large bloc, the Arabs might be more amenable to granting the Jews concessions on the Mediterranean coast.

There were, however, four disadvantages to the plan. There was nothing to indicate that it would appeal to any of the Arab countries concerned, especially since the British Minister Plenipotentiary in Jeddah had difficulty in seeing how Saudi Arabia could be part of any unity plan, since it had very little to contribute to or benefit from it. Moreover, Yemen would not be an active member of the union, and the Gulf Sheikhdoms were not yet ready to join. As to the difficulties involved in the Protectorate of Aden's participation in the plan, they needed no further elaboration.

The Committee concluded that a confederation that included Saudi Arabia, Yemen, the Persian Gulf states, Muscat and the Aden Protectorate would be impractical for many years to come. If there should be any progress towards a political union, it should start with the more advanced Arab countries further to the north.

Scheme II: This initiative was predicated on a more limited union involving Iraq, Syria and Palestine, without Saudi Arabia and other countries of the Arabian Peninsula. It was enough to say that the rivalry between the Hashemite family and Ibn Sa'ūd was such that Ibn Sa'ūd would view any union along these lines as a threat to his vital interests. For this reason, it would be better to start with Syria, Lebanon, Palestine and Trans-Jordan, and leave Iraq for a later stage.

Scheme III: This envisioned a union comprising Syria, Lebanon, Palestine and Trans-Jordan, based on a federal system that would deal with economic and political matters of interest to these four countries. The more successful such a scheme might prove to be, the greater the prospects for the resolution of the Palestine problem.

What made the adoption of this scheme possible was the fact that Syria, Lebanon and Palestine were once, under the Ottoman Empire, part of a union known as 'Greater Syria'. Their subsequent division was a historic mistake and the source of many problems, not to mention the fact that the borders between them were indefensible. The implementation of this plan, however, faced serious difficulties:

- The French had always been against Arab unity, and the Free French Government[5] would certainly be no less opposed to any union between Syria and Lebanon on the one hand, and Palestine and Trans-Jordan on the other. The French would see it as a manoeuvre to increase British influence in the Levant at the expense of their own.
- In regard to Palestine, the scheme would mean the end of the British Mandate, as well as the ensuing difficulty of finding a suitable alternative arrangement acceptable to both Arabs and Jews. In that context, it would be important that the future of the Jews in Palestine be part of the scheme from the very outset, and that both Jews and Arabs should demonstrate a certain readiness to cooperate and coexist.

- As regards Trans-Jordan, it would be difficult to sideline it from any scheme that included Palestine, Syria and Lebanon, though it would be equally difficult to include the Emir 'Abdullah in such a plan. Moreover, although it was conceded that 'Abdullah ought to be rewarded for his many services to Britain, by making him the King over the entire region, the idea was bound to meet with vehement resistance from Ibn Sa'ūd.

Scheme IV: This was a plan to develop the above-mentioned Treaty of Arab Brotherhood and Alliance between Iraq, Saudi Arabia and the Yemen (1936–7) in a manner to form the basis for an eventual Arab union, and encourage Syria and Lebanon to join after gaining independence. Measures would be taken to hold meetings, periodically, between representatives of the Treaty's signatories to deal with issues of common interest and formulate policies that promoted consultation among them, an arrangement that could eventually provide the basis for a federal system.

Although this particular scheme's advantage – according to those who formulated it – was that it built on a Treaty that the Arab rulers themselves had concluded, it rendered it more difficult for the British Government to have any influence over the federation. Furthermore, although it was clearly difficult for Palestine to join the 'Treaty of Arab Brotherhood' as long as it was under the British Mandate, to exclude it would only increase criticism of British policies and Jewish aspirations in Palestine. Moreover, there was no reason for Britain to encourage Syria and Lebanon to join the Treaty.

Scheme V: The alternative was to encourage the removal of economic barriers, beginning with Syria, Lebanon, Palestine and Trans-Jordan. The British Minister of State in the Middle East recommended the adoption of this particular scheme, and proposed taking charge of its implementation.

He believed that a purely economic scheme would be in the best interest of the four countries involved, and would remove reasons for the Free French Government to reject it. The dismantling of economic barriers could reduce the level of anger towards the existing artificial borders, especially since economic cooperation might eventually develop into some form of political cooperation.

In addition, the Committee adopted the suggestion of the British Ambassador in Baghdad which called for the closer coordination of academic curricula in Arab schools, and for holding regular cultural conferences, publishing newspapers of interest to all Arabs and arranging exchange programmes for higher education students.

Having adopted a scheme calling for the promotion of cultural contacts between the Arab countries, the Committee drew attention to Egypt's eventual re-entry into the picture since the Egyptians saw Cairo as the cultural centre of the Arab World. It said that it was not clear what the British Government could do in this regard, except welcome any initiative the Arabs might take in this regard.[6]

After evaluating the five schemes, members of the Committee decided that it was not the right time to include Saudi Arabia, Yemen and other states of the Arabian Peninsula. The schemes should be confined to countries further north, that is, to Syria, Lebanon, Trans-Jordan and Palestine, and start by establishing closer economic cooperation between them. On the political front, the British Government had no objection to Syria and Lebanon joining the 'Treaty of Arab Brotherhood and Alliance', and on the cultural front, British representatives in the region were to encourage all steps in that direction.

The Committee had reservations in two different regards: the first was concerning British interests in the region, and the second was over the Palestinian problem.

British interests in the Middle East revolved around communication routes and oil, as well as maintaining the naval, military and air facilities necessary to protect them. The Committee drew attention to the risks involved if the intended federation were to fall into the hands of extremists. To avoid such an outcome, the British Government ought to adopt a positive attitude from the very beginning, and steer the movement in a direction that would achieve Arab interests without jeopardising those of Britain.

In respect to Palestine, Arab unity should help find a proper solution to the problem by asking the federation's permission to transform it into a Jewish state in return for financial inducements. The idea of placing the Jews under the protection of Ibn Sa'ūd was considered, but was dismissed when the Committee realised that the man was unlikely to accept such a proposition. The alternative was to replace the British Mandate by a Palestinian Government acceptable to both Jews and Arabs. The Arabs could be made to accept the proposition by ending the Mandate and including Palestine in the Arab Federation, and the Jews by convincing them that the best hope for a future Jewish national home in Palestine would be through reaching an understanding with the Arabs within a federal framework.

The Committee concluded with a set of four recommendations regarding the policies that Britain ought to pursue vis-à-vis Arab unity, based on Eden's declaration.

- On economic cooperation: British representatives in the Middle East should be asked to submit their views on closer economic cooperation and the removal of economic barriers between Syria, Lebanon, Palestine, and Trans-Jordan. Once approved, their recommendations would be submitted to the Free French Government, and implementation could start immediately.
- On cultural cooperation: British representatives should be asked to specify what sort of non-political contacts they might encourage.
- There should be no objection to the eventual expansion of the 'Treaty of Arab Brotherhood' to include other independent Arab states such as Syria and Lebanon, although the implementation of such a proposition ought to be contingent upon the approval of the parties concerned.
- To conduct a study of British strategic post-war requirements in a manner that would reconcile French rights, Jewish ambitions and Arab aspirations.[7]

* * *

While officials at the War Cabinet were busy charting the course of British policies towards Arab unity in the aftermath of Eden's declaration, representatives of the Free French in Cairo were submitting a proposal to the British Minister of State in the Egyptian capital, concerning a joint statement on the issue. Under pressure from the war, the Free French had already issued a statement, on 8 June 1941, on ending the mandate and accepting the independence of Syria and Lebanon, based on the terms of a treaty to be signed at the end of the war.[8]

General Catroux proposed that Britain and France proclaim the independence of Syria and Lebanon 'an important step in the history of peoples of the Arab language and culture in the Middle East'. He suggested that the two countries declare that their policies towards peoples of the region were inspired by the same desire to give satisfaction to their aspirations for independence and liberty. He also suggested that the two countries state that they were

> prepared to consider with sympathy, in the spirit of Mr Eden's declaration, the desire shown by these people while maintaining the ties that their

common language and culture have created between them, and facilitate and foster closer economic and political relations.[9]

The British did not respond to these suggestions based on the belief that the Syrians and Lebanese were no longer interested in any further statements, but on French fulfilment of previous treaties from which it had cut itself off. British officials in Cairo were also suspicious of the way the French had formulated their statement, describing the Arabs as 'peoples of Arab language and culture in the Middle East', which seemed only to render it the target of attack.

In fact, to British policy-makers working to implement Eden's declaration, General Catroux's suggestion was akin to a rejection of that statement.

* * *

For its part, the Colonial Office submitted its own views regarding the implementation of Eden's declaration, in a long memorandum by Sir Harold MacMichael, the British High Commissioner in Palestine, dated 7 June 1942.[10] MacMichael had a more definite view of the policies Britain ought to pursue in the Arab region, and the concomitant measures it should adopt to protect its interests. By the term 'region', he meant the eastern coast of the Mediterranean in general; the port of Haifa and its hinterland, which was vitally important for the defence of the region; the new port of Aqaba and the Lake of Tiberias and the Dead Sea as landing sites for amphibian airplanes. The term 'region' also included areas in four different countries suitable for the construction of airports, namely in Syria, Lebanon, Palestine and Trans-Jordan, and the protection of the oil pipeline from Iraq to Haifa and Tripoli, as well as its refineries. He drew attention to railroad links between the four countries, and between those four and Egypt and Turkey, in addition to the Baghdad-Haifa road. He also included mention of the protection of the holy sites in Jerusalem, and proposed that a special mechanism be put in place to resolve disputes involving them. MacMichael addressed the issues of a national home for the Jews, protecting the Arab inhabitants of Palestine, and finally alluded to France's interests in the Levant.

The High Commissioner in Palestine also proposed a formula for the future union that was both unique and markedly influenced by the position he held. This included:

- The establishment of a Federal Council based on a proportional representation system that corresponded to the size of each of the populations of the four countries. Attention should also be paid to proportional representation within each of the delegations, including the Muslim Arabs, Christian Arabs, Jews and other minorities, such as the Druze.
- Selection of the capital where the Federal Council would be based, with his own preference being given to Haifa. His choice was based, among other factors, on the city's population of 112,000 being well distributed among Muslim and Christian Arabs, Jews and Europeans. It was also based on the fact that the city had never witnessed any religious or historic complications, not to mention its clement weather, sufficient water supply and efficient transportation system. All of the above, in addition to the city's central location on the Mediterranean coast and in proximity to the oil pipeline terminal, made Haifa a far superior choice to any other.
- Each country would have its own elected Legislative Council to deal with domestic issues, and representation in these Councils would be based on each group's share of the country's population.
- A number of ministries and departments should be integrated, including Education, Railways, Post and Telegraph, Customs, Higher Appeal Courts and Currency.
- Formation of a Higher Supervisory Council made up of representatives from Britain, France and the United States, as well as an Administrative Department made up of the Prime Ministers of Syria, Lebanon, Trans-Jordan and President of the Zionist Organisation.

The Foreign Office did not show much enthusiasm for the High Commissioner's plan, and its officials made a number of observations, mainly to the effect that it was fundamentally impracticable:

> Whatever the Arabs may mean when they refer to Arab federation, it is something very different from a system placing them under the supervision of three foreign states. It would be a political error of the first magnitude for His Majesty's Government to sponsor such a proposal. It must be remembered that we have promised the Syrians and Lebanese their independence, and they cannot be expected to agree to join such a federation as this, in which their independence would be subordinated to a British-French-American supervisory committee ... Their independence will presumably have to be embodied in international treaties on the lines of the treaties with Iraq or Egypt.[11]

The other comment by the Foreign Office concerned Britain's partnership with France and the United States. The belief was that the French were never really in favour of Arab unity, and always feared any project that entailed the end of French influence over the region in favour of Great Britain and the United States. It was also doubtful that the Americans would welcome such a scheme as it might burden them with considerable responsibilities towards the new federation, especially if military assistance were ever required.

* * *

It was then the turn of the India Office to voice its opinion in a memorandum by Colonel Prior, the India representative at the Middle East War Council in Cairo. He strongly opposed the entire Arab unity idea.[12] The Representative of India began by saying that unity among the Arab states, at that time, was impossible to achieve and warned against any moves in this direction. Any such move, he said, would put Britain in an unenviable position because it would revive hopes that it cannot fulfil, and Britain would ultimately have to pay the price for the inevitable failure.

He then proceeded to enumerate the obstacles that hindered the establishment of a close union between the Arab countries. These included the absence of any spirit of sacrifice on the Arabs' part – namely a lack of willingness to sacrifice one's personal interests for the sake of the public good, not to mention the ongoing conflicts stoked by different capabilities and cultures. He said that the history of the Arab race revealed that any attempt for closer relations would be unacceptable and impractical.

Colonel Prior underlined his opinion by stating that soon after its establishment the chances are that the union would lose its lustre. The military presence of troops from one of the countries in the union on the territory of another would be liable to cause severe apprehension in that country, bearing in mind that language alone was not considered a valid basis for unity, especially given the widely disparate dialects of these countries' inhabitants.

He, however, agreed with MacMichael regarding an experimental union between Syria, Lebanon, Trans-Jordan and Palestine, since they had once formed a single economic unit and their fragmentation into separate entities had brought untold miseries on their populations. On the other hand, Iraq was always racially and economically separate from Syria and, historically, its territory was a theatre of conflict between the Persians and Greeks, and subsequently the Umayyads and the Abbasids. Furthermore, and because it had the greatest mineral wealth next to Egypt, Iraq would be ill-disposed towards sharing it with Syria, Trans-Jordan and Palestine. He concluded by recommending a number of policies that Britain should pursue in this regard and specifically to not encourage any initiative towards unity, and to confine its role to the removal of economic and cultural barriers between the countries concerned.

As regards the first recommendation, Prior proposed a form of customs union along the lines of a Zollverein, although he cast some doubt on policies that sought to remove custom barriers, since they raised fears in wealthy countries that they might be obliged to share their resources with poorer ones. As for the removal of cultural barriers, although he believed that to be an easier undertaking altogether, he warned against France's possible objections in this regard given that the latter believed that any cultural union would ultimately weaken its own cultural ties with countries of the Levant.

Prior underscored his point by quoting an article that appeared in *The Egyptian Mail*, on 21 January 1942, saying that it reflected Arab public opinion towards the issue. The author of the article called for convening two conferences, one bringing together representatives of Arab broadcasting stations to discuss closer cooperation, and the other being a gathering of education experts to study the unification of school curricula. Prior was not very optimistic regarding the outcome of the first conference, but thought that the second was a more practical option. He proposed reducing postal and telegram charges between the Arab countries. However, the most important item in memorandum of the India Gnovernment's representative concerned the Gulf countries' position towards the proposed union, given his government's keen interest in Gulf-related issues.

Colonel Prior believed that the disadvantages that the Gulf countries would reap from the union would outweigh the advantages since a customs union would cost these countries most of their income from customs duties, and he doubted that countries like Bahrain, Kuwait and Qatar would agree to share their oil income with larger Arab countries. He also pointed out that the Gulf countries' distance from the Arab heartland, the small size of their populations and their 'backwardness' did not make them valuable additions to the Arab Nation, whereas they would still be expected to provide the union with substantial financial contributions.

Given the focus of Indian representatives on the interest of the Empire as a whole, Prior referred as well to a potential double impact that a future Arab federation might have on these interests:

First: The Indian presence in the Gulf: If its countries were to join a larger Arab federation, a front hostile to non-Arab interests would be formed, and the discrimination against the Indians that once prevailed in Iraq would find its way to the Gulf; the same kind of discrimination that had led to their migration to the Gulf region in the first place. Moreover, although it is true that climatic conditions would not encourage Syrians to come to the Gulf, it would not prevent people from Najd from coming in large numbers, and once there, from raising the slogan 'the Arabian Peninsula for the Arabs', as a ploy to get rid of their Indian rivals.

Second: British interests in the Gulf were so vital that Britain cannot afford to relinquish them. He listed these interests as the safety of air traffic, the protection of naval bases and that of the newly discovered oil fields that required further development, adding: 'These states should be encouraged to look to us and to no one else.' He seized the opportunity to sound the alarm in regard to Russian ambitions in the Gulf, if British influence there were ever destabilised.[13]

* * *

The matter was not constrained to knowing the opinion of officials at the Colonial and Indian Offices, but went well beyond it to the opinion of experts on the region, including Professor H. A. R. Gibb,[14] whose opinion was sought regarding the very central issue of Arab unity. The memorandum he wrote in response became the focus of considerable attention and criticism by British officials!

At the beginning of his report, Gibb puts the responsibility of taking the initiative regarding a potential Arab union on Britain's shoulders, especially since the prevailing situation in the region was a direct result of 'the opportunist policies adopted by the victors in the last war'. This implied that the British Government was duty-bound to implement this plan, especially in light of its close relations with the Pan-Arab Movement early in its inception. He seized the opportunity to warn officials that if they did not take an initiative in that direction, others probably would, and thus subsequently put the British Government under even more pressure.[15]

After specifying the guiding principles upon which the unity scheme should draw – namely avoiding complications, simplicity, flexibility, attending to Arab economic problems and taking their interests and independence into account – the famous professor addressed the ways and means by which Arab unity could be realised. He proposed that it be implemented in stages, starting with the cultural dimension, then the economic and, finally, the political, and he accused the current plan of being devoid of practicable bases. In his opinion, any joint economic institutions of a permanent nature should necessarily be founded on political grounds; any economic union based solely on an agreement between sovereign countries would be subject to pressure from conflicts of interests among the concerned parties, and this would soon lead to its demise.

Professor Gibb believed that one of the main obstacles facing the projected union would be in keeping the political borders drawn after the war, and the ideal solution would be the integration of all the old provinces into a single political entity. He listed these provinces as Basra, Baghdad, al-Jazeera, Aleppo, Damascus, Lattakia, Lebanon, Jabal al-Druze, Palestine and Trans-Jordan, which left the Syrian Desert that could be divided into northern and southern provinces.

He justified this particular point by saying that a federation along these lines would, on the one hand, overcome the potential problems arising from the different size of various provinces and, on the other, ensure that smaller entities would not pose a threat to the unified state. Moreover, such an arrangement would resolve the problem arising from the presence of a Sunni majority by giving minorities a measure of internal independence in regions where they constituted a considerable segment of the population, such as in the cases of the Shīʿites in Basra, the Kurds in Mosul, the ʿAlawites in Lattakia, the Christians in Lebanon and the Jews in Palestine. In addition, it would secure the interest of pastoral groups in the Syrian Desert: 'It will allow for differences in the infrastructure in each province without this affecting the central government. This approach would be flexible enough to allow the adherence of more provinces.'

According to its designer, however, the scheme would face two obstacles. The first would be in regard to the way in which the Kingdom of Iraq should be dismembered, a rather difficult undertaking to envision, with his solution being a division into three provinces that would join together in a federal union. The second obstacle would be Ibn Saʿūd's attitude towards the projected union; Professor Gibb believed that it would be difficult for the King of Saudi Arabia to oppose the union as long as the populations concerned wanted it. Moreover, King ʿAbd al-ʿAziz had several times stated his desire for Arab unity, and there was always the possibility that Saudi Arabia would enter into an alliance with, or perhaps eventually join, a confederation of united Arab states.

However, the real problem would arise when the issue of establishing a national home for the Jews came into play. Gibb seemed to presage what would transpire later on; he saw the future of this national home as being contingent on its ability to integrate:

> its incorporation as a positive cooperating element in the Federation and that the erection of Palestine into an independent Jewish state is entirely excluded. If any stable settlement at all is to be reached in the Middle East, it is essential that Palestine should not be allowed to become a discordant factor, pursuing a foreign policy different from and possibly antagonistic to that of its neighbours.[16]

Officials at the British Foreign Office were not ready to accept Professor Gibb's plan, and one of them, Mr Cassia, told him that two factors made it unacceptable. The first was the fact that the Iraqis would never accept their country's dismemberment and, second, it was highly doubtful that Jewish public opinion would accept the Jews in Palestine becoming one of the proposed federation's 12 provinces.[17]

On the other hand, Foreign Office officials thought that Professor Gibb's proposals were not only impractical, but also that the division of the Arab world into provinces would provoke the ire of the Arabs and create many complications. Their own solution was to deal boldly with the roots of the problem, to allow the Arab people to take control of the situation and to wait for the right moment to establish an Arab democratic state. With this comment, Professor Gibb's initiative was buried deep among the files on which the present study is based!

* * *

Despite all the back and forth consultations among various British Departments, there was still a need to hear an Arab voice, and the choice fell on Emir ʿAbdullah of Trans-Jordan. Among all the Arab rulers, he had the closest relationship with Britain at the time, especially given the active role he played in helping put down Rashīd ʿĀlī al-Gaylanī's movement in Iraq, in April 1941.

On Monday 30 November 1942, during a luncheon at the Emir's Palace in Amman, attended by a number of high-ranking officials in the region, headed by Mr Casey, Minister of State for Middle Eastern Affairs, and Sir Harold MacMichael, the British High Commissioner in Palestine, the Emir ʿAbdullah was asked his opinion on the proposed Arab union. They had forewarned him earlier that any steps in this regard would have to wait for the war to end, since the Allied leaders were preoccupied, for the time being, with prosecuting the war. They had also given him notice that the British Government intended to let the Arabs take the initiative in this regard.[18]

The Emir chose to respond the next day (30 November) by way of a letter to Prime Minister Winston Churchill in which he addresses him as 'my dear and very great friend'. At the beginning of his correspondence, he expresses his joy at recent British victories in the war, saying that thanks to Churchill's wise direction and excellent command, the light of dawn had appeared after the black darkness of war. Of greater importance, however, is the memorandum attached to the letter in which he gives his opinion on the subject.

He reveals a conversation that took place between his Prime Minister and the British High Commissioner, in Amman the preceding year, 1941, during which the former had voiced the national aspirations of the Arabs, and the latter had reassured him that Arab rights would be guaranteed. The Emir goes on to say: 'Of the several things which the present war has made so clear is the necessity of the maintenance of a strong and permanent friendship between the Muslims and the democratic nations; and in the forefront of these stand the Arabs.' He then summarised his proposal in four points:

1 To establish a union of Greater Syria, namely the complete union of the countries of the Levant, the paramount issue for the satisfaction of the Arabs.
2 The evolution of a cultural union between Iraq and the Syrian countries with a view to bringing the Arabs nearer to a general confederation.
3 Solving the Palestine problem within such a group, in a manner which would not prejudice the previous promises given by Britain, and will not, at the same time, expose the Arabs to the danger of a Jewish superiority.
4 Here the Emir was first keen to underline that he had no personal motives behind his fourth proposal which involved the creation of a system that would guarantee the contentment of the Muslim world, without allowing a religious minority to overrule a majority in all that this majority has inherited in the way of traditions and principles from the dawn of Islam up to the present day.

He concluded his letter with a historical review of the burden Britain has shouldered in the Arab World and gave a number of odd examples to illustrate his point. Among these were the British assistance to the Ottoman State against Bonaparte's attempt to capture Acre, and its assistance in putting down Muḥammad 'Alī's schemes and success in forcing him to return to the lands from which he had come. He also cited Britain's role in the Crimean War and in the compromise solution between Turkey and

Russia, as well as its intervention in Egypt after the Ottomans failed to suppress the 'Urābī Revolt. Finally, he thanked Churchill and the Minister in charge of Middle East affairs for having given him the opportunity to advise them on this very important matter.[19]

Since the Emir had asked during the meeting with British officials to represent his country at the Peace Conference, to be held after the war, and insinuated the possibility of his abdication if he did not receive satisfactory assurances to that effect, the Colonial Office decided that Churchill would answer the Emir in general terms and ignore his two requests. It was impossible to respond positively to his first request, since Trans-Jordan was under the British Mandate, and therefore could not be represented at the Peace Conference, or at any other Conference, given that the management of its external affairs was the mandatory power's responsibility.

Economic Cultural Unity

After all the studies, the memoranda and the solicitation of the opinions of concerned parties, the British decided to adopt the idea of encouraging some form of economic rapprochement and a cultural union, a decision reflected in their policies towards Arab unity over the following months. Specifically in regard to economic cooperation, the Department of External Research at Balliol College – Oxford University – was asked to prepare a study, which was completed in April 1942.[20]

According to its authors, the study's objective was to raise the standard of living in the Arab countries, and examine the best way to strengthen political ties between them. The report covered Arab countries over which Britain had influence, namely all the Arab Asian countries as well as Egypt and Barqah – the ultimate aim being to explore the possibility of uniting them into a single economic bloc.

To arrive at the desired goal, researchers at Balliol College turned their attention to identifying the problems that required solutions, and five such problems were identified:

1 The need for a comprehensive survey of agricultural products and the volume of trade between various countries of the region, to be able to answer the question as to whether encouraging domestic trade would yield any economic benefits, without radically altering current economic activities. In the course of answering this question, it would be useful to identify what could be gained by instituting customs tariffs

to allow preferential treatment among these countries, as well as a currency and a domestic transport policy.

2 The answer to the above question would probably be negative, requiring a re-examination of productive projects including the full utilisation of natural resources, especially land cultivation through irrigation, as well as the benefits of any industrial development. This required the identification of market shares to justify the funding of large industrial projects, to assess what Arab countries could offer in terms of resources and what they would likely need to import. It would also require studying the impact of any change on foreign trade.

3 There was also a need to know the position of Arab governments in regard to the above changes. The division of the northern Arab countries between French and British Mandate regions, and the right that Egypt had acquired, in 1930, to pursue its own protection policies, resulted in an upsurge of local activities. There was yet another obstacle in the face of progress towards some sort of economic union and that was the fear of Jewish commercial infiltration, particularly by way of Syria and Iraq. In addition to these issues, there was a need for adequate information about the nature of the Jewish economy in Palestine. Needless to say, economic relations between the Arabs and the Jews would depend on the nature of political relations between them. No doubt, the Arabs would wonder whether this economic union would make them dependent on Western capital, not to mention whether or not this would also expose them to ensuing interference in their domestic affairs.

4 It would be quite natural for the above suggestions to raise questions regarding whether a tighter economic union would mean more advantages for the beneficiaries. The following step, in this context, would be to define what sort of institutions needed to be established in order to implement what had been decided upon. The concept of an 'economic union' should be translated into institutions that would oversee economic relations between those Arab countries; institutions that would enjoy supervisory privileges over important and relevant aspects of people's lives.

5 Finally, it would be necessary to examine the impact that these regional relations might have, in the post-war period, on the nature of international development, and mainly on agriculture and trade. For example, the formulation of wide-ranging plans to control international investments would require a certain vision regarding the role

that the Arab countries would play in such an economic system. In any case, active foreign economic interests in the Arab world would undoubtedly play a role in forging future economic relations between the Arab countries, and the opposite would also be true. Changes that might conceivably take place as a result of the economic union between the Arab states would affect the nature of these interests.[21]

In comparison to this approach, a cultural union among the Arab states seemed less complicated, and it started with Egypt. A British document reveals that Ibn Saʿūd received an invitation from the Egyptian Government to take part in a new cultural cooperation bureau it intended to establish to promote cultural relations between the Arab countries. The Egyptian Government's invitation to the Arab governments stated that all they needed to do was send a representative to the said bureau's meetings, exchange information in the cultural and educational fields, and discuss the terms of a future cultural agreement between the Arab countries.[22]

The Iraqi Government was first to respond to the Egyptian invitation, raising Ibn Saʿūd's suspicion that Nūrī al-Saʿīd was behind the entire idea. Two officials from the Iraqi Ministry of Education arrived in Cairo on 1 August 1943 to discuss cultural relations between the two countries[23] and, at the end of two weeks of talks, the Egyptian Ministry of Education issued a statement announcing the conclusion of the cultural cooperation talks between the two countries. The communiqué said that two sides agreed on the terms of a cultural treaty involving exchanges of students, teachers, scientific publications and curricula. The agreement's terms also included a recommendation regarding the encouragement of scientific and literary publications in Arabic. The two parties agreed to establish a joint bureau to implement the agreement's provisions, with the stipulation that its next meeting take place in Baghdad, under the presidency of the Iraqi Minister of Education.[24]

It seems that the Wafd Government in power at the time was behind the encouragement of these relations. This became evident when the al-ʿUrūbah League, newly established at King Fu'ād I University and composed of students from the al-Wafd Party, began preparing for an Arab students' Conference, to be held under the presidency of Naḥḥās Pāshā, one of the main items on its agenda being the promotion of Arab unity.[25] In addition, the famous Egyptian jurist Dr ʿAbd al-Razzāq al-Sanhūrī Pāshā played a role in strengthening cultural ties between the two countries, whether through his role at the Faculty of Law in Baghdad, or via his contributions to drafting Iraqi civil laws.[26]

Not much time passed before other countries expressed their wishes to join the Egyptian-Iraqi Treaty. On a visit to Cairo in early November 1943, the Syrian Prime Minister discussed with the Egyptian Minister of Education the possibility of Syria becoming party to the Treaty. In fact, the two sides were in complete agreement about the bases on which any future cultural cooperation, between the two countries, should be established.[27]

British Government departments welcomed these cultural initiatives, although their attitude was politically motivated since various reports indicated that educated Arab classes were clearly behind the Axis Powers and supported fascist ideology, in general. This prompted the 'Middle East War Council' to recommend in a report that Britain assist the Arabs in the cultural field, with the hope that Arab intellectuals would welcome activities aimed at developing Arab thought along Western cultural lines.[28]

Of course, matters were not expected to hinge solely on cultural-economic relations alone; soon afterwards, therefore, the situation started moving towards a political orientation, especially in light of British successes in the war against the Axis Powers. In October 1942, the British Eighth Army scored a number of victories against the Axis forces in the Battle of Al-Alamein and maintained pressure on their enemies until early January of the following year, when they succeeded in forcing Field Marshal Erwin Rommel's troops to pull back some 1350 miles in a mere 82 days. The famous German commander withdrew behind the Tunisian border,[29] ending the German threat to North Africa, and to the Arab region in general.

The initiative came from the Iraqi Government and from Nūrī Pāshā al-Saʿīd, in particular, who began by asking the London Government's permission, which proved quite generous towards him. On 15 February 1943, Nūrī sent a memorandum to Lord Halifax writing that now that the end of the war and the ensuing peaceful settlement were drawing close, he believed it was an opportune time to discuss the issues of Arab independence and unity, in light of the developments of the previous 28 years. He attached a summary of his opinion on the matter,[30] including the need for the United Nations to issue a declaration announcing a union between Syria, Lebanon, Palestine and Trans-Jordan, otherwise known as Greater Syria, and allowing its people to choose their own form of government. The proposal also included an item regarding the establishment of an Arab League to which Syria, Iraq and any other Arab country would accede at once, and the formation of a League Council responsible, among other matters, for defence, foreign affairs, currency and customs.

Nūrī al-Saʿīd's proposal also included giving the Jews in Palestine some form of autonomy that would permit them their own education system and security service, under the supervision of the Greater Syrian State. For their part, the Maronites of Lebanon would enjoy their own administrative system, similar to the one they enjoyed under the Ottoman regime, guaranteed by the international community.[31] Nūrī Pāshā ended his exposé by arguing that the implementation of these recommendations was the only way to ensure peace in this part of the world.

Convening the Arab Conference

The response came in the form of another declaration by Anthony Eden in the House of Commons, on 24 February 1943, giving the Iraqi Prime Minister the go-ahead to proceed.

In Parliament, Mr Price asked the Secretary of State whether the British Government had taken any steps to encourage political and economic cooperation among the Arab countries with the aim of creating an Arab federation. The reply was:

> His Majesty's Government viewed with sympathy any movement among the Arabs to promote their economic, cultural and political unity, but that the initiative would have to come from the Arabs. So far as I am aware, no such scheme, which would command general approval, has yet been worked out.[32]

Therefore, one of the parties had to make the first move.

Having gained Britain's approval, the Iraqis embarked on their initiative with a visit by former Iraqi Prime Minister Jamīl al-Madfaʿī and Iraqi Minister Taḥsīn al-ʿAskarī to a number of Arab countries, in March 1943, ending in Cairo. Although on the surface it appeared as if the two Ministers were in the Egyptian capital to prepare for a royal visit to Egypt by King Fayṣal II and the Queen Mother, the real motive was to hold unofficial talks on the issue of Arab unity.[33]

In Cairo, however, there were apparent differences on the issue between the Egyptians and Iraqis. On 27 March during the talks between Naḥḥās Pāshā and his two Iraqi guests on the subject of holding a conference to which all the Arab countries would be invited, the latter were of the opinion that the conference should be both official and unofficial, while Naḥḥās Pāshā thought that it should only be at the official level.

It was probably due to this difference of opinion that the Egyptians decided to seize the initiative, as evident from the Egyptian Government's long statement in the Senate, on 30 March concerning its policy regarding Arab unity. The Minister of Justice, who delivered the statement on behalf of the Government, said that Naḥḥās Pāshā had long been involved in Arab issues, and that in light of Eden's recent declaration, consultations with all Arab governments would be held, and political contacts with each accelerated, to learn their views on the matter and coordinate them as closely as possible. Arab governments would then be invited to attend the Conference to be held in Cairo under the auspices of the Egyptian Government, to discuss this very issue and take a number of decisions with the aspirations of the Arab people in mind.

The statement mentioned the meeting between Naḥḥās Pāshā, and Taḥsīn al-ʿAskarī and Jamīl al-Madfaʿī, saying that the Egyptian Prime Minister had told them of his programme and already addressed an official invitation to Nūrī Pāshā al-Saʿīd, on the understanding that the next step would be to review Iraqi proposals relative to economic and political aspects, especially the latter. The statement added that Naḥḥās Pāshā would soon issue invitations to all Arab governments to attend preparatory talks, and if these proved successful, the Egyptian Government would invite all delegations to attend the Conference in Cairo.

The British Embassy in Cairo commented on the Egyptian statement by saying that Muṣṭafā Naḥḥās was anxious to wrest control away from Nūrī al-Saʿīd and, at the same time, to overcome any obstacle that King Fārūq might put in his path if he were to decide that the Conference should be unofficial.[34] British documents show that both the Iraqi initiative and the contacts in Cairo and Baghdad had stirred things up regarding Arab unity in Saudi Arabia, Trans-Jordan, Yemen, Syria and Lebanon.

In Saudi Arabia, Mr Wikeley, the British Minister in Jeddah, sent on 26 April to the Foreign Office and to British representatives in Baghdad, Jerusalem, Beirut and Cairo, a copy of a letter from King ʿAbd al-ʿAziz giving his opinion on Arab unity and Pan-Arabism, in general, as a comment on Eden's declaration at the House of Commons. At the beginning of his letter, the Saudi King draws attention to what he had already told the British representative in his country, regarding differences between the Arab leaders calling for the Conference. He added that he did not trust any of them because they were all using the invitation to strengthen their domestic positions and therefore did not advise the British Government to adopt the same approach!

ʿAbd al-ʿAziz then went on to say that he was aware of the fact that each of these leaders was seeking to win his support for his own plan, and although he knew that the British Government strongly supported the legitimate aspirations of the Arab people, he preferred to remain out of the fray. He intimated that he only trusted the British Government, and would only work in coordination with it. However, he added that if the latter believed that public interest required him to take part in the Conference he would then do his best. He would do so on condition that the British gave him the necessary assurances that such Conferences would not go against his interests.

In the event of a decision that he should attend, he would consult the British Government every step of the way, starting with the question of the policy he should follow if the projected Conference were to address the Palestinian issue in a manner contradictory to British interests.

He concluded by reiterating that

> unless His Majesty's Government wishes him to enter the arena, he will keep out of it, and will continue his policy of communicating to his Majesty's Government with the greatest friendship and frankness his views of the truth of these subjects. He will continue to advise the Arabs that their interest lies in cooperating with His Majesty's Government and in avoiding all matters which would embarrass it during the war.[35]

The London Government responded by sending instructions to its representative in Jeddah asking him to inform the King, after thanking him for his frankness, that the British Government's policy was clearly defined in Eden's declaration at the House of Commons, on 24 February. This policy encouraged any move on the part of the Arabs towards an economic, cultural and political union – provided the initiative came from the Arabs themselves. It goes on to say the British Government would have no objections to Arab governments and leaders holding discussions on the matter, although it believed that a Conference was not the ideal way to proceed, but they should rather begin with secret talks through diplomatic channels. The representative in Jeddah apprised the King that the British Government had already shared its opinion with the Iraqi Prime Minister, without any ambiguity.[36]

On a subsequent occasion, Ibn Saʿūd expressed his annoyance to the British Minister in Jeddah at being left out of the picture as far as Naḥḥās Pāshā and Nūrī al-Saʿīd's efforts to organise a Conference without consulting him were concerned. He said that he was in complete agreement with the British Government on the need to hold secret talks between Arab governments prior to convening the conference, and that, if Britain approved, he would be ready to take the initiative in this matter.[37]

At the beginning of June, in an interview with American *Life* magazine, King 'Abd al-'Azīz gave his candid opinion on the Palestinian issue, and said that he had been reluctant to do so for a long time to avoid coming under pressure from the Allies, but that the time had now come for him to do so. He concluded by saying that he was fully confident that Arab unity would be achieved with help from the Allies.[38]

King 'Abd al-'Azīz's doubts, however, increased in the wake of the Saudi-Iraqi talks that took place towards the end of April and the beginning of May. The King noticed that Nūrī al-Sa'īd had given a lot of importance to the unification of Syria and Palestine in one independent state and to his call on Arab leaders to do their best to make this prospect a reality. Nūrī al-Sa'īd claimed that Naḥḥās had agreed to both this plan and to a meeting to discuss the issue, and that he intended to send an invitation to the King to participate in the meeting.

The Iraqi Prime Minister added that an Arab Unity Conference could be held once a successful solution to the Palestinian-Syrian issue had been found. However, Ibn Sa'ūd did not agree with that, although he did believe that the issue was certainly important enough. He considered it the duty of the Arabs as a whole to help achieve the independence of these two countries and that it should be done quietly without fanfare, with the full agreement of Great Britain and the United States.[39]

In the middle of that same month of June, Ibn Sa'ūd wrote a lengthy letter to the British Government stating his opinion on Naḥḥās' address in the Egyptian Parliament and on Nūrī al-Sa'īd's subsequent attempts to forge closer ties with him. This had greatly upset the King, who believed that the two men should have consulted him on any action before Naḥḥās made his statement. He added that, under such conditions, he would not be able to cooperate with either Naḥḥās or Nūrī Pāshā.

The King added that if the said Conference were to go ahead, it would undoubtedly fail for the same reasons that had led to the failure of the Palestine Conference in London, regardless of whether he were to take part in it or not. Nūrī Pāshā, or anyone else, could deliver an anti-British speech to make the Arabs happy, in which case he would have only one of three options from which to choose: to simply listen without taking any action, which would be very difficult to do; to applaud, which would never happen; or start a fight, which would be very harmful to the Conference.

King 'Abd al-'Azīz expressed his astonishment at Iraq's invitation to him to cooperate on such important issues, despite the failure of the two countries to solve the many smaller problems between them. In actuality, by wondering about the benefit of cooperating on such substantial issues, the King was signalling his opposition to the proposed Arab unity plan.

In his comment on the King's letter, the British Minister in Jeddah said that Ibn Sa'ūd would not take part in the Conference unless he was certain that the British were genuinely interested in the matter, and only after the problems between him and Iraq were settled. Finally, he suggested that both Nūrī al-Sa'īd and Naḥḥās Pāshā do something to assuage the King's anger and heal his wounded pride.[40]

The British were even more annoyed by what happened after Naḥḥās Pāshā sent a private message to King 'Abd al-'Azīz, through the good offices of Sulaymān al-Ḥamad, asking him to acquaint himself with Nūrī Pāshā's proposals on Arab unity. The Saudi King's answer was rather provocative – asserting that Nūrī Pāshā's motive behind these proposals should be borne in mind. That is: first, there was his desire to use the occasion to achieve his personal ambitions; second, there was his plan to annex Syria and Palestine to Iraq; third, there were his efforts to incite trouble between Egypt and Saudi Arabia; and, finally, there were his attempts to strengthen the Hashemite family at the expense of Ibn Sa'ūd.[41]

In reaction to the Saudi King's angry response, the British Government sent a military envoy to Riyadh, where a meeting was held with King 'Abd al-'Azīz at the end of August in order to know where he stood on the issue of Arab unity. After the meeting, Colonel Hoskins sent a report to London containing the following points:

- At this point, Ibn Sa'ūd is unable to propose a specific union plan because it is difficult for him to predict, as of now, in what condition the Arab states will be after the war.
- Ibn Sa'ūd admitted that he could not ignore the cultural, linguistic and religious affinity that binds the Arabs together, and understands that some form of economic and political union was inevitable. He said that he would be glad to take part in achieving it, and was ready to play a role in the relevant negotiations. He believes, however, that the first step should be the establishment of an Arab joint entity along the lines of the North American states, followed perhaps by other steps towards a closer union.
- Although Ibn Sa'ūd expressed his willingness to cooperate fully in view of achieving Arab unity, he placed two conditions on his cooperation. The first was that the Hashemites should not poke their noses into the affairs of the Syrian and Palestinian governments, and the second was that measures to implement Arab unity should impede

neither the military efforts of the Allies nor the establishment of a just peace after the war.

- King ʿAbd al-ʿAzīz admitted to Colonel Hoskins that he had not been consulted regarding the steps that Naḥḥās and Nūrī al-Saʿīd had so far taken towards achieving Arab unity, even though he had recently received an invitation from the Egyptian Prime Minister asking him to send a representative to Cairo to transmit the King's opinion on the matter. The King responded by asking Naḥḥās Pāshā to send Riyadh a detailed explanation of his own plans in this regard, since he, the King, would not be able to expound on an issue he knows very little about.[42]

Naḥḥās Pāshā contributed to the goodwill campaign towards King ʿAbd al-ʿAzīz by sending him a letter in reply, explaining that the only reason a correspondence had taken place between Egypt and Iraq, about the issue of Arab unity, was Nūrī Pāshā's desire to share his thoughts on the subject with the Egyptian Government. From that point on, he said, it was only natural for this exchange to develop into a wider network of contacts involving other Arab governments. When the Egyptian Minister for Foreign Affairs handed the letter over to the Saudi Arabian delegation in Cairo, in order for them to transmit it to King Ibn Saʿūd, he asked them to inform the King that the fact that the talks had started with Iraq did not mean that the latter country had priority over other Arab states. Moreover, in an effort to placate the Riyadh Government, the Egyptian Foreign Minister confirmed to the Saudi representative in Cairo that Emir ʿAbdullah had tried to obtain Nūrī Pāshā's support for his nomination to the throne of Syria, but that the latter had not encouraged him in his quest.[43]

At the same time, Nūrī al-Saʿīd sent a long letter to King Ibn Saʿūd comprising two main points:

- After consulting a number of prominent personalities in Syria, Lebanon, Palestine and Trans-Jordan, he perceived a strong desire for a Greater Syrian union among the four countries. However, there were three obstacles on the path towards this objective: the French presence in Syria; the condition of minorities in Syria – a situation that would undoubtedly cause trouble eventually; and, finally, the Jewish presence in Palestine.
- In light of the above, Nūrī Pāshā proposes a campaign having two main lines of activities: immediate action to achieve the political unity

> of Greater Syria, to be followed by wider discussions regarding close relations among all the Arab states; and the possibility of a cultural, economic and political union between them.[44]

King 'Abd al-'Azīz reply was to say that Nūrī should have no doubts, whatsoever, that Ibn Sa'ūd was doing his best to secure the independence of all the Arab countries in a manner that preserved their respective individual characteristics, and ensured that no Arab state would ever attack another. He also said, however, that this could only be achieved by reaching some sort of equilibrium among the Arab states.[45]

While all eyes in London, Baghdad and Cairo were focussed on Saudi Arabia, in 1943, a new hero emerged on the scene in the form of none other than Emir 'Abdullah of Trans-Jordan, most of whose story with regard to Arab unity in that same year has now been revealed to us through British official documents.

* * *

In Trans-Jordan, the beginning came in the form of a telegram sent by Sir Kinahan Cornwallis, the British Ambassador in Baghdad, on 12 March stating that Emir 'Abdullah had called the High Commissioner in Jerusalem to request his permission to hold a Conference under his presidency, in Amman, attended by Egypt, Syria, Palestine, Iraq and the Kingdom of Saudi Arabia.

When Nūrī al-Sa'īd learned of the Emir's move, he warned Cornwallis against accepting 'Abdullah's request, since most of the countries involved were likely to reject the invitation. He said that the matter would depend largely on the intended conference's agenda; if it were confined to the issue of an Arab confederation, then there would be little hope that these states would acquiesce to take part in it. If, however, it involved issues related to the future governments of Syria and Palestine, or to the selection of a candidate to the throne, it would raise considerable suspicion. The Iraqi Prime Minister went on to say that, in any case, Emir 'Abdullah was not the right man to lead such a conference, and that raising the issue of nomination to the thrones of Palestine or Syria, at this point in time, would actually destroy the cause of Pan-Arabism. The Arabs would simply turn their attention away from the main issues towards disputes over thrones.[46]

Not long after making his proposal, Emir 'Abdullah took the next step once he realised that the first had gone nowhere. He issued a manifesto stating Arab objectives in general, though he concentrated on the division of Greater Syria and the need for its future unification. He addressed himself to the Syrian people from 'The Gulf of Aqaba, to the Mediterranean Sea to the Upper Euphrates River', by which he meant Palestine, Trans-Jordan, Syria and possibly Lebanon. The climax of the statement was an invitation to prominent personalities in Greater Syria to play a role in bringing about this Syrian unity, and to those who would participate in a special Syrian Conference, which he said he would be glad to host in his Kingdom's capital.

The Emir intended to broadcast his manifesto on the Near East Broadcasting Station in Jaffa, but the British official in Amman asked those in charge not to comply, upon which the censor in Palestine took it upon himself to do the rest, including preventing the manifesto from appearing in any newspaper. However, despite the above measures, some copies were leaked to Palestine, Syria and in a number of neighbouring countries.

More significant is that the British Resident in the Jordanian capital met the Emir on 21 April and, as he explains it, 'I consider it necessary that I should make it quite clear to him that he should not have issued a proclamation of the kind without first consulting the representative of His Britanic Majesty, as he is bound to.'[47]

Emir 'Abdullah admitted that he had made a mistake when he issued his manifesto without consulting the British Government, and added that he was very sorry. He, however, justified his move by saying that all he had wanted was to remind the British Government of his presence, and had he asked for permission to issue the manifesto, he would not have got it. The Emir recalled the events of the previous quarter of a century and complained that the Hashemite family had not got what it deserved, and that the British Government, despite his unwavering loyalty to it, had repeatedly and personally let him down and failed to keep promises made to him.[48]

Emir 'Abdullah did not desist from attempting to urge others to accept the Greater Syria project. This became clear when he sent his Prime Minister, Tawfīq Abul-Hudā, to Egypt, at the end of August, to put the matter to Egyptian Prime Minister Muṣṭafā Naḥḥās Pāshā – a visit that culminated in a joint statement on the subject in early September 1943.

The statement said that the two countries had taken into consideration the current situation in Trans-Jordan, and its aspirations regarding its relations with Syria, Lebanon, Palestine and the other Arab countries. It is obvious from the ambiguity and neutrality of the wording that the Egyptian side had not taken the bait, prompting Abul-Hudā to issue a statement to the press, upon his departure from Cairo, praising Naḥḥās Pāshā and addressing a number of issues other than the subject of their discussions. He expressed his hope that Naḥḥās Pāshā would discover what the position of Palestine was, and said that Syria would probably be the next country to be consulted.[49]

The meeting between Prince ʻAbd al-Ilāh, the Iraqi Regent, and Emir ʻAbdullah, at the Dead Sea airport where the former stopped on 28 October, reveals both the aspirations and apprehensions of Jordan's Emir. The Regent conveyed his discontent over the Egyptian Government's attitude towards Arab unity and at the fact that Naḥḥās Pāshā was trying to monopolise leadership. The Emir's response was that the leadership should remain in the hands of the Hashemite family, that Ibn Saʻūd supported Syrian intentions to establish a republic and that the Egyptians were seeking to improve their position. Emir ʻAbdullah also added that he had neither the money nor the men to influence matters, whereas the Regent had both.

The British High Commissioner in Palestine, Sir Harold MacMichael, commented on the meeting, saying:

> All this rings fairly true, except I assume the Amir did not fail also to point out to the Regent that he, the Amir, was the senior member of the House of Hāshim. Reference to Syria shows a welcome sense of realities – the Amir appears to have been slightly reassured by the above in respect of his previous fears that the Regent might be H. M. Government's candidate as Head of the Arab Federation.[50]

On 7 November 1943, the same member of the House of Commons, Mr Price, asked the Foreign Secretary if he could make a statement about the conference of delegates from Arab Middle Eastern countries that recently convened in Cairo. Contrary to his habit, Eden's answer came in a long statement:

> For your own information, the Iraqi Prime Minister visited Cairo in July to discuss this question of general cooperation between Arab states with the Egyptian Prime Minister. At their meeting, Nūrī and Naḥḥās agreed that Naḥḥās should enter into conversations with the governments of other Arab states, in order to ascertain what measure of agreement there was between their respective views. If the result of these discussions showed a sufficient measure of agreement between the Arab States it was proposed to hold a conference of all the states concerned, probably in Cairo to work out and endorse a common policy.[51]

This marked the beginning of the process to establish the Arab League.

Notes

1. F.O. 371/31337, War Office – Arab Federation Report, 9 January 1942. See Annex 6.
2. Britain had appointed a Minister of State in the Middle East, based in Cairo, to coordinate among various parties in support of the war effort.
3. The War Cabinet is a downsized ministry comprising the main government ministers responsible for urgent war-related decisions.
4. F.O. 371/31337, War Cabinet – Arab Federation Report.
5. The Government that General Charles de Gaulle formed in London after the fall of Paris to the Nazis.
6. F.O. 371/31337, Annex-Schemes of Arab Federation.
7. F.O. 371/31337, War Cabinet – Arab Federation Report.
8. J. L. Magnes, 'Palestine and Arab Union', *Bayot Hayom*, 25 July 1941.
9. F.O. 371/31337, Text of declaration proposed by General Catroux.
10. F.O. 371/31338, High Commissioner in Palestine to His Majesty's Principal Secretary of State for the Colonies, 7 June 1942.
11. F.O. 371/31338, Cassia (Foreign Office) to Boyd (Colonial Office), 9 June 1942.
12. India Office, Whitehall, London, to Foreign Office, 6 May 1942.
13. Report by Colonel Prior, Representative of India, Middle East War Council, Cairo, 26 January 1942.
14. Hamilton Alexander Gibb and Harold Bowen, *The Islamic Society and the West: A study of the impact of Western civilisation on Muslim Culture in the Near East* (London, New York: Oxford University Press, 1950–7).
15. F.O. 371/31338, Plan of Arab Federation by Professor Gibb (Royal Institute of International Affairs), 21 December 1942.
16. F.O. 371/31338, Plan of Arab Federation by Professor Gibb.
17. F.O. 371/31338, Minutes by Mr Caccia, 10 February 1943.
18. F.O. 371/31338, From Baxter (Foreign Office) to Sir Kinahan Cornwallis (Baghdad), 23 February.
19. F.O. 371/31338, From Edmond (Colonial Office) to Foreign Office, 23 December 1942.
20. F.O. 371/31338, A Note on the Proposed Equity into the Possibility of Closer Economic Association between the Arab Countries, 23 April 1943.
21. F.O. 371/31338, A Note on the Proposed Equity.
22. F.O. 371/34955, Egyptian proposal for a cultural bureau of Arab countries, 22 February 1943.
23. F.O. 371/35537, Weekly Political and Economic Report, from 29 July to 4 August 1943.
24. F.O. 371/35537, Weekly Political and Economic Report, from 12 to 18 August 1943.
25. Ibid.
26. F.O. 371/35537, Weekly Political and Economic Report, from 14 to 20 October 1943.
27. F.O. 371/3537, Weekly Political and Economic Report from 4 to 10 November 1943.
28. F.O. 371/34975, Resolutions adopted by the Middle Eastern War Council.
29. A. J. Grant and Harold Temperley, *Europe in the Nineteenth and Twentieth Centuries* (1789–1932), pp. 515–16.
30. F.O. 371/34958, Council of Ministers, Baghdad, to Viscount Halifax, 15 February 1943.

31. F.O. 371/34959, Memorandum on Arab Unity by the Naval Intelligence Department, 4 June 1943.
32. F.O. 371/34955, Parliamentary Question.
33. F.O. 371/35537, Weekly Political and Economic Report, from 18 to 24 March 1943.
34. F.O. 371/35537, Weekly Political and Economic Report, from 25 to 31 March 1943.
35. F.O. 371/34957, From Mr Wikeley (Jeddah) to Foreign Office, 26 April 1943.
36. F.O. 371/34957, From Foreign Office to Jeddah, 4 May 1943.
37. F.O. 371/34958, Ibn Sa'ūd and the proposed Conference, from Mr Wikeley (Jeddah), 29 May 1943.
38. F.O. 371/34958, From Wikeley (Jeddah) to Foreign Office, 27April 1943.
39. F.O. 371/34958, From Wikeley (Jeddah) to Foreign Office, 20 July 1943.
40. F.O. 371/34960, From Wikeley (Jeddah) to Foreign Office, 20 July 1943.
41. F.O. 371/34960, From Wikeley (Jeddah) to Foreign Office, 27 July 1943.
42. F.O. 371/34961, Arab Unity Conversation between Colonel Hoskins and King Ibn Sa'ūd at Riyadh, 30 August 1943.
43. F.O. 371/34960, From Wikeley (Jeddah) to Foreign Office, 29 July 1943.
44. Ibid.
45. F.O. 371/34960, From Wikeley (Jeddah) to Foreign Office, 3 August 1943.
46. 371/34955 Cornwallis to Foreign Office, 12 March 1943, Amir Abdullah's proposals for a Conference.
47. F.O. 371/34957, Colonial Office to Foreign Office, 21 April 1943, Emir Abdullah's manifesto on Arab Federation.
48. F.O. 371/34957, Colonial Office to Foreign Office, 29 April 1943, Amir Abdullah's manifesto on Arab Federation.
49. F.O. 371/35538, Weekly Political and Economic Report, from 2 to 8 September 1943.
50. F.O. 371/34963, From Sir H. MacMichael (Palestine) to Colonial Office, 3 November 1943.
51. F.O. 371/34963, Parliamentary Question by Mr Price.

Chapter 6

Britain and the Establishment of the Arab League 1943–5

In September 1943 discussions began about the convening of the conference that would give birth a year later to the Alexandria Protocol, and which a few months after that would lead to the proclamation of the Arab League Charter (March 1945). Although Egypt had taken the initiative in these discussions, British Foreign Office documents reveal that Britain was never far distant from its proceedings.

The Preparatory Meeting

'Alī Kāmil Ḥabīshah Bey, Secretary General of the Egyptian Prime Ministry and one of the officials close to Muṣṭafā Naḥḥās, leader of the Wafd Party, was the first Egyptian envoy to visit the Arab countries in preparation for the Arab Unity Conference. This marked the beginning of a fruitful endeavour that culminated, a year later, in the Antoniadis Conference in Alexandria, and in the Arab League Protocol, in September 1944.

Ḥabīshah Bey left Cairo Airport on 15 September 1943, with the full knowledge of the British Embassy in Cairo, which was completely aware of both his destination and mission. His first destination was Riyadh, capital of Saudi Arabia, and his mission was to consult with King 'Abd al-'Azīz on the next steps towards convening the Arab Unity Conference.[1]

Ḥabīshah Bey stayed at al-Bādīyah Palace in Riyadh, where he held several meetings with the Saudi King in the presence of British officials. It seems, based on information by the British representative in the Saudi

Kingdom, that the Egyptian delegate wanted to assure King 'Abd al-'Azīz that the intended conference would not be political in nature, and that all agreements reached would be confined to the cultural, social and economic domains.

The British representative in Jeddah noted that the Egyptian Government had sent its envoy only after consulting with the British Ambassador in Cairo, and that the Saudis were giving that same representative a systematic account of their meetings with the Egyptian envoy. The British Minister in Jeddah knew that the King had insisted to Ḥabīshah Bey throughout the talks that he would not put any pressure on Britain or the Allies while the war was still going on.

In a meeting between King Ibn Sa'ūd and Mr Jordan on 21 September, the latter explained that the British Government did not object to Arab unity, but believed that the Arabs should not pursue it hastily while the war was still ongoing in order to avoid any eventual unpleasant consequences for the Saudi Government. King 'Abd al-'Azīz had agreed with him on that point, and added that the war even made an eventual economic agreement less likely, thus leaving only the potential for a cultural union which he encouraged, and would do his best to promote. Ḥabīshah Bey's visit ended with a decision to send a Saudi envoy, Sheikh Yūsuf Yāsīn, to Cairo to work according to the Saudi King principles, spelt out in his meeting with the British representative.[2]

In Cairo, after several meetings between the Saudi envoy and the Egyptian Prime Minister, a joint communiqué was issued on 20 October, postponing the meetings until Sheikh Yūsuf Yāsīn had had the chance to consult with the King. The British Ambassador in the Egyptian capital commented on that, saying: 'It is obvious that there are remarkable differences in opinions concerning the initial steps to be taken prior to convening the Conference.'[3]

The last round of meetings between Naḥḥās and Sheikh Yūsuf Yāsīn took place in Cairo, on 2 November, during which the latter shared his master's opinion on the entire issue. He said that King Ibn Sa'ūd believed that it was still too early to address political matters, although he did not totally exclude any such discussions if they could produce positive results. A joint communiqué was issued after the talks to the effect that King Ibn Sa'ūd's advice, which emanated from a sincere desire to achieve prosperity for the Arabs and fulfil their aspirations, had been crucial to the success of the meeting. It added that the two parties had reached a complete understanding on the main principles and objectives.[4] It was a statement of a sort that its general terminology concealed more than it revealed.

At the same time, in October–November 1943, the Egyptian capital witnessed a surge of activities related to the Preparatory Meeting ahead of the proposed Arab Unity Conference. There was news that Imam Yaḥyā, the ruler of Yemen, was about to send a delegate to take part in the consultations, and that Sa'ad-Allah al-Jābirī Bey, the Syrian Prime Minister, had indeed arrived in Cairo with Syrian Foreign Minister Jamīl Mardam Bey and immediately held a meeting with Naḥḥās Pāshā.[5]

Sheikh Yūsuf Yāsīn seized the opportunity of the Syrian delegation's presence in Cairo to hold a round of consultations with them on the issue of Arab unity, based on the Saudi views on Syria that the Saudi King had enunciated during his meeting with the British Representative in his Kingdom. Yāsīn told the Syrians that these views stemmed from the long and cordial relationship between the two countries, especially since his country has no personal ambitions in the region, like the Hashemites have in Iraq, and that all he wanted for Syria was full independence from France.[6]

On 4 November, at the end of the meetings between the two sides, a joint communiqué was issued to the effect that all aspects of Arab unity and Arab cooperation had been reviewed in an atmosphere of sincere friendship, and that the meetings were characterised by the strong desire to see the Arab countries tied together in close cooperation. The Syrian Prime Minister also took the opportunity of his presence in Egypt to study, with the Minister of Education, the possibility of Syria joining the Cultural Treaty between Egypt and Iraq, and stated that an understanding had been reached on cultural cooperation between Egypt and Syria.[7]

At the same time, reports indicate that Egypt had sent an invitation to the Lebanese Government to send a delegation for talks on the same subject. King Fārūq had also sent 'Umar Fatḥī, his aide-de-camp, to Lebanon to congratulate its president, while the Government of Lebanon declared that it had accepted Naḥḥās Pāshā's invitation to send a delegation to the Egyptian capital for talks on the issue of Arab unity.[8]

On 24 November 1944 the London Government stated its position on the issue in the House of Commons once again, when a Member of Parliament, Mr Gallagher, addressed a question to the Foreign Secretary as to whether he had 'any information on the results of the conference recently held on Arab federation'. Eden replied:

> No general conference has recently been held on Arab federation. I understand that consultations have been proceeding for some months between representatives of the various Arab governments concerned, but there is no

> statement that I can make on the subject as I have no responsibility for these consultations, though His Majesty's Government follow them with sympathy and interest.[9]

A few days after making his statement, Nūrī Pāshā al-Saʿīd made a move in a different direction. At the beginning of February, he undertook a tour of Palestine and Syria and was warmly received in Beirut and Damascus. He agreed with the Syrian Government on the establishment of some kind of union in the fields of defence and foreign affairs, leaving the door open for other Arab countries to join, if they wished to do so. They also agreed that Damascus and Baghdad would ask Naḥḥās Pāshā to form a committee of one or two members from each of the countries concerned, before the beginning of March, in order to prepare the agenda for the main conference, scheduled for April in Cairo. The said Conference would be confined to official delegations who would decide on which sort of union they wanted, so that countries could begin preparing for it.[10]

The British Foreign Office was unhappy with Nūrī al-Saʿīd for having undertaken such an initiative without consulting it, and instructed its Ambassador in Baghdad to inform the Iraqi Prime Minister not to be too hasty in his quest. They cited two reasons for their request. The first was that what he proposed was closer to an alliance than a federation which contravened Article 1 of the Iraqi–British Treaty that had finally determined the issue of Iraq's defence; and the second was that any agreement concerning Syria should wait until after the war, to give the French time to put their affairs in order.[11]

After undertaking the necessary investigations and meeting with Nūrī al-Saʿīd, Cornwallis reached the conclusion that London's fears were not justified, and that Nūrī al-Saʿīd had not yet concluded any agreement with the Syrians. He also thought that the potential for such an agreement did not actually exist given the close relationship between the Syrian President and Ibn Saʿūd. The Ambassador wrote: 'It seems possible that Nūrī Pāshā derived a misleading impression of Syrian attitude from the Minister for Foreign Affairs.'[12]

At the same time, Eden sent instructions to Lord Killearn, the British Ambassador in Cairo, on that same subject, and asked him to monitor Naḥḥās' movements regarding the Conference. He also asked him to obtain sufficient guarantees that the Conference would not degenerate into a hostile demonstration against Britain, especially against its policy in Palestine. Lord Killearn did in fact succeed in receiving from the Egyptian Prime Minister an oral report on Egypt's consultations with Arab

Governments, over the previous period, though he did not voice any objections to the steps undertaken up to that time. Nothing warranted such a move on his part, since 'it would be very delicate to raise objection now, particularly in view of Foreign Secretary's declarations in Parliament. Gravely doubts, therefore, wisdom of any attempt to prevent Nūrī Pāshā's proposed conference.'[13]

Over the next few days, Nūrī al-Saʿīd accelerated efforts to convene the Conference, though both the British and the Egyptian governments preferred to move slower in this regard, a fact revealed by Lord Killearn, on 14 March, in a coded telegram to the Foreign Office in London. Although during that same period Taḥsīn al-ʿAskarī paid an official visit to Egypt to discuss that very subject, the British Ambassador in the Egyptian capital asked the parties not to be too hasty, and asked the British Ambassador in Baghdad to reign in Nūrī al-Saʿīd's enthusiasm in this regard.[14]

At the same time, other British officials, among whom was the Minister of State for Middle East Affairs, were holding talks in Cairo. The latter met with Sheikh Ḥāfiẓ Wahbah and Sheikh Yūsuf Yāsīn, both of whom were on a visit to Cairo, to relay to Naḥḥās Pāshā, Ibn Saʿūd's conditions for attending the Conference. These were:

1 That the Conference would recognise the King's status in the Arab world.
2 That the Conference take no decision that would pressure the British Government, or its Allies, while the war was still ongoing.
3 That the Conference would not propose, under any circumstances, the annexation of Syria, Lebanon or Palestine to either Egypt or Iraq.

Talks between Naḥḥās Pāshā and the Saudi envoys ended with the former agreeing to postpone the Conference until the issue of Palestine's representation was settled. Sheikh Yūsuf Yāsīn told the Egyptian Prime Minister that King Ibn Saʿūd wanted all participating countries to have equal status at the Conference in order to ensure that no country would have priority over Saudi Arabia. He also requested that if the Greater Syria project were ever to see light, that there would be no plans either to annex Syria, Lebanon or Palestine to Iraq or Egypt, or to integrate them in a Hashemite state.[15]

In the spring of 1944, the issue of Palestinian representation at the Conference imposed itself on the scene when Naḥḥās Pāshā sent a memorandum to the British Ambassador in Cairo, asking that his Government reconsider its decision to ban Palestinian leaders from travelling to Cairo.

He also asked for the release of Amīn Tamīmī and Jamāl Husaynī, so they could come to Cairo for talks on issues related to the Conference. Lord Killearn commented on the memorandum, saying that Naḥḥās Pāshā was trying to blame the British Government for hindering his Arab unity plan by preventing Palestinian representatives from travelling to Egypt to take part in the preparatory talks.[16]

After contacting his Government, the British Ambassador in Cairo asked Amīn ʿUthmān Pāshā to warn Naḥḥās against raising the issue of Palestine in the course of launching his invitation to the Conference, and to allow the Conference idea to unfold peacefully. Amīn ʿUthmān agreed to do so.[17]

The Antoniadis Conference

While British officials in the region were closely monitoring events relevant to the proposed Conference, the unexpected acceleration in the pace of activities gave them sufficient cause for worry, and provoked a major increase in the number of reports heading London's way.

On 22 April 1944, Mr Spears, British Minister Plenipotentiary in Beirut, sent a long memorandum to London in which he assessed Lebanon's position vis-à-vis the Conference. He said that Ibn Saʿūd's desire to postpone the Conference had had considerable impact on Lebanese politicians, especially the Christians and the President himself, who were not much in favour of it in the first place but could not say so openly. Circumstances were such that even Prime Minister Riyāḍ al-Ṣolḥ, the official most enthusiastic for the Conference, was unable to impose his own point of view.

As for Syria, the country's President Shukrī al-Quwatlī, who had very close ties to Ibn Saʿūd, would not be keen on the Conference if the King were not in favour of it; he had also, however, to take into consideration strong national feelings in his country. On the other hand, Jāmīl Mardam was fully prepared to play the role that Nūrī al-Saʿīd had played in speeding up preparations for the Conference, especially given his shaky loyalty to the President. Based on the foregoing analysis, Spears asked his Government to inform Naḥḥās Pāshā that Mardam Bey did not speak on behalf of the Syrian Government, that he was no more than Nūrī Pāshā's mouthpiece and not a man one could talk to in total confidence!

At the end of his report, the British Minister in Beirut said that it would not be necessary for his Government to oppose the Conference openly, since, in his opinion, a number of negative factors were sufficient to do the job. These include Ibn Saʿūd's position, his relationship with Quwatlī, conflicts within the Hashemite family and, finally, the hesitant attitude of the Lebanese Christians.[18]

What further complicated matters for the British was the memorandum that Egyptian Prime Minister Naḥḥās Pāshā had unexpectedly sent to General de Gaulle, on 22 April, through the French legation in the Egyptian capital. In it, Naḥḥās asked that the North African countries, including Libya, be allowed to participate in the ongoing negotiations on Arab unity. He also requested that these countries' imprisoned leaders be released, and that the independence of Algeria, Morocco and Tunisia be recognised.[19]

It is clear that Naḥḥās Pāshā had been influenced by the press campaign over the previous months in Egypt, calling for widening the circle of negotiations around the proposed union. Fikrī Abāẓah, the most famous journalist in Egypt at the time, wrote that, in his opinion, these negotiations had to pass through two different stages. The first involved consultations with representatives from Yemen, Palestine and the North African countries, and the second involved the convening of a general conference to arrive at practical results.[20] The daily newspaper insisted on the importance of the countries of the Arab Maghreb taking part in these negotiations.[21]

Soon afterwards, Dr Ṭāhā Ḥussayn gave a talk in which he said that the impact of any Arab union would not be sufficiently comprehensive without the participation of the Arab Maghreb countries. The British Ambassador in Cairo commented on this in his weekly report, saying that the notion was widely welcomed, and spread further afield by the Egyptian press.[22]

'Abd al-Majīd Ṣāliḥ Pāshā, a member of the Egyptian Senate, asked the Government a question concerning the participation of North African countries in the discussions around the issue of Arab unity. Naḥḥās gave an indecisive answer to the effect that the Egyptian Government would like to seize the opportunity to confirm its interest in ensuring all the Arab countries' wellbeing, without discrimination, including the North African countries.[23]

The British Government was not in favour of the Egyptian Government undertaking such an initiative and tried to ignore it until the Egyptian Ambassador in London asked for an audience with Anthony Eden. At the meeting, which took place on the afternoon of 5 May, the Ambassador submitted a memorandum from the Egyptian Prime Minister covering the gist of the message that Egypt had addressed to General de Gaulle. The British Minister was very astonished by the gesture, since neither the

French nor the British Governments would have approved of such a move. Eden told the Ambassador that there was nothing to indicate that the states mentioned in Naḥḥās' memorandum were ready for self-government, meaning that there was no use for the Egyptian Government memorandum at this time, and he suggested that Egypt first put its own house in order. The Ambassador had no choice but to tell Eden that he would relay to Naḥḥās Pāshā what had taken place at the meeting.[24]

It appears as if British anxiety reached its climax when it transpired that some of the Gulf countries would be participating in the Conference. This was made clear by the India Office's warning to the Foreign Office that the Sultan of Muscat, who was on a visit to Cairo at the time, had met with Naḥḥās Pāshā to discuss the impending Conference. The India Office was acting on information published in the Iraqi English-language newspaper, the *Iraq Times*, on 14 April 1944, although it did express some reservations regarding its veracity, saying it could be part of an Iraqi propaganda campaign,[25] a hunch that later proved to be well founded.

The foregoing developments prompted the British Ambassador in Cairo, Lord Killearn, to take the initiative, starting with an indirect warning to the Egyptian Prime Minister delivered by Finance Minister Amīn 'Uthmān Pāshā, known as Britain's man in the Egyptian Government. There were several dimensions to that warning: it cautioned Naḥḥās to slow down his activities towards holding the Conference, and to refrain from raising the Palestinian issue at any level, since it could prove extremely harmful. He also warned that holding such a conference would not be in the interest of either the British Government or that of Naḥḥās Pāshā, and that the idea should be left to die gradually. It was also an indirect threat to the Prime Minister that what he was doing could cost him his post, especially since the relationship between him and King Fārūq was at a nadir. It was well known at the time that the latter had not got rid of his Prime Minister simply because of concern for a possible adverse reaction from the British. Lord Killearn also cautioned that there was no longer reason to keep pursuing the Conference idea, since the competition over its implementation, between him and Iraqi Prime Minister Nūrī al-Sa'īd, had ended when the latter vacated his post.[26] At the same time, Killearn told his Government that Naḥḥās was under pressure from the Iraqis and Syrians, and wanted the British Government to instruct its representatives in Baghdad and Damascus to issue similar warnings to the Iraqi and Syrian governments.[27]

Anthony Eden's comment on Lord Killearn's telegram clearly exposes the broad contours of British Government policy on the issue. Eden felt that if the Conference, to which the British Government could not object openly, were convened its activities would have to be restricted to the issue of economic and cultural cooperation, something that the Arabs could successfully do. If, on the other hand, they were to allow themselves to become involved in the political aspects of the situation, this would mean raising contentious issues like the Palestinian problem or the French presence in the Levant.[28] Based on these comments, the British Foreign Office sent on 3 June a lengthy coded telegram to its representatives in Cairo, Baghdad, Beirut and Jeddah, with instructions regarding the Conference:

First: It admits that it would not be advisable to oppose the Conference openly, especially since not all those invited are certain to accept, or might doubt the benefit of holding such a Conference under the present circumstances. British representatives should confine their role to encouraging those who support its postponement.

Second: As for the instructions pertaining to Naḥḥās Pāshā, who had encountered some difficulties in his talks with different delegations, Lord Killearn had to convince him to restrict his contacts to the issue of economic cooperation, like coordinating different financial systems, facilitating transportation between Arab countries and reorganising passport, customs and commercial exchange procedures. In the cultural field, he should encourage the Arabs to increase cooperation in the fields of education, research and technology and to unify their laws. The main mission of the Conference should be to seek consensus among the Arabs.

Third: It was necessary to remind Naḥḥās Pāshā of the commitments he made during his meeting with the British Ambassador in Cairo, namely that the Palestinian issue would be addressed within reasonable limits. An assurance should also be obtained from Naḥḥās that the Conference would not discuss any issue relevant to France's past or future presence in Greater Syria, and that no decisions would be taken or public speeches delivered in this regard.

Finally, the British Ambassador in Cairo was instructed to caution Naḥḥās Pāshā against publicising the Conference at this stage because any failure by the delegates to produce tangible results would be highly detrimental, especially if details about the negotiations became a matter of public knowledge.[29]

British reports indicate, however, that Naḥḥās Pāshā did not heed these warnings and, at the end of June, he issued invitations to all Arab countries to send their delegations to the committee that would draw up the Arab Unity Conference's agenda. He proposed Cairo as the location for the meeting which he suggested should be held in early July. Soon afterwards, the Minister of Justice delivered a statement in the Senate, on behalf of the Prime Minister, stating that the Egyptian Government's consultations with Iraq, Jordan, Saudi Arabia, Syria, Lebanon and Yemen had ended, and the decision had been taken to form a committee to prepare for the upcoming General Conference.[30]

Reactions soon began arriving from various Arab capitals. On 10 August, MacKereth sent a report from Beirut concerning a meeting he had with Nūrī al-Saʿīd, during which the latter had said that he was speaking on his own behalf and that of the Syrian and Lebanese Prime Ministers. Mackereth said that Nūrī Pāshā wanted to know the British Government's position on the Arab Unity Conference, and that Nūrī came out from the talks with the impression that the British Government favoured postponing it until September, based on the belief that the proposed date was not convenient. Nūrī al-Saʿīd explained that he and his colleagues were ready to postpone the Conference if the British Government so desired, and expressed his belief that prospects for Arab unity depended entirely on the goodwill and pleasure of the British Government. He added that the Arabs would not push forward with their plans until they got the go-ahead from the British Government.

MacKereth went on to say that he got the impression that Nūrī al-Saʿīd had not strayed too far from the course of the Iraqi Foreign Minister. He added that he had learned from reliable sources that the Syrian President had suggested giving up the idea of holding the Conference for fear of dire consequences if the issue was discussed before post-war settlements were finalised, adding that it would be impossible for the Conference to ignore the Palestinian issue.[31]

The Foreign Office's response to MacKereth's report came without much delay. It asked him to thank Nūrī al-Saʿīd for his ideas and tell him that the British Government would not approve the Conference if there was any intention of raising the issue of Palestine during the meetings.[32] Most important for Britain was the Saudi position regarding Naḥḥās' invitation to the Conference, a position that attracted a lot of attention in London. In August and September 1944 the Saudi position also became the subject of back-and-forth discussions between Cairo, London and Riyadh, once the Egyptian Government decided to hold the Conference on 25 September, right after Ramadan – the Islamic month of fasting and the *ʿīd al-fiṭr* holiday which concluded it.

The memorandum sent to London on 3 August 1944 by Mr Jordan, head of the British Delegation in Jeddah, is highly significant for two major reasons. This is first due to the fact it shows how the policy of the London Government towards the Conference had developed and, second, because it reveals the Saudi position vis-à-vis the Conference – a unique position around which a feud seems to have ensued between Cairo and Riyadh.

Initially, and based on what Sheikh Yūsuf Yāsīn had told Mr Jordan, the Saudi attitude was that King ʿAbd al-ʿAzīz was of the opinion that the time was not right for the Conference and that, if allowed to take place, the Preparatory Committee Meeting was likely to do more harm than good to the Arab cause. The British representative welcomed the King's views, especially since Britain believed that if one or more Arab states stayed away from the Conference, Naḥḥās Pāshā would drop the whole idea. This belief was based on information leaked to the British Embassy in Cairo by Amīn Pāshā ʿUthmān regarding the Egyptian leader's opinion on the upcoming Committee Meeting, namely that he preferred a unanimity of views among the Arabs on the issue of attendance.

The British representative in Jeddah, however, was not entirely convinced by this view, and advanced the alternative possibility that enough Arab states might agree to send delegates to the Preparatory Committee Meeting and thus encourage Naḥḥās Pāshā to proceed with his plan to hold it on 25 September. He advised the Saudi King to take part so that he would have the chance to air his views and infuse the meetings with a climate of moderation. In this case, the British Government should ask that discussions about the issues of Palestine and the French presence in the Levant be kept within the limits agreed upon and that no public statements be made regarding either issue.

The British Government put the above conditions within yet another policy context which Mr Jordan shared with Sheikh Yūsuf Yāsīn. It included the requests that the Preparatory Meeting be postponed until after hostilities had ceased, that discussions be kept behind closed doors and that decisions regarding the General Conference be adopted by unanimous vote.[33]

After consulting with the King Ibn Saʿūd, Yūsuf Yāsīn replied that the latter was determined not to take part in the Preparatory Committee Meetings on 25 September. Yāsīn said that the King could not guarantee that the participants would avoid either the Palestinian issue or that of the French presence in the Levant, both propositions being highly detrimental to friendly relations with Britain. To keep this from happening, he preferred that there be no Committee Meeting at all, and he would do his best to win over Yemen and Lebanon to his side.[34]

It was not long before the British Mission in Jeddah received three different documents from Sheikh Yūsuf Yāsīn, in favour of the steps that the Saudi Government had undertaken to support the King's position in postponing the Conference. The first document was a letter the King had sent to Naḥḥās Pāshā in response to the invitation to the Preparatory Meeting. He began by saying that he was among those who preferred postponing the meeting either until after the war or until an understanding was reached with Britain on the Palestinian issue and the Arabs' relationship with the Allies. Regarding the issue of Palestine, the fact was that the Arabs would not be able to discuss the matter until they reach an understanding on how to ensure Arab rights and aspirations, and under the present circumstances, the Conference would not be able to agree on a reasonable resolution of these issues. If this were to happen, it would undoubtedly reveal the true extent of Arab differences, which would be extremely prejudicial to the Arab cause.

King 'Abd al-'Azīz added that although Naḥḥās had previously agreed with his aforementioned views, he failed to address any of these issues in his invitation to the Preparatory Committee Meeting. For all of these reasons:

> we therefore would like to apologise to you, in all frankness and clarity, for not being able to attend the meeting; we are fully confident that our decision is in line with the general bases and principles we previously shared with you, and thus do not see any benefit in our participation.[35]

The second document was a letter the King had sent to the Syrian and Lebanese presidents. It began with a sort of admonition for having told him that in response to the invitation they had sent Naḥḥās the names of their delegation members to the proposed meeting. He added that this had surprised him and confronted him with a fait accompli, and that he had no choice now except to say that each was the best judge of his own affairs. The King added that as far as he was concerned, Naḥḥās' invitation had come entirely unexpected. The latter had expressed complete agreement with his views during the talks that had taken place between the Egyptian official and the Saudi envoy in Cairo, especially with regard to the issues of Palestine and Arab relations with the Allies. Moreover, and although he had as yet not received an invitation like the one received by the two presidents, 'in the event that I do get one, I intend to refuse sending representatives from my country'. He ended his letter with three observations:

First: While keeping silent would be unfair at such a gathering, agreeing to what might take place would be highly embarrassing for him, given the trouble this expected failure was bound to bring him. Besides, he was not a Prime Minister who could just quit in case of failure, meaning that it was far better not to take part in something of no benefit whatsoever.

Second: He had not been told yet on which basis and according to which principles an Arab federation among states like Egypt, Iraq and Syria would be founded, since each of those countries had a particular programme it wished to implement.

Third: There were questions regarding the meeting's presidency, namely whether or not everyone would enjoy equal status or if someone, meaning Naḥḥās Pāshā, of course, would want to assume overall control. The question that begged itself was therefore:

> what would be our position at the meeting? You are personally well aware of this issue since you have previously used your good offices to overcome this obstacle, and have come to naught. Should I, in this case, remain silent and let matters proceed like one who lays bricks without using cement?

The King ended his letter by saying that although he was doing his best for the Arabs, he would sincerely not be able to take part in any activities prejudicial to the British Government with which he favours cooperation, consults regularly and maintains constant contact: 'I am not someone who seeks propaganda for himself, or tries to enlist the support of "X" or "Y"; my true purpose is to serve the entire Arab nation, and ensure prosperity for all.'[36]

The third set of documents contained three telegrams the King had sent to Imam Yaḥyā of Yemen, in response to a telegram from the latter informing him of Naḥḥās' invitation to the Preparatory Committee Meeting. He repeated what he said in the above letter, namely that he had written a letter to the Egyptian Prime Minister sharing his views on the subject and warning of the dire consequences if such a meeting were to take place. These were, once again, the Palestinian issue and the possibility of Palestinian participation in the meeting, as well as the attitude vis-à-vis the Allies – especially with respect to a solution of the Palestinian problem. He added that Naḥḥās had agreed with him regarding the need to find solutions to these two problems before resuming negotiations and on the need to postpone the Committee Meeting until those problems had been solved.

He then moved on to an issue he had mentioned in his previous letters to Naḥḥās and to the Syrian and Lebanese Prime Ministers, namely his intention to refuse any invitation that went against what had been agreed upon with the Egyptian Prime Minister. He said that he had recently received a message from the latter regarding the meeting's postponement to 25 September and that he had not responded either negatively nor positively yet.

King 'Abd al-'Azīz ended his telegrams to Sana'a, saying that he was not trying to influence the Imam Yaḥyā's decision in any way. He added:

> I do not ask you to follow the course I have chosen in this regard; I felt, in light of the brotherly relations between us, that I had to share with you all that has transpired in detail, and let you act as you see fit.[37]

On 11 August 1944, Yūsuf Yāsīn was in Cairo explaining the King's point of view to Naḥḥās, and straight from his meeting with the Egyptian Prime Minister he went to see Sir Walter Smart, the Eastern Secretary at the British Embassy. He told Smart that Naḥḥās had completely changed his mind and now felt that he must hold the Conference on 25 September as events made it impossible to postpone it any further. He gave Sheikh Yāsīn a letter to Ibn Sa'ūd to this effect, and Yāsīn wired a summary of it to the King asking for his instructions.

Meanwhile, Sheikh Yāsīn received a telephone call from Shukrī al-Quwatlī, President of the Syrian Republic, inviting him to Damascus for talks on the subject. Yāsīn told Smart that if the King approves his trip, he would urge Quwatlī and Riyāḍ al-Ṣolḥ to try to prevail upon Naḥḥās Pāshā to postpone the meeting. At the same time, however, he expressed his belief that Ibn Sa'ūd would remain firm in his stance and not change his mind unless the British Government wished him to do so. Sheikh Yūsuf Yāsīn then asked Smart as to what the position of the British Government was.

The response was that London had so far told Ibn Sa'ūd that they did not advise him to refuse an invitation. They, however, believed that 'despite this, Ibn Sa'ūd apparently thinks we would like him not to be represented'. Lord Moyne advised his Government to ask its representative in Saudi Arabia to correct this misapprehension, adding" 'If the meeting has to take place, it seems better for it to take place with the moderating pressure of Ibn Sa'ūd's delegate rather than without him.'[38]

In the first weeks of September, that is, just days before the opening of the meeting on 25 September, intense contacts were under way to urge all independent Arab countries to attend. Most of these contacts revolved round Saudi Arabia's attendance, contacts to which Britain was also a party, whether through its Minister and Embassy in Cairo or its Minister in Jeddah.

In Cairo, Sheikh Yūsuf Yāsīn, who had just arrived from Damascus, met the British Minister of State Lord Moyne, on 31 August, and informed him that the Syrians were insisting on attending the meeting and that unless the British Government advised Ibn Sa'ūd to attend, he would persist in his refusal.[39]

Once back in Jeddah, Sheikh Yūsuf met with Mr Jordan and told him that it would be extremely unfortunate if Ibn Sa'ūd, who was in a particularly difficult situation, was not represented at the meeting. This time he had a different suggestion for the British representative; Yāsīn had sensed during his talks with Naḥḥās and the Presidents of Syria and Lebanon that if the British Government were to suggest that the time was not opportune for holding the Conference, they would give up the idea.[40]

British officials did not agree with that. In Cairo, Lord Moyne believed that putting such pressure on Syria, Lebanon and Naḥḥās Pāshā would place the responsibility squarely on the British Government; moreover, given the enthusiasm for the Conference in Iraq and Syria, it meant that they would be extremely suspicious of British intentions.[41] The Foreign Office agreed with this view, and communicated to its representative in Jeddah that the British Government could not object to the Conference as long as the Arab states involved wished to go ahead with it. It added that if the Conference did take place, it would be better if Ibn Sa'ūd was represented, even if only as an observer.[42]

Up until a few days before the Preparatory Committee's meetings began, the Egyptians maintained the hope that Ibn Sa'ūd would change his mind at the last moment. Naḥḥās Pāshā sent a letter to the King urging him to attend and reminding him that he was the first to call for Arab unity, some ten years previously, when he had called for a meeting of Arab states after Saudi Arabia's war with Yemen was over. He assured him that his request that meetings be held behind closed doors and all press statements unanimously approved before publication would be acted upon.[43]

On 19 September, less than a week before the Conference convened, Naḥḥās received the King's answer, and a long one at that. In the first part of his letter, Ibn Sa'ūd said that although he was the first to call for Arab cooperation, he still believed that it would be humiliating to accept decisions already taken by others without consulting him. He then proceeded to enumerate cases where Naḥḥās had exceeded the limits of decency, as he saw it, in the letters addressed to him, adding that in his opinion such a conference would be useless before the war was over.

He then went on to enumerate his conditions for attending the Conference, which he said were never acted upon. These included defining the meeting's topics and objectives in an agreed-upon agenda; agreement on guaranteeing the rights of the Arab people of Palestine; and an a priori understanding with the Allies, especially Great Britain, on the extent of its relations with the Arabs – particularly concerning the Palestinian issue. The King's conditions also included knowing beforehand the opinion of Arab governments as headed by Egypt.[44]

Despite the King's unforthcoming answer, Naḥḥās sent him a telegram that sought to assuage his anger and urged him to send delegates to the meeting in any case. 'Abd al-'Azīz finally relented, accepted British advice, and decided to send Sheikh Yūsuf Yāsīn to attend the Conference as an observer.[45]

Meanwhile, political manoeuvres were under way in Greater Syria. A few days before the Conference convened, Emir 'Abdullah visited Damascus to promote the Greater Syria project, involving a union between his Emirate and Palestine, Syria and Lebanon, under his throne in his capacity as the eldest son of the Hashemite dynasty. However, Sa'ad-Allah al-Jābirī, the Syrian Prime Minister, was unhappy with the visit.

Al- Jābirī's position, as he himself told a British official, was that Syria would not relinquish its republican system; but it would not, however, reject a union with Trans-Jordan, provided a referendum was held to determine if the people wanted 'Abdullah as king, or if they preferred a republican system. It was only natural for the Syrians to be proud of their historical leadership of Arab Nationalism and the vital role they played in the revolt against the Turks.[46]

In turn, the British Embassy in Baghdad was closely monitoring Iraqi reaction to the Conference, as is now known from some of the information they succeeded in gathering at the time. It is documented, for example, that once it became known that former Prime Minister Nūrī al-Sa'īd would be a member of the Iraqi delegation, the Egyptian Charge d'Affaires asked that this decision be reconsidered, which was exactly what the Saudis had also wanted. The Iraqis, however, did not heed the requests, and saw these as interference in their internal affairs. What is also revealed is that the Iraqi Foreign Minister had promised officials at the Embassy that the Palestinian issue would not be addressed in a prejudicial way. He believed that although Naḥḥās Pāshā was openly extolling the virtues of Arab Nationalism, he was in fact out to advance Egyptian interests, especially the re-examination of conditions inherent in the 1936 Agreement, particularly those relevant to Sudan.[47]

Finally, the issue of Palestinian representation imposed itself on the Preparatory Committee, presenting a dual-faceted problem. First, Palestinian parties agreed on who should represent them at the meeting on 25 September, with the selection of Mūsā al-'Alamī and the leaders of the six parties[48] signing the relevant appointment documents taking place on the very same day the Preparatory Committee convened. The second problem involved 'Alamī's attendance as an observer. A Colonial Office report on the selection of Mūsā al-'Alamī shows that the British were reassured by the choice of a moderate representative. He was a scion of one of the most respected Palestinian families, a graduate of Cambridge University, a practical politician who accepted things as they were and someone without a strong enough personality to rally Palestinian politicians behind him.[49] With that, nothing stood in the way of the Preparatory Committee Meeting.

On 25 September, the Egyptian newspaper *al-Ahram*, which enjoyed the widest circulation, devoted most of its pages to historical, geographical and political information about each of the attending countries, and on the following day began publishing the minutes of the meeting.[50]

Those same minutes were also reaching officials at the British Embassy in Cairo thanks to their man in the Egyptian Government, Amīn 'Uthmān Pāshā. What they were most interested in, however, was Mūsā al-'Alamī's position on various issues of the agenda. They were reassured when the latter announced he did not represent the Palestinian Government and would not be part of the decision-making process, or a signatory to the decisions the Committee agreed upon.[51]

On 7 October, the Preparatory Committee of the Conference[52] published its final resolutions that stated:

> The Syrian, Jordanian, Lebanese and Egyptian delegations have unanimously adopted a number of vital decisions. For their part, the Saudi Arabian and Yemeni delegations have opted to postpone any decision on the said resolutions until they have had the chance to submit them to His Majesty King 'Abd al-'Azīz Āl-Sa'ūd, and His Majesty Imam Yaḥyā Ḥamid al-Dīn.

In point of fact, the Committee adopted five resolutions, the first being the establishment of the Arab League and its council (*majlis*), under the name of the Council of the Arab League, in which all Arab states would enjoy equal representation, and the resolutions of which would be binding on those who accepted them. The same resolution also states: 'It is also illegal to follow a foreign policy that would harm the policy followed by the League of Arab States or any of its Members.' The second resolution concerns cooperation 'in the economic, cultural, social and other domains'; and the third, the promotion of inter-Arab relations. The fourth concerns respect for Lebanon's independence and its sovereignty over its current borders; and the fifth, and last, concerns Palestine, and calls on Britain to put an end to Jewish immigration, protect Arab land, and work towards achieving the Palestinians' legitimate aspirations and rights.[53]

The London Government's first reaction to the Protocol was to make sure that the newly founded organisation would not contradict the plans of the Allies to reorganise the post-war world, and in particular the Middle East Regional Council and the United Nations, with officials at the Foreign Office failing to find any such contradiction. Concerning the first above-mentioned organisation, the impact of the new League would be that its members would join as a bloc, which was also what was about to happen at the United Nations, a move they deemed beneficial to Great Britain, rather than the contrary.[54]

The second reaction was to ensure that the organisation remained loyal to Britain, which is exactly what British Embassy officials in Cairo attempted to do when Mr Shone, the Eastern Consultant at the Embassy, hastily met with Nūrī al-Saʿīd to inquire about various trends at the Preparatory Committee, though he was reassured on that account. During the meeting, the former Iraqi Prime Minister gave the British official details about the proposed structure of the new organisation. As he explained it, this comprised the Arab League Council – in which all members would have equal rights – and the General Secretariat, which, in his opinion, was the organisation's most important body. He revealed that he intended to nominate a personality that both Great Britain and the Arab states trusted and to go over various issues with British representatives in secret before they were officially submitted to the League's Council. He thought Fāris al-Khourī would be the ideal candidate for the job and said that the League would also establish expert committees on foreign affairs, defence, finance, the economy, education, transportation and social affairs.[55] The most significant reaction, however, concerned Saudi Arabia's refusal to sign the Protocol; it took the country nearly three months to accept to do so, during which time a number of incidents took place.

In Egypt, Naḥḥās Pāshā's Government was dismissed the day after the Protocol was signed, and regardless of what sort of government was to be appointed in Egypt after that, it was clear that the Palace had decided to take over responsibility for issues relevant to the Arab League and deal with the matter of Saudi Arabia's signing in its own different way. On the one hand, ʿAbd al-Raḥmān Bey ʿAzzām, who was known for his good relations with the Saudis, was appointed Minister Plenipotentiary for Arab affairs at the Ministry for Foreign Affairs and, on the other, he was given charge of that year's Egyptian *ḥajj* delegation – meaning the opportunity to meet King ʻAbd al-ʻAzīz and convince him to sign the Protocol. At the same time, King Fārūq took a trip to the Red Sea on his yacht *al-Maḥrūsah*, and took the opportunity to visit the town of Yanbuʻ for a meeting with the Saudi King.

The news reached King ʻAbd al-ʻAzīz, who then consulted with the British and told them that he still objected to the League's establishment, giving three reasons for his objection. The first was that Arab interests lay in forming an alliance with Britain, and he, therefore, did not wish to take part in activities that could in any way be inimical to Britain. The second was that the agreed-upon Protocol did not suit Saudi Arabia; his country followed the law of Islamic *sharīʻah,* while the other Arab countries did not. The third and final reason was that, in his opinion, personal interests were the driving force behind the Protocol, a fact of which the Egyptians were well aware. Instead of the Protocol, he suggested a series of bilateral agreements along the lines of those he had signed with Yemen and Iraq.[56]

The British Foreign Office did not approve of the Saudi response to the Egyptians; to begin with, Article 1 of the Protocol did not prevent any member state from maintaining relations with other states. The Article in question states, 'every state shall be free to conclude with any other member state of the League, or other powers, special agreements which do not contradict the text or the present dispositions'. British officials believed that even if the other Arab states accepted the notion of bilateral agreements, they would still not give up on the Protocol. Moreover, this position would undoubtedly lead to Saudi Arabia's isolation from the other Arab states, since 80 per cent of these had already signed the Protocol.

Based on that, it was decided that the British representative in Jeddah would advise the King to tell the Egyptian envoy that now that he had had time to study the Protocol, he had found some issues on which he agreed and others on which he did not. The King should also tell the Egyptians that since all the other Arab countries had welcomed the Protocol, he would agree to take part in the relevant discussions. Finally, the British Foreign Office instructed its representative to inform the King that his Government placed a great deal of hope on his participation in the League's discussions, to put them on the right track.[57]

Acting on British advice, the Saudis ended their opposition to the League, and ʻAbd al-Raḥmān ʻAzzām sent the good news to the Egyptian Government in the form of a lengthy telegram to the Prime Minister which appeared in newspapers on 8 January 1945. The telegram stated at the outset:

> Today, talks between myself and the Government of Saudi Arabia ended with what the Arabs most wish to hear, thanks in great part to the wisdom of His Majesty King ʿAbd al-ʿAzīz, May God keep him ... His Majesty has instructed his representative at the Preparatory Committee, Sheikh Yūsuf Yāsīn, to sign the Alexandria Protocol on behalf of the Saudi Government.[58]

On 16 January, Saudi Arabia did indeed sign the Alexandria Protocol, and although on the surface the credit seemed to go to ʿAzzām Bey, British documents reveal otherwise. It was *British* advice that had prompted the King's change of heart![59] With this, all obstacles to the Arab League Charter had been removed.

Issuing the Charter

On 24 February 1945 the Preparatory Committee's Sub-Committee[60] met at the Ministry for Foreign Affairs in Cairo to prepare the draft of the Charter of the Arab League. Although the Sub-Committee's task took more than one month to complete, the British Embassy monitored the negotiations with extreme diligence and gave the London Government step-by-step accounts of the proceedings.

After the first meeting, the Sub-Committee issued a statement announcing the decision to invite Mūsā al-ʿAlamī to take part in the sessions as the representative of Palestine.[61] However, despite Naqrāshī's statement at the end of the second meeting, concerning the agreement over the basic principles where he stated that the talks were proceeding in a friendly atmosphere, the British Embassy learned from a source inside the Committee that a crisis had erupted among certain members. It had started when ʿAbd al-Raḥmān ʿAzzām made a remark regarding the Islamic character of the proposed Arab federation, prompting the Lebanese delegate to protest against raising the issue of the *sharīʿah*, on the grounds that it was a religious matter. ʿAbd al-Raḥmān ʿAzzām's response was that it was impossible to ignore the issue since the overwhelming majority of Arabs were Muslim. The Lebanese delegation was, however, reassured when the matter of the *sharīʿah* was dropped from the Cultural Committee's agenda.[62]

The British Embassy in the Egyptian capital received news about another crisis precipitated over Article 1 of the Protocol, which states: 'The Council will intervene in every dispute which may lead to war between a member state of the League and any other member state or power, in order to reconcile them.' While some wanted arbitration to be compulsory, others thought it should remain optional; the two main protagonists in the crisis being the Iraqi and Saudi representatives. 'Azzām Bey, however, told the Embassy that the crisis had finally been resolved.[63]

At the beginning of March, Naqrāshi Pāshā announced that the Sub-Committee had finished drafting the Charter and was on the verge of submitting it for the Preparatory Committee's approval. Thanks to 'Abd al-Raḥmān 'Azzām, the British Embassy soon had its own copy of the draft, and a summary was already well on its way to London.

In particular, the summary focussed on Article 3, which defines the functions of the League, among which is 'solicitude for the affairs and interests of all Arab countries and the establishment of means of cooperation with whatever international institution may be formed to organise the future peace of the world'. Lord Killearn said that this particular sentence was inserted thanks to his personal intervention, based on a dispatch he had received from the Foreign Office. Articles 4 and 5 lay down the extent and methods of cooperation in non-political matters, and Article 6 names Cairo as the permanent headquarters of the Arab League Council, although it could convene at any other location. Articles 8 to 11 deal with the administrative machinery of the League and propose the appointment of 'Abd al-Raḥmān 'Azzām to the post of Secretary General of the League. The British report then pauses to reflect on the personality of the latter, saying:

> Although he is generally popular among the Arabs, Arab delegates during the recent sittings of the sub-Commission have been frankly apprehensive of his lack of responsibility and his amateur methods. According to an agent in contact with the Palace, 'Azzām Bey has got the ear of King Fārūq in Arab matters, and it is no doubt 'Azzām Bey's influence which has inspired King Fārūq with the idea of playing the leading part in an Arab League which is to bring under its fold not only the present independent Arab states, but also other Arab states at present under foreign domination.

Officials at the British Embassy wrote a report reviewing various articles of the Charter, and giving their opinion on each. They noted that Articles 12 and 13, which deal with procedures that the League would follow in case of conflict between two member states, exclude anything related to the independence, sovereignty and territorial integrity of member states. The next article deals with the possibility of an alliance between two or more member states, and Article 15 expresses Saudi Arabian and Syrian fears of

Hashemite attempts to establish a Kingdom in Syria. The article subsequently ensures the right of member states to withdraw from the League at any time of their choosing, and Article 18 obligates member states to implement all decisions that the League adopts unanimously. Those adopted by majority vote obligate only states that have voted for them.

The two annexes of the Charter responded to issues that the British Embassy in Cairo deemed dangerous. The first concerned Palestinian representation and the second the status of non-independent Arab countries; however, the Charter did not adequately respond to the British need.[64] Egypt expressed certain reservations on the issues of Baraqah and Tripoli, and stated its objection to Italy's return to these territories as this would expose them to great danger. It asked that they be represented at the League. There was also the intention to ask Mūsā al-'Alamī to sign the Charter on behalf of Palestine.[65]

On 10 March new instructions arrived at the British Embassy in Cairo warning about the two aforementioned issues, and asking Lord Killearn not to encourage any attempt to raise the matter of non-independent Arab States at the Preparatory Committee Meeting. The instructions stated:

> In the interests of the Arabs themselves, it is important that the Arab League, at the moment when it is making its first appearance in the world, should avoid any hasty or ill-considered action such as might cause world opinion to doubt the wisdom and statesmanship of its members.

As for Mūsā al-'Alamī signing the Charter, the British Government could not see the wisdom of such a move; they thought it illogical to place a Palestinian who occupies no official position on equal footing with the Prime Ministers of Egypt and the representatives of independent Arab States. They said that Mūsā al-'Alamī had no authority to speak on behalf of the Palestinian administration or to make any commitments on behalf of the Arab citizens of Palestine.[66]

This last issue revolved round the meeting that took place between Naqrāshī Pāshā and Lord Killearn on 17 March, in which the former stated that although since the very beginning the British Government did not object to the presence of a Palestinian representative at the Preparatory Committee Meeting, the issue of the Charter's signature was a purely technical matter. Although Naqrāshī agreed that 'Alamī did not hold an official position, he thought that any decision on the legal matter of his signature was better left for 'Abd al-Ḥamīd Badawī Pāshā, the famous Egyptian jurist who helped draft the Charter, to decide, a proposition with which Killearn did not agree.[67]

That same day, the Preparatory Committee was meeting at al-Zaʿfarān Palace to hear Naqrāshī Pāshā's exposé on the Sub-Committee's work in which he said that the Charter had taken into account the particular circumstances of each country. Killearn reported that he continued to warn the Egyptian Minister, up to the very last minute, regarding the two issues over which Britain was most concerned.

Officials at the British Embassy in Cairo also noticed that neither Judge Ḥussayn al-Hilālī, the Yemeni delegate who arrived late, nor Mūsā al-ʿAlamī, who reported sick, had attended the Zaʿfarān Palace meeting, and that, no doubt, their absence was very reassuring to them. They also noted that the participants had not dwelled long on the issue of the non-independent Arab states, thanks to Naqrāshī's statement that the League was intent on promoting cultural and economic relations with them.[68]

The great celebrations following the signing of the Charter on 22 March 1945 signalled the end of one stage and the beginning of another in Arab history. At the same time, they also marked the end of the influential role Britain had played over the previous three decades in regard to Arab unity.

Notes

1. F.O. 371/35538, Weekly Political and Economic Report, from 9 to 15 September 1943.
2. F.O. 371/34962, Record of Conversations between Ibn Saʿūd, Sheikh Yūsuf Yāsīn and His Majesty's Minister on Arab Unity, 20 September 1943.
3. F.O. 371/35539, Weekly Periodical and Economic Report from 14 to 20 October 1943.
4. F.O. 371/ 35539, Weekly Political and Economic Report, from 28 October to 3 November 1943.
5. F.O. 371/35539, Weekly Political and Economic Report, from 21 October to 28 October 1943.
6. F.O. 371/34962, Record of Conversations between Ibn Saʿūd, Sheikh Yūsuf Yāsīn and His Majesty's Minister on Arab Unity, 20 September 1943.
7. F.O. 371/35539, Weekly Political and Economic Report, from 4 to 10 November 1943.
8. Ibid.
9. F.O. 371/39987, Parliamentary Question by Mr Gallagher, 23 January 1944.
10. F.O. 371/39987, Sir K. Cornwallis (Baghdad) to Foreign Office, 8 February 1944.
11. F.O. 371/39987, From Foreign Office to Baghdad, 18 February 1944.
12. F.O. 371/39987, Arab Unity: Nūrī Pāshā's talks in Damascus, 21 February 1944.
13. F.O. 371/39987, From Lord Killearn (Cairo) to Foreign Office, 24 February.
14. F.O. 371/39987, Projected Arab Conference in Cairo from Lord Killearn (Cairo) to Foreign Office, 17 March 1944.

15. F.O. 371/41317, Weekly Political and Economic Report, from 23 to 29 March 1944.

16. Ibid.

17. F.O. 371/41317, Weekly Political Report, from 1 to 7 June 1944.

18. F.O. 371/39988, From Mr Spears (Beirut) to Cairo, 22 April 1944.

19. F.O. 371/39988, Participation of North African countries in Arab Union discussions, Killearn to Foreign Office, 22 April 1944.

20. *Al-Muṣawwir*, 24 January 1944.

21. F.O. 371/41316, Weekly Political and Economic Report, from 20 to 26 January 1944.

22. F.O. 371/41316, Weekly Political and Economic Report, from 10 to 16 February 1944.

23. Minutes of Senate Session, 29 February 1944.

24. F.O. 371/39988, from Mr. Eden to Lord Killearn, 5 May 1944.

See Annex 8.

25. F.O. 371/39988, Arabic Union project-Sultan of Muscat's interview with Naḥḥās Pāshā, from India Office to Foreign Office, 1 May 1944.

26. F.O. 371/39988, From Lord Killearn (Cairo) to Foreign Office, 5 June 1944.

27. F.O. 371/39988, From Lord Killearn (Cairo) to Foreign Office, 22 June 1944.

28. Ibid.

29. F.O. 371/39988, From the Foreign Office to Cairo, 3 July 1944.

30. F.O. 371/41318, Weekly Political and Economic Report, 6 to 12 July 1944.

31. F.O. 371/39989, From Mr MacKereth (Beirut) to Foreign Office, 8 August 1944.

32. F.O. 371/39989, From Peterson (Foreign Office) to Mr MacKereth (Beirut), 12 August 1944.

33. See Annex 9.

F.O. 371/39989, From Jordan (Jeddah) to Sir Anthony Eden, 3 August 1944, Enclosure I, aide-memoire.

34. Enclosure II, in: Ibid.

35. Enclosure III, in: Ibid.

36. Enclosure IV, His Majesty's letter to President of the Syrian Republic; similar letter to the Lebanese Prime Minister, in: Ibid.

37. Enclosure V. Text of three telegrams sent by Ibn Sa'ūd to Imam Yaḥyā, in: Ibid.

38. F.O. 371/39989, From Lord Moyne (Minister Resident in Cairo) to Foreign Office, 11 August 1944.

39. F.O. 371/39990, From Lord Moyen (Cairo) to Foreign Office, 31 August 1944.

40. F.O. 371/39990, From Mr Jordan (Jeddah) to Foreign Office, 4 September 1944.

41. F.O. 371/39990, From Lord Moyne to Foreign Office, 7 September 1944.

42. F.O. 371/39990, From Foreign Office to Jeddah, 11 September 1944.

43. F.O. 371/39990, From Mr Jordan (Jeddah) to Foreign Office, 14 September 1944.

44. F.O. 371/39990, From Resident Minister (Cairo) to Foreign Office, 19 September 1944.

45. F.O. 371/39990, From Mr Ellison (Jeddah) to Foreign Office, 25 September 1944.

46. F.O. 371/39990, From Colonial Office to Foreign Office, 13 September 1944.

47. F.O. 371/39990, From Mr Thompson (Baghdad) to Foreign Office, 13 September 1944.

48. Rāghib Nashashībī from the Defence Party, Tawfīq Ṣāliḥ al-Ḥusaynī from the Arab Party, 'Awnī 'Abd al-Hādī from the Independence Party, Ḥussayn al-Khālidī from the Reform Party, 'Abd al-Laṭīf Ṣalāḥ from the National Block and, finally, Ya'qūb al-Ghuṣayn from the Youth Party. *Al Ahram*, 26 September 1944.

49. F.O. 371/39990, From Mr Eastwood (Colonial Office) to Mr Baxter (Foreign Office), 3 October 1944.

50. See *al Ahram* on 25 and 26 September. Its headlines on the following day read: 'Opening of the Conference Preparatory Committee Meetings – welcoming the Arab delegations – party at Antoniadis Palace – hopes for the arrival of King 'Abd al-'Azīz and Imam Yaḥyā's representatives – mission of Palestine's representative at the Committee – happiness in the Arab countries!'

51. F.O. 371/41318, Weekly Political and Economic Report, from 28 September to 4 October 1944.

52. The Preparatory Committee held under the leadership of Naḥḥās Pāshā comprised five Arab delegations. The Syrian delegation was led by Prime Minister Sa'ad-Allah al-Jābirī, accompanied by Foreign Minister Jamīl Mardam; the Jordanian delegation by Prime Minister Tawfīq Abd al-Hudā; and the Iraqi delegation by Prime Minister Ḥamdī al-Pāchachī, accompanied by Foreign Minister Irshād al-Ḥumarī and former Prime Minister Nūrī al-Sa'īd. In addition to Naḥḥās, the Egyptian delegation included Minister of Education Najīb al-Hilālī, Minister of Justice Ṣabrī Abū 'Alam, and the Undersecretary of the Ministry for Foreign Affairs, Muḥammad Ṣalāḥ al-Dīn.

53. Text of the Protocol is in:
Al-Ahram, 8 September 1944.

54. F.O. 371/39991, Foreign Office Minutes, 30 December 1944.

55. F.O. 371/39991, From Mr Shone (Cairo) to Foreign Office, 1 November 1944.

56. F.O. 371/39991, From Mr Jordan (Jeddah) to Foreign Office, 14 November 1944.

57. F.O. 371/39991, From Foreign Office to Jeddah, 28 November 1944.

58. *Al-Ahram*, 8 January 1944.

59. F.O. 371/45930, Weekly Political and Economic Report, from 25 to 31 January.

60. The Committee was headed by Naqrāshī Pāshā, with Syria represented by Jamīl Mardam, the Foreign Minister; Jordan by Samīr al-Rifā'ī, the Prime Minister; Iraq by Nūrī al-Sa'īd, the former Prime Minister; Saudi Arabia by Khayr al-Dīn al-Zarkalī, consultant to the Saudi Legation in Cairo; Lebanon by Henry Far'awn, the Foreign Minister; and, finally, Egypt by 'Abd al-Raḥmān 'Azzām, Minister Plenipotentiary at the Egyptian Ministry for Foreign Affairs, and the Committee's dynamo.

61. F.O. 371/45930, Weekly Political and Economic Report, from 8 to 14 February 1945.

62. F.O. 371/45930, Weekly Political and Economic Report, from 15 to 21 February 1945.

63. F.O. 371/45930, Weekly Political and Economic Report, from 22 to 28 February 1945.

64. F.O. 371/45737, Lord Killearn (Cairo) to Foreign Office, 9 March 1945.

65. Ibid.

66. F.O. 371/45737, From Foreign Office to Cairo, 10 March 1945.

67. F.O. 371/45737, Lord Killearn (Cairo) to Foreign Office, 17 March 1945.

68. F.O. 371/45930, Weekly Political and Economic Report, from 15 to 21 March 1945.

Conclusion

By closely monitoring British policy vis-à-vis Arab unity during the period covered by this study, that is, from the Versailles Conference (1919) to the end of World War I, we arrive at the following conclusions:

- Great Britain and its various official departments, including the Foreign Office, Colonial Office, India Office, the War Cabinet that had been formed as a result of the conditions of World War II and the Resident Minister for the Middle East in Cairo (formed for the same reasons), was the imperialist country with most influence on the issue of Arab unity.
- The situation was different for the other powers, mainly France, whose political presence in the Arab Mashreq had waned considerably after the withdrawal of the French Campaign from Egypt in 1801. Its impact had all but disappeared save for a few attempts by the Paris Government to undermine British control in the region, especially in Egypt; attempts that came to an end after the signature of the Entente Cordiale in 1904.
- The settlement that followed World War I had brought the French back to the region with a Mandate over Syria and Lebanon. However, because their presence was never unproblematic, they had not had the opportunity Britain had enjoyed to form a comprehensive perspective of the Arab world.
- If this was the situation for a major imperialist power like France, one could only imagine what it must have been for a mid-level power like Italy, whose presence in the region was confined to Libya, straddling the two regions under the control of the two imperialist powers – Britain to the east and France to the west. We do not believe that such a position qualified it in any way to play a significant role regarding Arab unity.

- Although Britain was the hegemonic power in the Arab Mashreq, the region always represented for it a major strategic necessity as the main access route to its Eastern Empire in India. This is perhaps what allowed imperial planners in London and Bombay to form a wider and more comprehensive view of the Arab world than others, especially those in France.
- It is only by viewing the situation through this lens that one is able to understand the difference between British and French policies towards Arab unity, especially given the restricted focus of the latter power on narrow interests in Arab areas under its control.
- It is clear that the decision-making process on matters concerning Arab unity went through several channels, the most important of which, in our view, was configured by the scrutiny of British representatives in the region. The latter were not merely tools of policy implementation; all worked for the same objective and differed only as far as implementation methods were concerned.
- Finally, the British had agents everywhere; a tactic that not only allowed them to know what was going on in various Arab government departments, but also helped them formulate their plans in a manner that best served their interest as this study has demonstrated in numerous cases.

APPENDICES

Appendix 1 British Foreign Office Document of the "Arrangement of May 1916, commonly known as the Sykes Picot Agreement".

FO 371/5066 31003

APPENDIX D.

Arrangement of May 1916, *commonly known as the Sykes-Picot Agreement.*

[ENGLISH TEXT.]

IT is understood between the French and British Governments—

1. That France and Great Britain are prepared to recognise and uphold an independent Arab State or a Confederation of Arab States in the areas (A) and (B) marked on the annexed map, under the suzerainty of an Arab chief. That in area (A) France, and in area (B) Great Britain, shall have priority of right of enterprise and local loans. That in area (A) France, and in area (B) Great Britain, shall alone supply advisers or foreign functionaries at the request of the Arab State or Confederation of Arab States.

2. That in the blue area France, and in the red area Great Britain, shall be allowed to establish such direct or indirect administration or control as they desire and as they may think fit to arrange with the Arab State or Confederation of Arab States.

3. That in the brown area there shall be established an international administration, the form of which is to be decided upon after consultation with Russia, and subsequently in consultation with the other Allies, and the representatives of the Shereef of Mecca.

4. That Great Britain be accorded (1) the ports of Haifa and Acre, (2) guarantee of a given supply of water from the Tigris and Euphrates in area (A) for area (B). His Majesty's Government, on their part, undertake that they will at no time enter into negotiations for the cession of Cyprus to any third Power without the previous consent of the French Government.

5. That Alexandretta shall be a free port as regards the trade of the British Empire, and that there shall be no discrimination in port charges or facilities as regards British shipping and British goods; that there shall be freedom of transit for British goods through Alexandretta and by railway through the Blue area, whether those goods are intended for or originate in the red area, or (B) area, or area (A); and there shall be no discrimination, direct or indirect, against British goods on any railway, or against British goods or ships at any port serving the areas mentioned.

That Haifa shall be a free port as regards the trade of France, her dominions and protectorates, and there shall be no discrimination in port charges or facilities as regards French shipping and French goods. There shall be freedom of transit for French goods through Haifa and by the British railway through the brown area, whether those goods are intended for or originate in the blue area, area (A), or area (B), and there shall be no discrimination, direct or indirect, against French goods on any railway, or against French goods or ships at any port serving the areas mentioned.

6. That in area (A) the Bagdad Railway shall not be extended southwards beyond Mosul, and in area (B) northwards beyond Samarra, until a railway connecting Bagdad with Aleppo viâ the Euphrates Valley has been completed, and then only with the concurrence of the two Governments.

7. That Great Britain has the right to build, administer, and be sole owner of a railway connecting Haifa with area (B), and shall have a perpetual right to transport troops along such a line at all times.

It is to be understood by both Governments that this railway is to facilitate the connection of Bagdad with Haifa by rail, and it is further understood that, if the engineering difficulties and expense entailed by keeping this connecting line in the brown area only make the project unfeasible, that the French Government shall be prepared to consider that the line in question may also traverse the polygon Banias–Keis Marib–Salkhad Tell Otsda–Mesmie before reaching area (B).

8. For a period of twenty years the existing Turkish customs tariff shall remain in force throughout the whole of the blue and red areas, as well as in areas (A) and (B), and no increase in the rates of duty or conversion from *ad valorem* to specific rates shall be made except by agreement between the two Powers.

There shall be no interior customs barriers between any of the above-mentioned areas. The customs duties leviable on goods destined for the interior shall be collected at the port of entry and handed over to the administration of the area of destination.

9. It shall be agreed that the French Government will at no time enter into any negotiations for the cession of their rights and will not cede such rights in the blue area to any third Power, except the Arab State or Confederation of Arab States, without the previous agreement of His Majesty's Government, who, on their part, will give a similar undertaking to the French Government regarding the red area.

10. The British and French Governments shall agree that they will not themselves acquire and will not consent to a third Power acquiring territorial possessions in the Arabian peninsula, nor consent to a third Power installing a naval base either on the east coast or on the islands of the Red Sea. This, however, shall not prevent such adjustment of the Aden frontier as may be necessary in consequence of recent Turkish aggression.

11. The negotiations with the Arabs as to the boundaries of the Arab State or Confederation of Arab States shall be continued through the same channel as heretofore on behalf of the two Powers.

12. It is agreed that measures to control the importation of arms into the Arab territories will be considered by the two Governments.

Appendix 2 Memorandum from W.H. Deedes of 22 December 1922 to the British High Commissioner in Jerusalem.

Fo 371 / 9001

COPY.

39977

SECRETARIAT

GOVERNMENT HOUSE

JERUSALEM.

22nd December, 1922.

High Commissioner,

I have the honour to submit the following memorandum on the question of the establishment of a "Confederation of States" in those portions of the late Ottoman Empire South of Anatolia separated from the Empire as a result of the Great War.

1. (a) The political situation at present obtaining in Palestine is unsatisfactory, and gives cause for anxiety.

The Arab Delegation has gone to Lausanne, but from information hitherto received Arab aspirations are little likely to be supported in any material fashion by the Government of Mustapha Kemal, whose first concern must presumably be the consolidation of Anatolia.

The Delegation will probably next apply to London where it is hoped the new Government may make a change in the Policy in Palestine. These hopes, it is believed, will not be realised.

On the return of the Delegation to Palestine there will then ensue either serious trouble or a continuance of the present state of hostility between the communities and consequent insecurity, which is so prejudicial to the economic development, and general stability, of the country.

(b) The true state of affairs in Iraq is not known here. But there is reason to believe that the Political situation is not wholly satisfactory. An important political factor is the Turkish menace both to Arab Nationalism and to British interests

(c) In Syria the situation gives cause for anxiety

the French directly, and indirectly to the British Authorities in Palestine.

(d) In Trans-Jordania an attempt is being made to arrive at a solution satisfactory both to His Majesty's Government and to the Emir Abdullah, but the factors which make for unrest and insecurity are by no means absent.

(e) In the Hedjaz King Hussein appears neither to be satisfied with, nor able to give satisfaction to, His Majesty's Government.

(f) Finally, in Central Arabia there exists an independent Arab Potentate who, acting on interior lines, appears to be in a position (and willing) to embarrass the States surrounding him.

To examine this generally unsatisfactory condition of affairs from the point of view of the interested parties:-

(a) The Arabs:

In Iraq and Trans-Jordania something near complete autonomy has been established. But the Arabs feel that they are more divided than they were under the Turkish regime. Syria is under a French Mandate. Palestine is under a British Mandate (Both Mandates are for different reasons unpopular). Trans-Jordania has a separate Administration from Palestine; and Iraq is again a separate State with a completely separate administrative system. The boundaries which have been set up between the different Arab countries appear to be so many obstacles deliberately created in order to thwart Arab unity.

(b) The Jews:

After a long period of waiting the Jews had at last the satisfaction of seeing the Mandate ratified in July last, but owing to the agitation set on foot by the Arabs and by a certain portion of the British press, and an influential number of British politicians, the task of carrying out the Mandate in a manner satisfactory to Jewish ambitions has been rendered more difficult. The area too in which the Policy can be applied has by force of circumstances been relegated to Palestine itself.

Owing to the hostility felt towards them, the Jews are now regarded in neighbouring and distant Arab countries with so much aversion and suspicion that the Policy of "No Jew need apply" is almost universal.

Trans-Jordania is virtually closed to them.

It is understood that in Syria and Iraq Jews fear to give vent to Zionist sentiments lest they call down on themselves the displeasure of the local Administrations

In a word Zionism has perforce had to assume an "intensive" as opposed to an "extensive" form. True, the National Home Centre would never be anywhere but in Palestine, but had events turned out differently other Arab countries might have offered a most valuable field of colonization for the thousands of Jews anxious to flee from persecution in Eastern Europe.

Great Britain:

Although the Jews are most grateful for what His Majesty's Government has done for them, yet neither they, nor the Arabs, are fully satisfied. British prestige throughout the whole area has suffered, and discontent has been aroused amongst Indian and other Moslem British subjects. The expenditure of British money is still considerable. The spectacle of a number of States artificially divided and burdened with Customs barriers, Passport Regulations, and Frontier Defence Forces, can afford little satisfaction to a country the watchword of whose Colonial Policy is Freedom; and so artificial and unnatural an arrangement can not be durable.

The enthusiasm once felt by the Arabs for their British Liberators is rapidly vanishing.

The gulf between Jew and Arab which Sir Mark Sykes hoped would be bridged by our policy of Zionism is as deep, and even deeper than ever.

Finally, the establishment of good relations between Great Britain and France has been rendered even more difficult by reason of our Middle Eastern Policy.

Although the immediate object of this memorandum is to attempt to find a solution for Arab and Jewish disagreement in Palestine, it has been found impossible to avoid alluding to the considerations above mentioned.

It must at once be stated that the solution offered is very far from being perfect; its application, if adopted, would be more difficult. It presupposes a desire on the part of both Jews and Arabs to find a satisfactory solution. It presupposes also the existence of men on both sides possessed of Statesmanlike views. Amongst the Jews they exist. Do they amongst the Arabs?

The greatest difficulty of all undoubtedly is the Arabs. There is no unanimity amongst the Arabs as to who the individuals are who would be competent and authorized to speak on behalf of the different Arab countries interested; secondly, no guarantee that those representatives would agree; and thirdly, that if they did agree they would be willing and able to carry out their engagements.

But some assumptions must be made; let it be assumed that the above difficulties can be surmounted.

The Plan:

(a) That there be constituted a Council composed of representatives of each of the States concerned:- Syria, Iraq, Palestine, Trans-Jordania, the Hedjaz, and such of the States of Central Arabia as care to join, empowered to deliberate upon such matters as are referred to it by any one or more of the States Administration, or to initiate discussions on any matter to which it desires to draw the attention of those Administrations.

(b) That these deliberations be instituted with a view to a co-ordination of legislation and administra tion in respect of the subjects so referred, and their ultimate Control by the Council.

The following are some of the subjects which might be so referred:- (A) Economic matters, such as the removal of Customs barriers, the removal of Passport restrictions, the single management of the Hedjaz Railway, the execution of certain Public Works, such as the development of the Jordan hydro-electric scheme, and the unification of Postal and Telegraph rates.

(b) Matters of cultural concern; the system of primary and secondary education throughout the Arab Countries, the establishment of one or more higher professional colleges, and the foundation of an Arab University which would give expression to the feeling for a revival of Arab civilization.

(c) Law:

Personal Law, which more particularlyconcerns the Moslem Arabs, it might be possible to secure unity of development by the formation of a Supreme Moslem Council for the whole of the Arab countries. That Council would replace the authority of the Sheikh El Islam, Constantinople, which, under the Turkish Regime, controlled all the Moslem Religious Courts.

Secular Law: There are certain subjects on which an attempt might be made towards approximation to uniformity in such matters as Commercial Law and Mining Law..

The organization sketched above would constitute the beginning of a Confederation of Arab Countries which in time might develop into a regular political Confederation, similar in some respects to the

Confederation of the German States in the Nineteenth Century. The institution of such an organization would, it is believed, inspire the Arab people with some confidence in the Mandatory Powers, and would reconcile to some extent, their leaders to the presence of foreign Administrations by manifesting the willingness of those foreign Administrations to foster and assist the unity of the Arab countries. At the same time it might help to better the relations between Arabs and Jews. At present the Jewish question is restricted to Palestine, and this restriction tends to make the feeling on both sides intenser and more bitter. If the question of a Jewish National Home were envisaged as part of the revival of Eastern civilization in which both Arab and Jewish national life were to be fostered by England and France, there would be more hope of co-operation and good understanding. The Arabs would recognize that Jewish finance amd Jewish enterprise can assist in economic development and might, therefore ,be prepared to admit a Jewish representative on such a Council.The Jewish Agency, of course, would have no place on any Council or Board concerned with cultural and educational questions, nor with any Council concerned with the management of the Hedjaz Railway, but if a beginning could be made for the co-operation of the Zionists in the development of the Middle East as a whole, it would help the recognition of the Jews as a permanent factor in the Arab countries, and relieve the acute stage which the problem of Jewish -Arab relations has reached in Palestine.

(Sgd) W.H.Deedes.

Chief Secretary.

Appendix 3 British Foreign Office Confidential Report on the 'Attitude of His Majesty's Government towards the Question of Arab Unity' of 13 June 1933.

FO 371/16855 XC/A/023637

No. 8. ARCHIVES.

EASTERN (GENERAL). June 13, 1933.

SECRET. SECTION 2.

[E 3119/347/65] No. 1.

Attitude of His Majesty's Government towards the Question of Arab Unity.

THE phrase "Arab unity" is an extremely vague one, which has been used in many different senses.

2. It is generally most in evidence on such occasions as Arab or Moslem congresses, and was freely bandied about during the Moslem Congress at Jerusalem in the autumn of 1931. On such occasions it is generally used extremely loosely as a popular rallying cry against either "Western imperialism" or the Zionist movement; but in actual fact it seldom amounts to much more than a rather undigested idea of co-operation between Arabic-speaking people in matters of education and propaganda, and possibly also in such politico-religious questions as that of the Hejaz Railway, the future of the Holy Places, &c. Arab unity in this sense is something rather akin to pan-Arabism, and appears to have no more practical significance than the rather shadowy pan-Islamic movement of which so much was heard some twenty years ago.

3. From the political and practical point of view, "Arab unity" should mean the union, either in a single State or in a confederation of autonomous States, of all former Ottoman territories, south of present-day Turkey, which have a predominantly Arab population. This would limit the application of the idea to the north-western half of Arabia, *i.e.*, to the Arabic-speaking territories north-west of a line drawn from the middle of the Persian Gulf to the southern end of the Red Sea. It is, in fact, only to this area that the idea can be regarded as properly applicable, and it is therefore mainly from this point of view that the question is discussed in the present memorandum. But attempts may well be made to extend the idea of Arab unity to the Persian Gulf States and to Southern and South-Eastern Arabia generally. It is thus not possible to consider the problem without touching on its possible relation to these areas also.

4. The idea of Arab unity, as applied to the former Ottoman territories, *i.e.*, to the Arabic-speaking areas north-west of the line mentioned in the preceding paragraph, was the ultimate aim of the Arab revolt during the war, and was the ideal for which the Hashimites, under Hussein and Colonel Lawrence, strove during the war and armistice periods. There is no doubt that the remaining members of the Hashimite family—Feisal, Ali and Abdullah—have never abandoned this dream, although subsequent developments have rendered it impracticable.

5. The most important of these subsequent developments, from the purely Arabian point of view, has been the rise to power of Ibn Saud, and his conquest of the greater part of the Arabian Peninsula, including the former Kingdom of the Hejaz. The dynastic rivalry between the Hashimites and the Saudis renders it almost inconceivable that there could be any close or organic combination between the territories respectively ruled by them. It is true that King Feisal of Iraq has come to terms with King Ibn Saud and is now in friendly relations with Saudi Arabia, and that we are working hard—with at last a fair hope of success—to secure a similar rapprochement between Ibn Saud and the Amir Abdullah of Transjordan. But the rivalry between the two family systems is still a basic factor in the situation, and unless one group were virtually to disappear, there seems no prospect whatever of any effective combination of the territories at present ruled by Ibn Saud (*i.e.*, the greater part of the Arabian Peninsula, including the former Kingdom of the Hejaz) with those at present ruled by the Hashimites (*i.e.*, the independent Kingdom of Iraq and the mandated territory of Transjordan). While the Arabs are themselves divided into these two camps, any talk of Arab political unity in the wider sense must be illusory.

6. It would, moreover, be impossible in present circumstances for His Majesty's Government to support either of these groups against the other, since they are bound by special obligations to each. Apart from the support which the Hashimites gave to the Allied cause during the Great War, King Feisal and the

Amir Abdullah have in the past shown themselves to be well disposed towards His Majesty's Government. It is not necessary to enter into details but two cases in which the Amir Abdullah, by his co-operation, materially assisted His Majesty's Government are those of the Druse rebellion of 1925 and of the Palestine disturbances of 1929. Moreover, His Majesty's Government have a special responsibility to support the Amir Abdullah's régime, which has been set up in Transjordan under their direct protection as mandatory. His Majesty's Government are no less closely bound to King Feisal of Iraq by the Anglo-Iraqi Treaty of Alliance of 1930. On the other hand, His Majesty's Government are also bound by special ties to King Ibn Saud in Saudi Arabia. They have maintained friendly and, indeed, cordial relations with Ibn Saud ever since the conclusion of the Treaty of Jedda in 1927. King Ibn Saud has not only continued and developed these friendly relations, but has proved himself one of the very few rulers capable of establishing and maintaining a stable and ordered Government in Arabia. Further, it is important for His Majesty's Government, with their great Moslem interests in India and elsewhere, to remain on friendly terms with the ruler of the Holy Places of Islam. In these circumstances the policy of His Majesty's Government is to hold the balance evenly between the Hashimites on the one hand and the Saudis on the other, and, while doing all in their power to promote friendly relations between the two, to refrain from any action which might lead to the predominance in Arabia of either House at the expense of the other.

7. Apart from this major difficulty, there are also other elements in Arabia proper which are unlikely to be capable of combination in any unified system. The most important of these are the independent Kingdom of the Yemen, whose ruler (the Imam Yahia) is short-sighted and quarrelsome, and on uncertain terms both with Ibn Saud and King Feisal, though he ostensibly has treaties of friendship with both, and the various minor Arabian rulers, such as the Sheikhs of Koweit, Bahrein, Qatar and the Trucial Coast, who are extremely jealous of each other and of their own independence, and have never shown any sign of capacity for political co-operation. The Sultanate of Muscat and Oman, and the Aden Protectorate need not for the moment be considered in this connexion. On the other hand, if the protagonists of the political idea of "Arab unity" were ever to succeed in translating their ideal into practice, it is probable that they would exercise strong pressure on the sheikhdoms of the Persian Gulf and of Southern Arabia, and on the Sultanate of Muscat and Oman, to join in furthering their aim. Such sheikhdoms as Koweit and Bahrein are in close touch with Iraq and Saudi Arabia, both commercially and politically. Moreover, all these States, including Muscat, maintain a link with Saudi Arabia through the annual pilgrimage to Mecca, which is attended by many members of their ruling families. The pilgrimage offers exceptional opportunities not only for religious and cultural, but also for political, propaganda; and if Mecca were at any time to become a political centre of a united Arabia, or of a great Arabian confederation, it is possible that the political ideal for which it would stand might exercise a considerable attraction over the Arab rulers of the South Arabian and the Persian Gulf States, and stimulate them to a greater desire to co-operate with the leading States of Western and Northern Arabia, at any rate from the negative point of view of combating Western political and cultural influence in the Middle East.

8. As regards the minor Arab States of the Persian Gulf, an important consideration is the fact that, save in the case of the Sultanate of Muscat and Oman (where, however, we exercise a dominating influence), the foreign relations of the rulers concerned are by treaty exclusively conducted by His Majesty's Government, and that His Majesty's Government are bound by a series of treaties to give these States varying degrees of protection against foreign aggression and to assist them to maintain their independence. Apart from these treaty obligations, it is a basic principle of the policy of His Majesty's Government in the Middle East that these States should not be absorbed by any of their powerful neighbours, but should remain as far as possible separate units under effective British control. The development of inter-imperial air communications, both civil and military, has in the last few years given this well-established principle a new importance. In the case of Koweit, both King Feisal of Iraq and King Ibn Saud of Saudi Arabia have at various times shown signs of wishing to acquire a hold over this territory, which would be a useful acquisition to either.

Both on treaty grounds, however, and on grounds of imperial policy, it is important to us that Koweit should not be absorbed by either Saudi Arabia or Iraq. Similarly, as regards Bahrein, apart from our treaty obligations to protect the Sheikh against aggression, it would be definitely against British interests that the islands should be absorbed by either Saudi Arabia or Persia. King Ibn Saud has already, by article 6 of the Treaty of Jedda, specifically recognised the special relations of His Majesty's Government with the Arab States of the Persian Gulf, and is not likely, therefore, to seek to annex Bahrein. Meanwhile, it is one of our main objects in our negotiations with Persia to obtain a similar recognition by Persia of our special relations with Bahrein, &c., and the abandonment of the antiquated Persian claims both to Bahrein and to certain other Arab islands in the Gulf. In these circumstances it would clearly be impossible for His Majesty's Government to acquiesce in the incorporation of any of the smaller independent Arab States, whether in the Persian Gulf or in Southern Arabia, in a wider Arabian political combination.

9. Meanwhile, in the north and west, any project for Arab unity in any practical sense of the term must come into conflict with the mandatory system in the French Levant States and in Palestine, with all that that system implies. The French, even if they were prepared to agree on certain conditions to the emancipation of the State of Syria proper, have made it clear that they have no intention of relinquishing their hold on the predominantly Christian State of the Lebanon, or, for the present at any rate, on the curious non-Arab enclave of the Jebel Druse. His Majesty's Government are equally precluded from allowing Palestine to be absorbed in any way in any kind of predominantly Arab union, if only in view of their deep commitment to the policy of the Jewish national home, quite apart from their obligations to the other non-Arab or non-Moslem communities and interests in Palestine proper.

10. From the point of view of practical politics, therefore, the question of Arab unity resolves itself into the possibility of some kind of combination between Iraq, Transjordan and the State of Syria.

11. As regards Transjordan (the union or combination of which with Iraq would at first sight seem easiest, since Transjordan is at present a purely Arab State, and since its ruler is the brother of King Feisal), an initial difficulty is presented by the fact that Transjordan is covered by the mandate for Palestine, of which it technically forms an integral part. It would therefore be necessary, before any effective combination between Transjordan and Iraq could be brought about, that His Majesty's Government should arrange for the release of Transjordan from the mandate. Transjordan does not, however, at present fulfil any of the conditions which have been laid down by the League of Nations as justifying the release of a territory from the mandatory régime. Even if Transjordan did to some extent fulfil these conditions, a factor which might militate against her liberation from the mandate is the possibility that there may at no distant date be a Jewish settlement in Transjordan. While there can be no question of extending to Transjordan the articles of the Palestine mandate which relate to the establishment of the Jewish national home, the existence of a Jewish minority in Transjordan would certainly increase the difficulties in the way of bringing the mandatory régime in that territory to an end.

12. As regards the State of Syria, there is no doubt that the French are seriously contemplating the possibility of its emancipation, and that King Feisal of Iraq, and Arab nationalists generally both in Iraq and in Syria itself, are considering the possibility of a union of Syria and Iraq, perhaps under the rulership of a single individual. There are, however, various grave difficulties and objections to such a project.

13. In the first place, the French are unlikely to release their hold on Syria completely. Even if Syria were to be released from the mandate, it is probable that the mandate would be replaced by a Franco-Syrian Treaty of Alliance on the lines of the Anglo-Iraqi Treaty of 1930. The position would then be that the Syrian portion of the new State, or confederation, whether it took the form of a republic or of a monarchy, would be bound to France, and would remain under predominantly French political and cultural influence, while the Iraqi portion would be bound to this country under the Anglo-Iraqi Treaty of 1930 and would remain under predominantly British influence. This might well lead to a situation of international rivalry which would produce serious international complications.

[8732]

14. Again, Syria is at present in a higher state of development than Iraq. Although its people are perhaps less virile, its towns are larger and more flourishing, and its culture and civilisation are more advanced. In any case, it is a far more agreeable country to live in. It is probable, therefore, that Iraqis would be increasingly attracted to the Syrian towns of Damascus and Aleppo, and thus, perhaps, also to the even more definitely French district of the Lebanon or town of Beirut, and that Syrian—and thus French—influence would tend to establish itself increasingly in Iraq proper. The capital of the new State might even be moved to Damascus, which is an infinitely pleasanter town than Bagdad, and as a result Franco-Syrian influence might spread eastwards until the whole character of Iraq and of the political relationship between His Majesty's Government and that country might be transformed. It is clear that the immediate interests of His Majesty's Government, particularly in regard to the safety of inter-imperial communications, which have been so carefully protected by the Anglo-Iraqi Treaty of 1930, would suffer serious injury as the result of such a development.

15. The questions dealt with in paragraphs 12, 13 and 14 above were considered by the Ministerial Middle East Sub-Committee of the Committee of Imperial Defence on the 17th November, 1931, and the relevant conclusions then reached ran as follows:

(1) That the outcome most likely to be to the advantage of His Majesty's Government would be the constitution of Syria as a republic with a Syrian as President.

(2) That for a single individual to hold the crowns both of Syria and Iraq would be most undesirable, and would, in any case, be likely to prove unworkable.

(3) That any attempt by King Feisal to transfer his crown from Iraq to Syria would be contrary to British interests.

16. Even were all these immediate dynastic and political obstacles to be surmounted, it is very doubtful whether real Arab unity could ever be achieved, even between the major States, such as Saudi Arabia, Iraq, &c., if only for purely geographical reasons. In actual fact, notwithstanding its apparent homogeneity and compactness, there is no geographical unity in Arabia. The northern countries, such as Iraq, Syria, Palestine and Transjordan, all differ widely from each other in configuration, soil, climate and general character. Southern Arabia, although it appears to possess a certain unity from a first glance at the map, can really more accurately be described as an archipelago of human settlements in a sea of desert, inhabited by tribes who are driven by the exigencies of desert life into becoming, as it were, land pirates ceaselessly preying on each other. Any idea of unity or confederation based on the ordinary European conceptions which such words suggest is quite inapplicable to an area of this kind.

17. But from the point of view of general international co-operation and understanding, of cultural development, and of economic prosperity, His Majesty's Government can naturally only view with sympathy any movement which tends to bring the peoples of the Arabian countries into closer and more friendly relations with each other, provided that it is not incompatible with their special treaty relations and responsibilities towards certain of the States concerned. They have, indeed, always done whatever has been possible to this end. The improvement in the last few years of relations between Iraq and Saudi Arabia has been mainly due to the efforts of His Majesty's Government, who brought about the reconciliation between King Feisal and King Ibn Saud on board H.M.S. *Lupin* in February 1930. His Majesty's Government are now actively engaged in trying to bring about a similar improvement in relations between Saudi Arabia and Transjordan, and hope that these may lead to the conclusion of a treaty settlement, including treaties of friendship and *bon voisinage*, between King Ibn Saud and the Amir Abdullah, corresponding to the treaty settlement concluded between Saudi Arabia and Iraq in April 1931. His Majesty's Government have, moreover, always sought to further the close co-operation of the Arab countries in economic matters, and have succeeded in securing for Iraq and Transjordan, by suitable provisions in the relevant instruments, the right to accord specially favourable tariff treatment to neighbouring Arab States, notwithstanding their most-favoured-nation obligations to other countries.

18. If—as appears likely—the question of the attitude of His Majesty's Government towards the problem of Arab unity is raised in the course of King Feisal's impending visit to this country, it is submitted that it should be explained to His Majesty that the general attitude of His Majesty's Government will be one of friendly sympathy towards any constructive proposals for peaceful economic co-operation and for the development of close and friendly cultural relations among the leading States of Arabia; King Feisal could be left to explain in greater detail exactly what he has in mind; but, since it is not possible for His Majesty's Government, for the reasons explained above, and especially in paragraphs 6, 8, 9, and 15, to support any policy designed to bring about the *political unification* of Arabia, it seems desirable that any suitable opportunity should be taken to discourage King Feisal emphatically from identifying himself with, or committing himself to, such a project. Such discouragement might, for instance, take the form of advising His Majesty, as Sir Francis Humphrys has already done, that he can best serve the Arab cause by concentrating his energies on the peaceful development of his own country's resources and institutions, so that the Government of Iraq may serve as a model and a source of encouragement to other Arab States.

G. W. RENDEL.

Foreign Office,
June 13, 1933.

Appendix 4 Report from Sir A. Clark Kerr to Mr. Eden of 6 June 1936.

EASTERN (GENERAL). ARCHIVES June. 6, 1936.

CONFIDENTIAL. SECTION 1.

[E 3284/381/65] Copy No. 8

Sir A. Clark Kerr to Mr. Eden.—(Received June 6.)

(No. 260.)

Sir, *Bagdad, May* 28, 1936.

I HAVE read with interest the report on the pan-Islamic Arab movement enclosed in Sir Miles Lampson's despatch No. 223 of the 24th February last, which came to me under cover of your despatch No. 229 of the 15th April, and I venture to submit some observations on this subject derived from my own contact with it in this country.

2. In the first place, I think it is perhaps a little misleading to use the term pan-Islamic when discussing the modern movement which springs from Arab nationalism. The efforts which have been made in recent times to quicken the spirit of Islam have been fundamentally religious and universal in their aims, while the manifestations of Arab nationalism have been political and regional. There are, of course, points at which the two movements meet, but these are, I feel, too few to justify their being dealt with as connected phenomena.

3. The Islamic world has not yet recovered, and may, indeed, never recover, from the shock of the Turkish abolition of the Caliphate in 1924. If, in their hour of victory, the Turks had not thrown aside Islam and the Caliphate and declared for a purely secular and nationalist State, a new unity might have developed among Islamic peoples. As it was, Islam was rejected by the one State that might have assumed the rôle of leader, and the Mahometan world was deprived of the one central institution (apart from the Haj) which stood above the regional interests of its diverse peoples. Appreciation of the gravity of the situation led to a movement in some quarters to revive the Caliphate, but the proclamation of King Hussein as Caliph in 1924 and the Caliphate Congress in Cairo in 1926 were both failures. The Congress of the Islamic World summoned by King Abdul Aziz Al Saud at Mecca in the summer of 1926 was equally barren of results. The General Islamic Congress founded in Jerusalem in December 1931 has also failed to establish its authority as a central directive body for Islam, and it now appears to be moribund. It should also be noted that, although its conception owed much to the idea of the Mufti of Jerusalem that the congress could be used to bring to the Palestinian Arabs the help of the Moslem world in the Wailing Wall dispute with the Jews, the congress itself was careful to resist all efforts to convert it from a pan-Moslem into a pan-Arab gathering.

4. The failure of this last effort to organise Islam was very largely due to the aloofness of all the Islamic Governments. The Turkish and Persian Governments regarded it as reactionary and obscurantist. The Arab Kingdom of Iraq and Saudi Arabia were suspicious of any organisation in which they could not enjoy a predominant influence. Egypt stood aside and Afghanistan was too distraught by internal disorders to have time to spare for the outside world. Only the Yemen accepted officially the invitation of the organisers. The line of cleavage was clear. National interests had usurped the allegiance once given to the faith. Henceforward, the peoples of Islam were to rally under their national flags rather than under the banner of the prophet.

5. The modern history of the movement to attain some form of political unity among the Arab peoples follows a different course. The spectacular manifestation of Arab national sentiment which was brought about by the Amir Feisal and T. E. Lawrence in the Hejaz (which, it must be remembered, was a revolt against the Caliph) did not evoke universal response in other Arab countries. In the heart of Arabia, in Nejd and in Hail, the princes and the people were quite unmoved. In Mesopotamia the revolt in the desert was scarcely

[731 f—1]

known, and Egypt had not then made up her mind whether she was really Arab at all. In Syria and Palestine the Hashimite rebellion won more adherents, but these two countries were too strongly held by the Turks for the Arabs there to give effective support. The vicissitudes of King Feisal's career need not be recapitulated here. So long as he lived, some of the ambitions, which his father claimed to have been recognised in the MacMahon correspondence, survived, but the Hashimite conception of Arab unity had in reality ceased to be practical politics when King Abdul Aziz conquered the Hejaz in 1925. With the death of King Feisal the last dream of a Hashimite hegemony over Arabia finally passed away. For a while there was nothing to take its place, but although King Feisal was dead, the men who had led his troops and who had been his Ministers still remained, and before long they began to evolve a new plan for Arab unity. It is this revised conception of the older ideal which is now being developed and which is the characteristic feature of the pan-Arab movement of to-day.

6. The heart of the movement is now in Iraq, where the political leaders have become masters of their country's destiny and are free to turn to wider issues. Palestine and Syria are still shackled by mandates, and until these shackles are broken the attention of the Arab leaders in these countries will inevitably be focussed on their local struggle for independence. Saudi Arabia is free from foreign domination, but is too backward and too self-centred to be able to take the lead. Egypt, like Palestine, is at present preoccupied with the settlement of her relations with Great Britain. It has therefore fallen to Iraq to inspire and direct the revival of the pan-Arab movement.

7. I have reported some of the chief indications of this revival in my despatch No. 101 of the 24th February last. Since then other events have continued to reanimate national sentiment. Another semi-official Iraqi delegation has been vociferously welcomed in Syria, Palestine and Egypt, a treaty of Arab Brotherhood and Alliance has been concluded between Iraq and Saudi Arabia to which it is open to all other independent Arab States to accede, and a significant rapprochement has taken place between Egypt and Saudi Arabia. The disorders in Palestine and the struggle of the Arabs for a positive limitation of Jewish immigration have at the same time evoked strong feelings in Iraq.

8. The immediate objective of the leaders appears to be the steady strengthening of a common national feeling among all Arab peoples. Their methods are incessant propaganda and the fullest possible personal intercourse between the leaders and publicists of the principal Arab countries, Iraq, Egypt, Saudi Arabia and Palestine. Their ultimate aims are less easily defined. They are no longer dreaming of an Arab Empire under one ruler or ruling family. They think more in terms of some form of close federation which would leave a wide autonomy to each individual State and which might perhaps stretch some day from the Persian border to the Atlantic.

9. The essence of their ideals was, I think, revealed in the negotiation of the Iraq–Saudi Arabia Treaty, in which a defensive alliance between all Arab States, a common Arab foreign policy, a common Arab culture and economy and the facilitating of intercourse between all Arab countries were at first the main issues discussed. For a variety of reasons provisions concerning all these points could not in the end be embodied in the treaty, but I suggest that they may be accepted as the objectives which the leaders of the pan-Arab movement are striving ultimately to reach.

10. The attitude of these leaders towards Great Britain is not, I believe, unfriendly. Bitterness about the alleged failure of His Majesty's Government to fulfil the so-called MacMahon pledges to King Hussein is now a thing of the past, and the straightforward honesty of British policy in Iraq, our friendship with Ibn Saud, our stand for Abyssinia and the present hopefulness of the situation in Egypt are all facts which encourage confidence in the goodwill of His Majesty's Government. In Syria, I am told, the Arab nationalists constantly eulogise the success of Great Britain's work in Iraq. It is only the Jewish question in Palestine which tends at present to embarrass our relations with the pan-Arabs; and the best of the leaders in this country and, I believe, elsewhere (although I cannot speak for Palestine) have not yet lost confidence in the desire and in the ability of His Majesty's Government to devise an equitable solution of this problem. If this can be done, I see no immediate reason why the pan-Arab movement should be in any way hostile to Great Britain, or why its aims should be inimical to British interests. On the other hand, if the situation in Palestine continues to deteriorate, there may be, I fear, uncomfortable consequences for British interests in the principal Arab countries.

11. I am sending copies of this despatch to His Majesty's High Commissioners at Cairo and Jerusalem, to His Majesty's Minister at Jedda and to His Majesty's consular officers at Beirut, Damascus and Aleppo.

I have, &c.

ARCHIBALD CLARK KERR.

Appendix 5 Administrative Memorandum of the British Foreign Office on 'Arab Federation' of 28 September 1939.

(15727)

Memorandum ... FO371 23239 8079

Arab Federation

The independent States which are commonly called the "Arab States" are Egypt, Iraq, Saudi Arabia and the Yemen, the first and second of these four being allies of the United Kingdom. To these must be added Syria, the Lebanon and Transjordan, which are administered by their own Governments under the guidance of a Mandatory Power (France in the first two cases and the United Kingdom in the third), Palestine, which is directly governed by a Mandatory Power (the United Kingdom), the British Colony and British Protectorate of Aden, the British-protected States of Koweit, Bahrein, Qatar, Kalba and the six Trucial Sheikhdoms, and Muscat, which is juridically entirely independent, but in practice subject to a considerable degree of British influence. To make the picture absolutely complete mention must be made of the Kuria Muria islands, which are British territory, and certain islands in the Red Sea of which the sovereignty is at present indeterminate. The inhabitants of Tripolitana which is part of the Italian Empire, and other territories of North Africa are sometimes referred to as Arabs, but the fate of these countries lies outside the scope of the present memorandum. So does the Sudan, which is under the condominium of Great Britain and Egypt, for although Arabic is spoken there, it cannot be called an Arab country.

2. It is doubtful whether even the most enthusiastic Pan-Arabs regard the union of all the Arab countries in Asia, together with Egypt, in a single Empire or federation as anything but a distant dream, although now that wireless and the motor-car have solved many problems of distance and communication, and the discovery of oil has gone a long way towards solving the problem of finance, there is no intrinsic reason why the whole of the Arabian peninsula as far north as the Anatolian and Iranian plateaux should not

amalgamate into a single political unit. Egypt would always be likely to remain apart, although in the past it has on more than one occasion formed a part of great Empires which embraced Syria, Mesopotamia and parts at any rate of the Arabian peninsula.

3. Pan-Arabs usually begin with more modest schemes and these schemes usually contemplate:

(a) the federation of Syria and Iraq (this was the form of federation most discussed in earlier years, a common idea being that there should be a dual monarchy under the King of Iraq)

(b) the federation of Syria (and possibly the Lebanon) Palestine and Transjordan, or

(c) the federation of Palestine, Transjordan and Iraq, (this has been advocated by General Nuri-al-Said, the present Prime Minister of Iraq).

4. The idea of closer union of one kind or another among the Arab States on the lines of one of these three schemes, or even on more ambitious lines, has at first sight much to

recommend it, and must seem especially natural to those older men who remember the days when they all belonged to one country, even though that country was under alien rule. For instance, Palestine and Transjordan are geographically, economically and strategically somewhat unnatural entities, which only exist as the result of external support. The same is true of Syria and the Lebanon. The four territories are geographically a single area and some kind of union between them ought to increase the prosperity of each of the four. Some kind of union between Iraq and Syria (especially if Syria were enlarged by the addition of the Lebanon), Palestine and Transjordan, would also be natural. On the other hand, any kind of union between Iraq, Transjordan and Palestine, without Syria, would not be very natural. In short, there is nothing inherently permanent about most of the present boundaries of the Arab countries. Apart from Egypt, and to a lesser extent Iraq, few of them correspond to natural geographical or economic divisions. A tendency to re-arrange their political divisions and groupings in future years is only, therefore, to be expected.

5. Small States find it increasingly difficult, moreover, in the world of today, to maintain their independence. Directly or indirectly they must rely upon the aid and support of some more powerful neighbour. A single large State could aspire with greater prospects of success to independence in the fullest sense of the word.

6. Finally, there is throughout the Arab countries, including even Egypt, a common language (despite local forms and dialects), for the great majority, except in the Lebanon, a common religion (which upon the whole transcends sectional differences) and a common culture (all allowance made for vast differences in development, education and sophistication). It would be tempting to add that there was a common racial origin, but there is probably nothing of the kind. On the other hand, Sunni Arabs regard themselves as forming one large community, and whether this sentiment is scientifically justifiable or not, they are in consequence the main standard-bearers of Pan-Arab ideals.

7. As a result of these factors, of more extensive education and of easier communications, there is unquestionably a growing sense of

solidarity among the Arab peoples. This sense of solidarity has been intensified in the case of Iraq, Syria and Palestine by the struggles of each country to gain its independence. It may also have been exploited by political leaders for reasons of their own and it has unquestionably been stimulated enormously in all Arab countries by the troubles in Palestine. But many national movements have been similarly exploited and stimulated and are none the less real on that account. In the case of the Arabs this sense of solidarity may ultimately overcome, at any rate temporarily, the personal jealousies of their rulers and politicians, as well as narrower local patriotisms, just as German nationalism eventually led to the German Empire and the Third Reich despite the opposition of the German Princes and Austrian politicians.

8. But meanwhile all such ideas are beset by formidable obstacles, which may be classified as the divergent interests of:

(a) the rulers of the various States
(b) France,
(c) Turkey, and
(d) Great Britain.

9. The jealousies among the rulers are intense. The strongest and most influential man among them is Ibn Saud, although his territory is one of the most backward and until its oil and gold resources can be developed certainly also the poorest. He is determined that if there is to be any outstanding leader among the Arabs, it shall be himself and no one else. He is particularly jealous of the Hashimite family which formerly ruled in the Hajaz and is now represented in Iraq and Transjordan, and the propsect of either the young King Faisal II or the Emir Abdullah extending his rule over Syria or Palestine appears to ~~him~~ Ibn Saud as a direct threat to his interests. The Royal families in Iraq and Transjordan no doubt repay his dislike with interest. Moreover, the Emir Abdullah and his relations in Iraq are rivals in various matters,

especially that of the nebulous throne of Syria. Another aspirant to leadership in the Arab and indeed the Moslem world is King Farouk of Egypt, whose ambitions in the direction of the Caliphate have already made him suspect to Ibn Saud at least. The Imam Yahya of the Yemen is an old man ~~for~~ to whom suspicion is second nature and the mere suggestion of dependence or subordination an outrage. Even the little Sheikhs of the Aden Protectorate and the Persian Gulf, although they may not like British control for its own sake, prefer it to absorption by stronger neighbours.

10. The jealousies of the Arab rulers are reflected, though less strongly, in their Governments. The Ministers and officials composing the administration of such a country as Iraq are like Ministers and officials elsewhere in that they try to make the best political and economic bargains they can for the community which they represent, without letting sentimental ideas about Arab

brotherhood interfere over much with their aims or reflecting too closely upon the precise composition of that community. For instance, the Sunni element to which allusion has already been made is actually out-numbered in Iraq by the Shiah Arabs and the Kurds, although it is politically predominant. Moreover, Arab brotherhood is soon forgotten whenever the Iraqi Government, for example, employ a Syrian or a Palestinian or an Egyptian for a post which an Iraqi ~~thinks he can~~ he himself could fill. Again, there is a genuine national sentiment at least in Egypt and, of recent years, in Iraq. In the other Arab countries national feeling in the wider sense can hardly exist. An Arab from Damascus, or the Hejaz, or the Hadramaut may and probably does have a fellow-feeling for those of the same local origin as himself and a feeling of loyalty – if he is a tribesman – for his tribal chief, ~~if he is a tribesman.~~ But it is unlikely that his emotions are profoundly stirred by the Republic of Syria, or the Kingdom of Saudi Arabia or the Sultanate of Shihr and Mukalla.

11. Finally, whatever the wishes of the Arabs may be (and notwithstanding the fact that a single large State or federation might, as already suggested, be better able to stand on its own feet than a number of small ones) the difficulties inherent in administering such a large, sparsely populated and backward country, in which Iraqis for instance, will still look on Syrians as effete and Syrians still look on Iraqis as boors, make it most unlikely that even a single Arab State or union of Arab States could, at any rate for a long time to come, dispense with friendly help and support from outside. In fact the best advice which sympathisers with Pan-Arabism can give to its supporters is that each Arab State should first learn how to

become strong and prosperous, so that it can bring strength and prosperity to the eventual federation, instead of weakness and poverty.

12. The French attitude towards Arab federation and *a fortiori* towards any closer form of union has been expressed emphatically and categorically on many occasions.(1) The French Government are definitely and implacably opposed to it as something which may weaken their position in Syria and even in the Lebanon. They maintain that it is in the interest of both Great Britain and France to stabilise as soon as possible the existing situation in the Arab world. Why the French Government attach so much importance to their position in the Middle East is not always easy to understand. The retention of Syria and the Lebanon under Mandate cannot be of any particular advantage economically, except in so far as it provides employment for a number of French officials. Although use is often made of the argument that it is cheaper to maintain troops in the Mandated territories than in France, the defence of territories so remote from other

---

(1) See Annex for some examples.

French territories must on the whole be an anxiety and a commitment rather than a source of strength. The reason is no doubt partly to be found in the historic cultural connexion of France with the Levant and in memories of the French rôle of protector of the Christians in the East: in fact a matter of pride and prestige, rather than of solid benefit.

13. Jealousy of Great Britain also plays its part in deciding the French attitude. Since the area in the Middle East where British influence is predominant is much larger than the area under French control, and since, moreover, His Majesty's Government have always been regarded as more sympathetic to Arab aspirations than the French Government, it is assumed in France that French influence in a united Arab State or federation would be much less powerful than British influence. Any sympathy shown by His Majesty's Government for Pan-Arab aspirations is consequently not regarded as being wholly disinterested, and in so far as it is considered to be a subtle attempt on the part of His Majesty's Government to rob France of her share in the spoils of the last war, it causes considerable resentment.

14. In any case, the France of today is determined to maintain an effective hold upon Syria and the Lebanon, whatever their precise status may be, and if there is one part of the world more than another where French Governments and officials have in the past been suspicious and resentful of British rivalry and where even today His Majesty's Government must pay more than ordinary regard to French susceptibilities, it is here.

15. There is not much that can be said about the position of Turkey. The Turkish Government have repeatedly declared that they harbour no territorial ambitions. But there are many people who refuse to believe this, especially since the absorption of the Hatay (the Sanjak of Alexandretta), and these people maintain that sooner or later Turkey will take steps to obtain control of Aleppo and Mosul, if not of areas further south. Although it is unlikely that Turkey will take these steps so long as her political interests

her to Great Britain and France, the existence of latent ambitions of this kind is probable enough. If these latent ambitions do exist, an Arab federation might indeed appear to Turkish eyes as a prospective obstacle to Turkish interests, although it would be difficult for the Turkish Government to say this openly.

16. There remains to be considered the position of Great Britain. His Majesty's Government are sometimes exhorted to have a "comprehensive policy" for the Middle East[2] and to formulate and pursue this policy on a "long view". This is admirable advice, but of a kind which it is seldom possible to follow effectively in practice. There may be an "ideal" Middle East, a grouping of States or political systems which would suit British interests better than any other. But it would be difficult to find any two persons to agree

---

[1] This term is used here to cover the Arab countries mentioned in paragraph 1, with the addition of Persia. It is usually held to embrace Turkey too, but Turkey lies outside the problem here under discussion. It might also be held to include Afghanistan, whose main importance is her position as a buffer between India and the Soviet Union.

on what form this ideal should take and even if the ideal were self-evident it would probably be ~~almost~~ most difficult if not impossible ~~difficult~~ to bring it into being. For the purposes of day to day diplomacy it is necessary to be less ambitious, to take the Middle East as it is and to endeavour to adopt the existing scheme of things to the more obvious needs of British Imperial policy.

17. The fundamental British interests in the Middle East are, as it happens, ~~pretty~~ well defined. They are communications and oil. Great Britain has two main lines of communication from the Mediterranean to India, Australia and the Far East. The first, which is primarily a sea-route, runs through the Suez Canal and the Red Sea to the Indian Ocean; the second, which is primarily an air route, runs from the Mediterranean Coast, through Palestine, Transjordan and Iraq, to the Persian Gulf and thence down its western shore to the Indian Ocean. The principal sources of oil are Persia (Iran) and Iraq, with Bahrein and Saudi Arabia

making rapid progress. The Persian oil is shipped by way of the Persian Gulf. The Iraqi oil is shipped from Tripoli and Haifa, on the Mediterranean Coast. In years to come increases in the range of air-craft, the discovery of oil in large or larger quantities in the United Kingdom or Canada or other developments may alter the strategic basis of the British Empire and make it possible for British policy to be less ~~wash its~~ concerned with developments in ~~hands more or less completely of~~ the Middle East. But, until that day comes, Great Britain must in some form or other - not necessarily the precise form of today - conduct her relations with the Middle Eastern countries, through varying degrees of protection, influence, alliance and friendship, so as to ensure that her essential interests shall continue. In particular she must maintain effective control, whether direct or indirect, of certain vital points like Haifa, the Suez Canal, Aden, the Persian Gulf and the Basra-Haifa air route, and she would not care to see any European Power less friendly than France established in Syria and the Lebanon.

18. Judging their needs by this standard His Majesty's Government do know ~~pretty~~ fairly well what they want from each of the Arab countries; and in spite of German and Italian rivalry and an unpopular policy in Palestine they have ~~continued~~ contrived until now to maintain their position as the predominant Power in the Middle East. It is impossible in pursuing any policy, "consistent" or otherwise, to please all the Middle Eastern countries and peoples equally. When one can only be pleased at the cost of displeasing another, all that can be done is to balance the major against the minor interest.

19. How then, in the light of all this, ought His Majesty's Government to regard the question of closer Arab union?

20. It is sometimes supposed by advocates of Pan-Arab ideas that Great Britain

must necessarily be opposed to these ideas for much the same reasons as France opposes them, and particularly because a single State embracing all the Arab countries would not be amenable to British influence in the same way as a number of small and weaker States. The invitations extended to the Arab States to be represented at the Conferences on Palestine may have shaken this belief to some extent, but there is some truth in it, and it is unlikely that His Majesty's Government would of their own accord ever wish actively to promote and encourage Pan-Arab ideas, even if the attitude of the French Government left them free to do so, and even if their relations with the various Arab rulers were of such a kind that they could support a policy which seemed to favour one among them without causing offence to the others.

21. At the same time, as has been said in earlier paragraphs, there is nothing inherently permanent about most of the existing boundaries of the various Arab countries, while Pan-Arabism is a phenomenon in the politics of the Middle East which has probably come to stay. This being so, any attempt to oppose the idea which it embodies, as opposed to any particular manifestation of that idea, or to treat it with open lack of sympathy, would be not only ineffective, but extremely unwise. His Majesty's Government have therefore taken the line, when the question has been discussed in the past, that while they would be unwilling to take any initiative and think that this initiative should and must come from the Arabs themselves, they would if the point were to arise endeavour to avoid displaying active opposition or open lack of sympathy, and would instead endeavour to guide the movement along lines which should ensure that the ensuing federation or union was friendly to Great Britain.

These views have been expressed to the French Government on more than one occasion and they probably represent the least, and also the most, that His Majesty's Government can decide or do for the moment.

22. This memorandum is not intended to be an exhaustive examination of the different forms which Arab union might take and somewhat vague terms have therefore purposely been used. But union can naturally take many forms, from alliances to complete amalgamations under a single administration. Iraq, Saudi Arabia and the Yemen are already parties to a Treaty of Arab Brotherhood and Alliance, which is not, in point of fact, an alliance in the true sense of the word, but a consultation pact. So far this treaty represents almost the only step taken by the Arabs towards the realisation of Pan-Arab ideas. So far as is known, no attempt has yet been made to give effect even to the limited obligations assumed under this treaty. It is not, therefore, a very long

step, but it may prove the beginning of a long march.

23. In conclusion, some reference must be made to the interest which the Zionist leaders take in the question of Arab federation. It has often been suggested to His Majesty's Government by these leaders and their sympathisers, as well as by other persons of no marked Zionist sympathies who nevertheless wish to find a solution of the Palestine problem, that an effort should be made to promote the union of Palestine and Transjordan with Iraq, or Syria, or both, because the Arabs of this larger State would have less objection to the immigration of Jews than the Arabs of Palestine alone; and the inducement held out to His Majesty's Government to make this effort is that they would be laying up for themselves treasure in Heaven by earning the lasting friendship and gratitude of the Arabs.

24. It is conceivable that His Majesty's Government might be able to win the friendship

and gratitude of the Arabs in this way. But it is unlikely that any assistance given by His Majesty's Government and the French Government to the union of the Arab states would lead the Arabs generally to agree to any really substantial increase of Jewish immigration either into Palestine or into the Arab area as a whole.

25. It is also possible that continued German or other propaganda in favour of Pan-Arabism may lead to pressure being put on His Majesty's Government to declare themselves in the same sense.

26. It is hoped, however, that enough has been said in this memorandum to show that a spontaneous attempt by His Majesty's Government to promote Arab federation, from whatever motives, would be a very risky experiment, from the point of their relations with the existing Arab countries, as well as their relations with France and possibly Turkey; and that a positive declaration on the subject should be avoided as long as possible.

Changes in the Arab world are doubtless bound to come, possibly changes in the direction of closer union. The present Middle Eastern edifice is slightly ramshackle and His Majesty's Government may sooner or later have to help in repairing it. But it will be better for them to wait until the play of natural forces has shown how their assistance and support can most usefully be applied. To add to the present edifice a further storey, with nothing but theory for use as mortar, ~~may~~ might merely bring it tumbling to the ground.

Eastern Department,
FOREIGN OFFICE,
28 September 1939.

Annex.

The French Government have always been opposed to any idea of a federation of Arab States, and have on many occasions made their views known to His Majesty's Government. In a memorandum referring to the Peel Commission Report of July, 1937, the French Ambassador drew attention to certain points in it which seemed to indicate that federation was a possible solution. He pointed out that such suggestions tended to encourage Pan-Arab aspirations and had a disturbing effect on the situation in Syria. He urged that it would be to the interest both of Great Britain and France to stabilise as soon as possible the existing situation in the Arab world. The French Government themselves were doing their best to stabilise Syria.

In October 1938, before the issue of the Woodhead Report, the French Ambassador again spoke about allusions in the press to the idea that some form of Arab confederation might receive the blessing of His Majesty's Government. This had greatly disconcerted the French Government, who were always desirous of being of help to His Majesty's Government in those areas. In this instance they hoped most earnestly that nothing of this nature would materialise. Their own position *vis-à-vis* Syria was always difficult, and any idea of a confederation could not but add to their difficulties. Even were the inclusion of Syria not contemplated - and to this the French Government attached the utmost importance - nevertheless such a confederation would act as a magnet and augment disquiet and agitation in Syria.

Officials of the Quai d'Orsay spoke in the same sense at the same time. They explained that the French Government wish Syria and the other States to remain as individual entities within their existing frontiers; they would not favour any idea of a large conglomerate Arab State under a sort of joint Franco-British mandatory régime such as had been mooted in the British press.

Appendix 6 War Cabinet and Standing Official Subcommittee for Questions Concerning the Middle East "Arab Federation Report" of 9 January 1942.

FO371/31337 7112

SECRET

Copy No. 15

M.E. (O) (42) 4

January 9, 1942

TO BE KEPT UNDER LOCK AND KEY.

It is requested that special care may be taken to ensure the secrecy of this document.

WAR CABINET

STANDING OFFICIAL SUB-COMMITTEE FOR QUESTIONS CONCERNING THE MIDDLE EAST

ARAB FEDERATION

REPORT

Great George Street, S.W. 1

ARAB FEDERATION.

REPORT.

1. The following is an extract from the minutes of a meeting of Ministers held at the Foreign Office on the 26th September, 1941, (M.S.C. (41) 14, Item 5):—

> "The Middle East Official Committee was invited to examine forthwith the various forms which a scheme of Arab federation might take and to report on their advantages and disadvantages and their practicability. In making this examination the Committee would pay special regard to the help such a scheme would afford to a solution of the Palestine problem."

It was made clear in the course of the meeting that the Committee was expected to proceed on the assumption that, in the view of His Majesty's Government, "Arab federation" was a development calling for favourable consideration on its own merits, quite apart from its bearing upon the question of Palestine.

2. We think it right to reproduce, at the beginning of our Report, the words used by Mr. Eden in his speech at the Mansion House on the 29th May, 1941, in which the attitude of His Majesty's Government towards Arab federation has been defined. In the course of this speech, Mr. Eden said:—

> "It seems to me both natural and right that the cultural and economic ties between the Arab countries, and the political ties, too, should be strengthened. His Majesty's Government, for their part, will give full support to any scheme that commands general approval."

3. No doubt as a result of this speech, the Saudi Arabian Minister in London suggested to Mr. Eden in August that it would be desirable for His Majesty's Government to take the lead in preparing a scheme for Arab federation without awaiting the end of the war. It was afterwards ascertained that the Minister had acted without instructions from Ibn Saud, and, indeed, that his suggestion did not correspond to Ibn Saud's wishes. The British Ambassadors at Cairo and Bagdad, the British Minister in Saudi Arabia, and the High Commissioner for Palestine were invited to put forward their observations on the Minister's suggestion. One and all expressed the strong opinion that it would be unwise for His Majesty's Government to promote a scheme for political federation at the present time, and they recommended that, if any action was to be taken, it should be confined to encouraging closer co-operation in the economic or cultural spheres.*

4. The Committee can only endorse the view that this is not the time for endeavouring to formulate and carry through a scheme of political federation. It is not without regret that we have reached this conclusion. From certain points of view it would appear that our means of influencing political developments in the Arab world are stronger now than they are likely to be in future years. Ibn Saud, the proved friend of this country, is perhaps the only Arab statesman with whom a satisfactory solution of many complicated problems might be reached. There is much to be said for taking the initiative while he is

* Since those views were expressed the record of a conversation at Cairo on the 28th November, 1941, between General Catroux and Mr. Oliver Lyttelton, Minister of State, has become available. Discussing the future of the Arab world, General Catroux said that he was not one of those who believed that Arab Federation in any ambitious form was a practical possibility for as far ahead as one could see. The most that could be done in the measurable future was to look for some form of closer economic ties.

Mr. Lyttelton expressed his entire agreement with this view: the dynastic, geographical, social and other differences between the Mohammedan countries were too great for any Arab Federation to be realised in the lives of ourselves or our grandchildren. The only progress that could be made was on the basis mentioned by General Catroux. He was glad to find that they were thinking on the same lines. It was most important that British and French policy on this question should be in concert.

still at the height of his power. A second argument in favour of taking the initiative at present is that we now have in the Middle East a much stronger military force than we can ever hope to maintain there in time of peace, with the result that, for the moment at any rate, British influence is greater now than it is likely to be after our troops have been withdrawn. Thirdly, the grant of independence to Syria and the Lebanon, and the supersession (to that extent) of the Syrian Mandate, may be expected to stimulate Arab aspirations elsewhere, particularly in Palestine and Trans-Jordan, where, as time goes on, there may be increasing agitation against the continued maintenance of the Mandatory régime. If it were practical politics to carry through some scheme of Arab federation which would also comprise a satisfactory solution of the Palestine problem, there would be much to be said in favour of immediate action, without awaiting the end of the war.

5. There are, on the other hand, strong arguments against an endeavour to promote a political federation of Arab States at the present moment. In the first place, there is nothing to show that Arab opinion is yet prepared for any scheme of federation.* Secondly, we believe that any scheme would in practice arouse such contentious issues that its discussion would inflame political passions throughout the Arab world, and probably also throughout the Jewish world. Thirdly, we are convinced that any scheme sponsored by His Majesty's Government would be received with suspicion, and would probably arouse much unnecessary anti-British feeling, at a time when it is essential not to take any incautious step which might give our enemies in the Arab world an opportunity for exciting agitation against us. It is mainly for these reasons that our representatives in the Arab countries have unanimously recommended that the main problem should be allowed to lie dormant until the present imminent dangers of war in the Middle East have passed.

6. As regards Arab opinion, we are given to understand that "federation" has never represented a fixed or genuine aspiration on the part of the Arab States or the Arab peoples as a whole, and must not be taken as one of the fundamental aims of the Arab national movement. So far as we are aware, there is at the present moment no Arab scheme of "federation" in existence. There is no evidence that, if His Majesty's Government were to put forward such a scheme, it would meet with favour in any quarter. It is not always remembered that three at least of the Arab territories, viz., Iraq, Saudi Arabia and the Yemen, have enjoyed a full measure of independence for a number of years past. If they had wished to federate, there was nothing to prevent them; certainly there was no opposition or lack of goodwill on the part of the British Government. In fact, the three States have taken a certain step in this direction which merits closer examination. A treaty of "Arab Brotherhood and Alliance" was concluded between Iraq and Saudi Arabia in 1936, to which the Yemen acceded in the following year. The object of this treaty was "mutual co-operation and understanding in regard to matters affecting the interests" of the three Kingdoms, with a view to safeguarding the integrity of their territories; and the spirit actuating the contracting parties was based on "the ties of the Islamic faith and racial unity" which bound them together. The Articles included a number of undertakings for consultation and co-operation, but no attempt was made to set up any new political machinery or any form of joint political or administrative authority. This treaty (which has so far produced few tangible results in practice) is a fair measure of the Arab desire for unity as envisaged by the Arabs themselves. They have no desire to be absorbed in a single State or federation of States. Each unit is tenacious of its own individuality and its own independence. They may be willing to co-operate, when necessary, for a common

* It is interesting to note what Colonel T. E. Lawrence wrote on the subject in 1928:—

"When people talk of Arab confederation or empires, they talk fantastically. It will be generations, I expect—unless the vital *tempo* of the East is much accelerated—before any two Arabic States join voluntarily. I agree their only future hope is that they should join, but it must be a natural growing-together. Forced unions are pernicious: and politics, in such things, should come after geography and economics. Communications and trade must be improved before provinces can join."

(See the *Letters of T. E. Lawrence*, page 577.)

purpose, but none of them will recognise the hegemony of any other or subordinate local interests and aspirations to those of a larger whole.*

7. Any scheme of federation which we could devise would also raise many long-standing difficulties which are probably best left alone at this moment. There are difficulties arising from the intense jealousies among the rulers of the Arab States, between Ibn Saud and the King of the Yemen, between Ibn Saud and the Hashimite rulers of Iraq and Trans-Jordan. There are difficulties due to rivalries between the inhabitants of the Arab States themselves, between Damascus and Bagdad, between Sunni and Shiah, Moslems and non-Moslems, desert-dwellers and townsmen. There are the strong objections which the French have always manifested towards any question of closer Arab union. Moreover, Arab suspicions have been aroused by the interest recently displayed by the Zionists in the project of Arab federation. At the present moment, the Arab States are quiet and are busied with other questions than that of federation. Neither in Palestine, nor in Syria, nor in Iraq, have the Arabs manifested any desire that His Majesty's Government should take the initiative. Ibn Saud, for his part, told us not long ago that in his view all our efforts should for the present be devoted to winning the war, and that speculation on future political forms in Arab lands is only a distraction from the main aim. Still more recently, in conversation with a British Political Officer, he again laid emphasis on Arab disunity as a fatal obstacle to any successful plan of federation.

8. Nevertheless, while it may be undesirable for His Majesty's Government to put forward at the present moment a wide scheme of political federation, it does not necessarily follow that no action whatever should be taken in connexion with the vague Arab wishes for some form of closer co-operation between the Arab States. On the contrary, it appears to us that His Majesty's Government might suitably take action in two directions without awaiting the end of the war. In the first place, since Arab nationalism, and the wish for a closer unity between the Arab States, is almost certain to grow, it is very desirable to examine carefully the question of what our own future policy should be, and what form we should prefer that any future Arab co-operation should take. Secondly, we believe that there are certain restricted measures which might usefully be taken even at the present juncture with a view to encouraging closer co-operation between the Arab States. In general, we accept the conclusion of His Majesty's representatives in Middle Eastern countries that it would be useful to study now some restricted measures of co-operation, with a view to showing practical sympathy with the Arab cause, and willingness to assist in removing some of the barriers which now separated the Arab States.

9. We have examined, as instructed in our terms of reference, a number of schemes of Arab federation, details of which are summarised in the Annex to this Report. We would point out that, in drawing up these schemes, we have ruled out any idea that some particular project should be imposed on the Arabs by force. We cannot contemplate, for example, a scheme for a federation under the supreme control of Ibn Saud to whom all the other Arab States would be invited, and in the last resort, compelled to subordinate themselves. The Ministerial meeting on the 26th September recorded the view that " We could not force the Arab States into federation." We can only record our full agreement with this conclusion.

10. As a result of our examination of these schemes, we have formed the opinion that Saudi Arabia, the Yemen and the other States of the Arabian Peninsula, are even more unsuited to participate in a scheme of federation than

* The following is an extract from a Memorandum prepared by Mr. George Antonius, a prominent Palestinian Arab, at the invitation of the High Commissioner for Palestine, in October, 1940:—

When Arabs speak of (Arab unity) they have in mind a somewhat looser association of separate States than is conveyed by the term Federation, an association which is to be achieved, first by attainment of independence and the removal of artificial (sc. imposed) frontiers and divisions, then by the strengthening of cultural and economic ties, and lastly, in some more or less immediate future, by the conclusion of such political conventions between the separate independent Arab States as time and trial may show to be in the best interests of the collective family of Arabic-speaking peoples. The conventions now in force in Iraq, Saudi Arabia and Yemen are examples in point, and their conclusion is universally regarded in the Arab world as a substantial realisation of their ideal of (Arab unity)."

the less backward Arab countries further north. We are satisfied that if experiments in federation are to have any prospect of success they must at first be confined to Syria, the Lebanon, Palestine and Trans-Jordan. For the present our main action should be in the direction of securing closer economic co-operation between these four territories, and the British representatives in the Middle East should be invited to draw up a scheme on this economic (not political) basis for consideration by His Majesty's Government and, if approved by them, by the Free French authorities. On the political side, we should have no objection to the now independent Syria and the Lebanon adhering to the existing treaty of "Arab Brotherhood and Alliance." On the cultural side, our representatives in the Middle East could be asked to consider what non-political projects of a cultural nature, designed to establish closer harmony between the Arab States, are deserving of encouragement.

11. We have given attention, when examining these problems, to the difficult question of how British interests and British strategic needs can best be safeguarded if, as we believe is probable, the Arab Nationalist movement grows in importance, and Arab federation becomes a more immediate problem than it is at present. Unfortunately, the pan-Arab movement, the more extreme form of Arab nationalism, is largely inspired by anti-foreign motives. The Arab desire for a closer union, in so far as such a desire exists, is in effect a wish to form a block of Arab States which will be strong enough to secure what are considered to be Arab rights in Palestine and Syria, and to present a united front to foreign Powers, especially Great Britain and France. It may easily be supposed that the movement for Arab federation is likely to degenerate into an anti-British, anti-French and, above all, an anti-Zionist and anti-Jewish movement. This is a very real danger. It is for this reason that it is so important that His Majesty's Government should not content themselves with a purely negative policy, but should show positive sympathy towards the movement and endeavour to guide it so far as possible, on lines which are both advantageous to the Arabs themselves and not incompatible with British interests.

12. It is important, in any case, that those responsible for British policy in the Middle East, if they are to endeavour to guide the movement on lines which are compatible with British interests, should bear in mind British strategic needs in the Arab States. Essential British interests in the Middle East have been defined as communications and oil. It is clear that we shall at least require to maintain those naval, military and air facilities which are essential to protect those interests. These are all points which will call for full consideration at the proper time.

13. We have also considered, as required by our terms of reference, how far a scheme of Arab federation might assist a solution of the Palestine problem. On this point proposals have been put forward in various quarters which, in our view, fall entirely without the range of practical politics. It has been suggested, for example, that Ibn Saud, in return for British support for some scheme of Arab federation under his own supreme control, and in consideration of certain financial inducements, might be persuaded to give the Jews a free hand in Palestine and allow them to turn Palestine into a Jewish State. We cannot regard such a suggestion as deserving of serious consideration. It is quite certain that a man of Ibn Saud's high spirit and honourable character could not be bribed or cajoled into taking a step which every Arab would regard as a shameful surrender of Arab interests.

14. At the same time, we do not rule out all possibility that a scheme of Arab federation might assist in a solution of the Palestine problem. It is necessary, however, to be clear exactly what we mean by the phrase "a solution of the Palestine problem." What we have in mind is the replacement of the Mandate by some permanent system of Government in Palestine, which shall be acceptable alike to both Jews and Arabs. The prospects of both communities agreeing on such a solution are admittedly very slight. Nevertheless, it is just conceivable that the Arabs, if they wish to secure the disappearance of the Mandate and the participation of Palestine in an Arab Federation, might be willing to acquiesce in a greater degree of Jewish penetration than they would otherwise contemplate, and that the Jews of Palestine on their part might come

to understand that the best prospect for the future of the Jewish National Home lies in a genuine endeavour to come to terms with the Arabs within the framework of a scheme of federation.

15. The formation of a joint Arab-Jewish State was the solution contemplated by the White Paper of 1939 (Cmd. 6019). There is an alternative solution, viz., that based on the establishment of a distinctively Jewish State in a part of Palestine. Unfortunately it cannot be supposed that such a reversion to the partition proposals of 1937 would ever be acceptable to the Arabs. The latter would never agree to allow the Zionists unrestricted control of Jewish immigration. Nor is it conceivable that a Jewish State, confined within a part of Palestine, and exercising only restricted control over its own immigration, would be accepted by the Jews.

16. Our general conclusion is that, while it might be possible to find a solution of the Palestine problem within the scope of a federal scheme, there is no great likelihood that any scheme for political federation which would include Palestine could be successfully launched unless the Arabs and the Jews in Palestine had acquired a greater readiness for compromise and collaboration than exists at present.

17. Our recommendations regarding further action may be summarised as follows :—

(*a*) *Economic co-operation.*—British representatives in the Middle East should be invited to draw up a scheme for closer economic co-operation, and removal of economic barriers, between Syria, the Lebanon, Palestine and Trans-Jordan. If their recommendations are approved, they should be put to the Free French, and an endeavour should be made to bring them into force.

(*b*) *Cultural co-operation.*—His Majesty's representatives should be invited to consider what non-political cultural contacts between the Arab States are deserving of encouragement.

(*c*) No objection should be raised to the extension of the "Treaty of Arab Brotherhood" by the adherence of other independent Arab States, such as Syria and the Lebanon; and, indeed, encouragement might be given to such a proposal if it were initiated by the parties concerned.

(*d*) A study could, if necessary, be made of our post-war strategic requirements in the Arab States, and of the means by which they can best be reconciled with French rights, with the aspirations of the Jews and Arabs, and with our existing obligations. It will, however, be realised that such a study cannot, at this stage, be other than of a very general nature.

Signed on behalf of the Committee :

J. E. SHUCKBURGH, *Chairman.*

Great George Street, S.W. 1,
January 9, 1942.

ANNEX.

Schemes for Arab Federation.

A.—*Political Federation.*

The territories concerned are—

(*a*) The Kingdom of Egypt.
(*b*) The Kingdom of Saudi Arabia; the Kingdom of the Yemen; the Sheikhdom of Koweit; the Sheikhdom of Bahrein; the Sheikhdoms of Qatr and Trucial Oman; the Sultanate of Muscat; the Colony of Aden and the Aden Protectorate.
(*c*) The Kingdom of Iraq.
(*d*) The Republics of Syria and the Lebanon (each independent, but still under French Mandate); the British Mandated territories of Palestine and Trans-Jordan.

As regards Egypt, Sir M. Lampson reminds us that she considers herself the natural leader of the Arab world and would probably want to play some part in schemes of Arab federation. The chance of Egypt being willing to limit her own political independence by joining a confederation of Arab States seems, however, to be so remote that it has not been thought necessary to pursue this suggestion in further detail.

Scheme I.—Federal scheme on a comprehensive scale covering the whole Arabian Peninsula, Iraq, Syria, Palestine, &c. (*i.e.*, all the territories named in (*b*), (*c*) and (*d*) above).

The constituent States would retain their independence of each other, and could maintain their separate treaty and diplomatic relations with foreign Powers, if desired. They would send delegates to a federal assembly. The presidency of the confederation might be held in rotation; or, preferably, Ibn Saud might be president for life. The federal assembly would have power to deal with certain specified questions, and federal laws would on these questions take precedence of those of each individual State. The constituent States would have a number of votes on the assembly, roughly in proportion to the size of their population.

Each constituent State would remain responsible for keeping order in its own territory. There would be federal machinery available for settling disputes between the constituent States, but, if hostilities broke out, there would be no obligation on other members of the confederation to join in the hostilities. External aggression against one of the constituent States would, on the other hand, be the concern of the federation as a whole. The confederation could not stand alone, and would require a military guarantee from His Majesty's Government, who would in return require guarantees safeguarding British interests and British strategic needs.

As part of the new arrangements, an endeavour should be made to secure Arab and Jewish consent to a solution of the Palestine problem, involving the abolition of the Mandate, new arrangements for Trans-Jordan, and for the Jewish National Home.

Advantages.

(1) Such a comprehensive scheme would show Arabs that we are taking seriously their talk about "unity."

(2) It would show the world at large that His Majesty's Government were taking a wide view of post-war settlements.

(3) An Arab organisation of this magnitude might be more prepared to make concessions to the Jews on the Mediterranean seaboard.

Disadvantages.

(1) There is good reason to suppose that any such scheme would make no appeal to the Arab rulers concerned, *e.g.*, Ibn Saud, the King of the Yemen or the Emir Abdullah of Trans-Jordan. Nor is there reason to believe that it would be supported at present by any of the Arab States.

(2) His Majesty's Minister at Jedda has pointed out that it is difficult to see how Saudi Arabia could usefully participate in any scheme of federation. That backward country has little contribution to make to a federation and could not derive any advantage from federation.

(3) The Yemen is an even less promising member, nor are the Sheikhdoms of the Persian Gulf at all qualified.

(4) The difficulties of fitting in the Aden Protectorate are obvious.

Practicability.

A confederation which would include Saudi Arabia, the Yemen, the Persian Gulf States, Muscat and the Aden Protectorate is likely to be impracticable for many years to come. If there is to be any progress towards political federation, a start will have to be made in the more progressive Arab countries further north.

Scheme II.—A federal scheme on a more restricted scale, covering Iraq, Syria, Palestine, &c., but omitting Saudi Arabia and the other States of the Arabian Peninsula.

It is sufficient to say that rivalry between Ibn Saud and the Hashimite family is such that Ibn Saud would regard a federal scheme on these lines as directly opposed to his vital interests. For this reason alone, it would be best to make a start with Syria, the Lebanon, Palestine and Trans-Jordan, leaving Iraq out of the picture until a later stage.

Scheme III.—A federal scheme applying only to Syria, the Lebanon, Palestine and Trans-Jordan.

The essence of this scheme is that federal machinery should be established to deal with political, as well as economic, matters affecting the four territories. The greater the powers which could be given to the federal machinery, the greater chance there would be that the scheme might assist towards a solution of the Palestine problem.

All Middle Eastern experts are agreed that, if Arab federation is to be brought about, Syria, the Lebanon and Palestine are by far the most suitable territories, and a start might well be made there. "Greater Syria" was a single unit in the past, under Turkish rule. Its separation into Syria, the Lebanon and Palestine was (as the High Commissioner for Palestine has pointed out) a defiance of history and has been responsible for much trouble. There is, in fact, an underlying unity between the three territories. The present boundaries between them are unnatural and indeed indefensible on any accepted principles.

The difficulties are, however, very great.

(*a*) The French have always objected strongly to Arab federation. The Free French will certainly oppose any far-reaching scheme for closer political union between Syria and the Lebanon on the one hand and Palestine and Trans-Jordan on the other. From the French point of view, this might be regarded as a manœuvre for increasing British influence in the Levant at the expense of French influence.

(*b*) As regards Palestine, the scheme would involve the termination of the British Mandate, and the difficulty would lie in replacing the mandatory régime by some arrangement acceptable to both the Arabs and the Jews. It is arguable that there may be, under this federation, a better chance of solving the question of the Jewish National Home; at any rate, it would provide a larger and different framework within which to find a solution, when the prospects of finding one within the smaller limits of Palestine alone are not favourable. It is important, however, to remember that the termination of the Mandate, and the future arrangements with regard to the Jews in Palestine, would have to form part of the scheme from its inception. The successful launching of the scheme, with the goodwill, or at least the acquiescence, of both Arabs and Jews, would thus seem to require a greater readiness for compromise and collaboration than has yet developed in Arab-Jewish relations.

(*c*) As regards Trans-Jordan, it would be difficult to leave Trans-Jordan out of any scheme which included Palestine, Syria and the Lebanon, but it would be equally difficult to fit the Emir Abdullah into any such scheme. We should have to show in some way that we recognised the Emir Abdullah's loyal services to us for the past twenty years. Any proposals, however, that the Emir Abdullah should become King of the whole area would be strongly resisted by Ibn Saud.

For these three reasons, viz., French suspicions, the necessity for a solution of the Palestine problem, and the Emir Abdullah's position, it is considered essential to confine our proposals, at all events at first, to the economic sphere (see Scheme V below).

Scheme IV.—A development of the Treaty of Arab Brotherhood and Alliance.

This Treaty, which provides for consultation and co-operation, was concluded in 1936 between Iraq and Saudi Arabia. The Yemen acceded in 1937. The suggestion now for consideration is whether this Treaty might be extended, and its provisions reinforced, to provide the basis for Arab federation. For example, Syria and the Lebanon, now that they have acquired their independence, might be encouraged to accede to the Treaty. Then, in due course, arrangements might be made for representatives of the parties to the Treaty to meet from time to time to discuss questions of joint interest, and put into effect the provisions regarding consultation between the parties to the Treaty. In this way, regular federal machinery might be gradually developed.

Advantages.

There would be advantage in building upon the foundation of an existing treaty, particularly on a treaty concluded between Arab rulers on their own unprompted initiative.

Disadvantages.

It would be more difficult for His Majesty's Government to exercise any guiding influence if federation were to take this form. It is clear that, so long as the British Mandate continues, Palestine could not adhere to a "Treaty of Arab Brotherhood"; and its exclusion might tend to give the federation an increased tendency to criticise and oppose British policy and Jewish aspirations in Palestine. It is to be noted, however, that so far the existing "brotherhood" has taken little or no effective action; and it is possible that increased membership would not lead to greater activity.

If Syria and the Lebanon should wish to adhere to the Treaty of Arab Brotherhood, there is no reason why His Majesty's Government should not encourage the movement.

B.—*Economic Co-operation.*

In general, the removal of economic barriers should be encouraged, but it would seem best to make a start with Syria, the Lebanon, Palestine and Trans-Jordan.

Scheme V.—Economic Co-operation between Syria, the Lebanon, Palestine and Trans-Jordan.

The Minister of State has recommended that British representatives in the Middle East should be instructed to draw up such a scheme. This suggestion should certainly be approved. In the meanwhile, no attempt has been made in London to work out detailed proposals.

Advantages.

A purely economic (not political) scheme would seem to be in the general interests of the four territories mentioned, and there seems no reason why the Free French should necessarily object. It is to be hoped that the removal of the economic barriers may reduce the unnecessary inconvenience arising from the present artificial frontiers.

It should be noted, however, that measures of co-operation in the economic sphere are likely to lead to a desire for measures of co-operation in the political sphere, viz., a scheme started on these lines might develop on the lines of Scheme III above.

C.—***Cultural Co-operation.***

The British Ambassador at Bagdad wrote as follows in a recent despatch :—

> "Cultural barriers could possibly be removed by establishing closer harmony in school curricula, by periodical cultural conferences, by the publication of journals of common interest to all, by the exchange of students in higher educational institutions and similar devices."

There seems to be no objection to British representatives in the Middle East being authorised to encourage such cultural contacts between the Arab States. It is perhaps worth noting that it is in these matters within the cultural sphere that Egypt comes into the picture. Cairo is regarded by the Egyptians as the cultural centre of the Arab world. It is not certain how far it would be wise for His Majesty's Government to take the initiative in cultural questions affecting the Arab States, but we can at least show ourselves ready to welcome and support any initiative taken by the Arabs themselves.

Appendix 7 Memorandum on 'Arab Unity' from the Naval Intelligence Department's Weekly Intelligence Report of 4 June 1943.

FO371/34959

8077

Registry Number E 3421/506/65

FROM Mr. Humphrey Bowman (Research Department) to

No. Mr. Hankey.

Confidential.

Dated 4th June, 1943.

Received in Registry 15th June, 1943.

E: General.

Arab unity.

Encloses a copy as requested of the memorandum on Arab Unity which he wrote for the Naval Intelligence Department Weekly Intelligence report.

Last Paper.

E 3416

(Minutes.)

Read with much interest. This shld be useful for reference.

RMAH. 18/6.

References.

(Print.)

(How disposed of.)

(Action completed.) 19/6

(Index.) 21/6

Next Paper.

CONFIDENTIAL-

RESEARCH
DEPARTMENT,
FOREIGN OFFICE.

4th June, 1943.

E 3421

Dear Hankey.

I enclose a copy, as requested, of the Memorandum on "Arab Unity" which I wrote recently for the N.I.D. Weekly Intelligence Report.

Yours sincerely
Humphrey Bowman.

The Hon.
R.M.A.Hankey,
Eastern Department,
FOREIGN OFFICE.

ARAB UNITY.

The Arab movement for liberation began in the latter part of the 19th Century, when secret societies were formed in Syria with the object of spreading Arab nationalism in all those provinces of the Turkish Empire where men of Arab race lived and spoke the Arabic tongue. In fact, their activities were confined to the Asiatic provinces. Egypt was already beginning a nationalist movement of her own, while the Arabs of North Africa were too remote or too much occupied with their own affairs to be affected by a movement that had its roots in Syria.

At an Arab congress held in Paris in 1913 resolutions were passed not indeed for separation from the Turkish Empire but for political rights and an effective share in the administration of the Empire. But the Imperial decree that professed to meet these demands remained a dead letter, and the outbreak of war in 1914 effectively put a stop to any thought of reform by the Government at Constantinople.

The war of 1914-1918 brought to the Arab nationalist movement an opportunity which it could scarcely have enjoyed in days of peace. Conversations had taken place in the spring of 1914 between Lord Kitchener, then His Majesty's Agent General in Egypt, and Abdullah, second son of the Sherif Hussain of Mecca, on the subject of Arab aspirations. They were another example of Kitchener's prophetic instinct. These conversations, which at the time seemed to have only an academic interest, gave birth, on the outbreak of war with Turkey, to an idea of far-reaching importance. They led directly to those negotiations with the Sherif Hussain which culminated in the MacMahon correspondence and the Arab Revolt. It is of interest to note that throughout the negotiations the Sherif Hussain envisaged a single Arab State, covering the whole of that territory of Western Asia inhabited by people of Arabic speech, namely Greater Syria (including Palestine and Transjordan) Iraq and the Arabian Peninsular. Throughout the war too the claim to set up a single Arab State was maintained, and in November, 1916 the Sherif was actually acclaimed "King of the Arab countries". This title, however, was never officially accorded him, and in January, 1917 he was recognised by the Allies as King of the Hejaz. Nevertheless, the claim for a single Arab State continued to be put forward during the Peace Conference, and even in the so-called "Agreement" between the Amir Feisal and Dr. Weizmann (January, 1919) reference is made throughout to "the Arab State" on the one side and "Palestine" on the other.

The first formal reference to separate Arab States was made in the Resolutions passed at the General Syrian Congress held at Damascus in July, 1919. This congress was attended by elected delegates, Moslem and Christian, from Syria and Palestine, who demanded an independent Syrian State, to include the Lebanon and Palestine (on both sides of the Jordan), with the Amir Feisal as

King; and an independent Iraq, with no economic barriers between the two countries. The proposed mandatory system was rejected out of hand, as were the Sykes-Picot Agreement and the Balfour Declaration. But the decision of the Peace Conference to impose the mandatory system in Syria, Palestine and Iraq, followed by the outbreak of hostilities between Ibn Saud and King Hussain, ending in the Hejaz forming part of the new kingdom of Saudi Arabia, prevented the furtherance of political union.

By this time, the territories of Najd and the Hejaz, now combined in Saudi Arabia, and also the Yemen had acquired independence. Since then, action has been mainly devoted to regional efforts to secure local independence in the other Arab countries - efforts which have met with success in Egypt and Iraq. Transjordan has an Arab Amir and an Arab Government. Syria and Lebanon were declared independent by the proclamation made on behalf of General de Gaulle in June, 1941, and, though these States are still technically under French mandate, steps have recently been taken to arrange for elections and a return to constitutional government. It is possible that the French will later make a treaty with the Levant States on the lines of our treaty of alliance with Iraq. As to Palestine, its independence by 1949 is envisaged by the White Paper, the relevant article (Article 8) of which reads: "His Majesty's Government will do everything in their power to create conditions which will enable the independent Palestine State to come into being within ten years".

Meanwhile the pan-Arab movement has never ceased to live, though the struggles of individual countries have taken the front of the stage. That movement has always looked forward to a political union of the Arabic-speaking States. The most authoritative definition of this objective is given in the first article of the Arab Covenant formulated at Jerusalem on the 13th December, 1931: "The Arab lands are a complete and indivisible whole, and the divisions of whatever nature to which they have been subjected are not approved nor recognised by the Arab nation". By Article 2 of the same Covenant Arab nationalists are pledged to direct their efforts in every Arab country "towards the single goal of their complete independence, in their entirety and unified", and "every ideal which seeks to limit the sphere of action to local and regional politics" is condemned.

But there was no agreement or clearly devised plan for the details of an Arab Federation. The outbreak of the present war put an end for the time being to such discussions: the Arab States were too much preoccupied with the danger of invasion and the stress of food shortages to allow their attention to dwell on any but their own problems. More recently talk of Arab unity has revived, especially since Mr. Eden's statement at the Mansion House on the 29th May, 1941, when the Foreign Secretary said: "The Arab world has made great strides since the settlement reached at the end of the last war, and many Arab thinkers desire for the Arab peoples a greater degree of unity than they now enjoy". In this they hoped for our support, and no such appeal should go unanswered. "It seems to me both natural and right that the cultural and economic ties between the Arab countries, and the political ties too, should be strengthened. H.M.G. for their part will give their full support to any scheme that commands general approval". Mr. Eden's second statement on the subject, made in the House of Commons on the 24th February, 1943, that "H.M.G. would view with sympathy any movement among the Arabs to promote their economic, cultural or political unity" received even closer attention in the Middle Eastern countries, and was everywhere warmly received. His view that the initiative must come from the Arabs themselves was also favourably noted. But it still remains to be seen if there is sufficient agreement among the leaders of the Arab countries concerned to take the intiative and to elaborate a scheme that will "command general approval".

Individual action has already been taken by three Arab leaders. Nusi Pasha Said, Prime Minister of Iraq, was the first to put forward definite proposals in the form of a confidential memorandum. These include a declaration by the United Nations that Syria, Lebanon, Palestine and Transjordan (i.e. Greater or Geographical Syria) shall be reunited into one State; that the form of government of this

State shall be decided by the peoples themselves; the creation of an Arab League to which Syria and Iraq will adhere at once, and which can be joined by other Arab States at will; and the getting up of an Arab League Council to be responsible for defence, foreign affairs, currency, customs etc. The Jews in Palestine would be given "semi-autonomy", with the right to maintain their own educational, health and police services subject to general supervision by the Syrian State. The Maronites of the Lebanon would be granted a privileged régime, should they demand it, such as they enjoyed under the Turks; and both their régime and the position of the Jews in Palestine would rest on international guarantee. Nuri Pasha followed this up by sending an emissary to the Levant States, Palestine, Transjordan and Egypt, to discuss the possibilities of unity with political leaders in those countries.

The second move was taken by Nahas Pasha, Prime Minister of Egypt, whose statement on the subject was read in the Egyptian Senate on the 30th March, 1943. Nahas while avoiding all details merely outlined procedure. He suggested that the question should first be examined by the Arab Governments concerned, and that the Egyptian Government should than take steps to ascertain and unify their points of view. His Government would then invite them to attend a friendly meeting in Egypt, where discussion directed to an effective union might begin. If agreement was reached it would then be possible to convene a Congress under the presidency of the Egyptian Premier, to reach final decisions.

The third Arab leader to enter the arena was the Amir Abdullah, who also proposed that a congress should be held for the same purpose, but with Amman as its milieu and under his own presidency. There seems little doubt that this proposal was connected in the Amir's mind with his pretensions to the Syrian throne; and it does not appear to have found much favour elsewhere.

The most influential leader in the Arab world, Ibn Saud, has little to say in favour of any of these suggestions. He believes that they are put forward not from disinterested motives nor for the sake of Arab interests as a whole, but because each of the leaders in question is anxious to magnify his position among his own people, and that of his country among others of the Arab world. His traditional dislike of the Hashimite dynasty is enough to alienate his sympathy for any proposal to unite the Arab States under Iraqi leadership; for the same reason he would contemplate with even less favour a united Syria under the kingship of Abdullah. He would equally resent Egyptian aspirations to the leadership of the Arab world, partly because he does not regard Egypt as properly belonging to it, partly perhaps because he is aware of King Farouk's alleged pretensions to the Caliphate. Ibn Saud indeed does not think that the time is ripe for political unity. He may be willing to participate in the activities of the Egyptian-Iraqi "Bureau for cultural co-operation", whose first task is to draft a cultural treaty between Egypt and

Iraq, and, if Ibn Saud agrees, Saudi Arabia. (Other States may also be invited later). Nor would he object in principle to the unifying of "Greater Syria", provided it was in the true interests of all concerned and was not placed under any Hashimite ruler. He is even willing to take part in preliminary discussions on the subject of Arab unity on a larger scale. But he is against the immediate convening of a conference for the purpose, and would certainly oppose any form of union of which either Iraq or Egypt was the acknowledged head. His two principal aims in life, second only to "his trust in God", as he has repeatedly asserted, are to serve the interests of Arabs of whatever State, and to maintain his friendship for H.M.G.

Whether the present discussions will bear any immediate fruit it is too early to say. Nuri's suggestion, which is also that of Abdullah, of a unified Greater Syria obviously cannot be achieved until the Palestine problem is solved. Dr. Magnes, Chancellor of the Hebrew University in Jerusalem, and well known as the chief spokesman of cultural as opposed to political Zionism, believes that a bi-national Palestine can be fitted in to such a federation. Dr. Weizmann too is believed to favour a scheme by which Jewish Palestine, with frontiers more or less on the lines recommended by the Peel Commission, but enlarged so as to embrace a wider extent of territory, could form part of a group of neighbouring Arab States. This would not of course satisfy the extreme Zionists such as Mr. Ben Gurion, whose aim is to constitute a Jewish Commonwealth in Palestine, with unrestricted immigration to all parts of the country. Nor is such a proposal likely to be accepted by the Arab nationalists, to whom any partition of Palestine is abhorrent. Meanwhile the policy of H.M.G. is that laid down in the White Paper, which looks forward to an independent Palestine in 1949.

A union limited to Syria and Lebanon only is more easily envisaged in the near future, even if the French mandate technically remains till the end of the war. Even if political union of these or any other of the Arab States may not be practicable in the near future, some form of economic and cultural union embracing "Greater Syria", Iraq and even Saudi Arabia may be achieved. An economic union, with a common currency and customs system, and a joint organisation for the planning of regional development, should not be beyond the bounds of practical statesmanship. The advice and co-operation of the Middle East Supply Council, which has done such admirable work in the years of war, might possibly be invited to help towards a solution. In the educational sphere it might be possible to extend the activities of the Egypto-Iraqi Cultural Bureau by holding periodical conferences in all the States concerned, by the exchange of teachers, and by some form of matriculation examination common to all. But whatever may be done in these or other directions it is clear that, when the war is over, the United Nations cannot disinterest themselves in the future of the Arab world.

Appendix 8 Secret Communication from Mr. Eden to Lord Killearn (in Cairo) on the demand for Arab Unity, 5 May 1944.

TOP SECRET. Copy No. 8

[E 2793/2793/G]

Mr. Eden to Lord Killearn (Cairo).

(No. 220.)

My Lord, *Foreign Office, 5th May,* 1944.

THE Egyptian Ambassador asked to see me this afternoon, when he gave me the enclosed document from the Egyptian Prime Minister. I expressed some surprise at its contents. It did not seem to me conceivable that the French would agree to what was here proposed, nor at a first reading could His Majesty's Government recommend that they should do so. Apart from any other consideration, I had no evidence that the States mentioned were in a position to undertake self-government. I added that I found it surprising to receive a document of this kind from the Egyptian Prime Minister at this time. I should have thought that Egypt would have been better occupied setting her own house in order.

2. The Ambassador seemed a little puzzled by my remarks, so I asked him whether he had not received any information of the recent events in Egypt. His Excellency said that he had heard nothing. I then gave him some account, whereupon he expressed due horror at the idea that Hassanein Pasha could have been a successful Prime Minister.

3. Reverting to the document, I commented that while it spoke in eloquent terms of a union of Arab States, so far as I was aware we were still far from such a desirable state of affairs; and as for the active help that the Arab States had given us, we here had not yet forgotten Raschid Ali's rebellion.

4. The Ambassador did not defend his Prime Minister's document with any great vigour and asked me what he was to say to Nahas Pasha. I suggested that it would be enough if he should reply that he had delivered the document to me. His Excellency also mentioned that copies of this had been sent to the French National Committee, the United States Government and the Soviet Government.

I am, &c.
ANTHONY EDEN.

Enclosure.

Son Excellence le Principal Secrétaire d'État
de Sa Majesté Britannique pour les
Affaires Etrangères, Londres.

Excellence, *Le Caire, le* [16] *avril* 1944.

LES leçons de la guerre et la révolution des esprits ont amené les États et les individus à considérer comme une nécessité absolue l'établissement d'un monde meilleur. En effet, tous les peuples pour qui cet avenir est en fonction d'une démocratie épurée et sincère envisagent, à la fois avec espérance et anxiété, la réalité d'une paix qui, non seulement doit mettre fin aux violences de la guerre, mais organiser l'existence des nations et des individus dans l'entente, la confiance et la solidarité.

2. Dans les tragiques circonstances que nous traversons et à cette heure qui précède l'aube de la paix, il est du devoir de chaque homme responsable de prendre une part active à l'élaboration du monde futur, d'exprimer son opinion avec franchise et d'émettre avec netteté ses suggestions. Pour l'Égypte, que des considérations historiques et sociales placent en tête des pays arabes et musulmans, et qui, par sa position géographique et son évolution sociale, est plus que jamais désignée à servir d'agent de liaison, d'entente et de paix entre l'Occident et l'Orient, c'est un devoir, qu'elle ne saurait esquiver, d'élever la voix et de défendre la cause de l'Union arabe, qui est en même temps une cause de coopération entre Etats et peuples liés par d'étroites affinités culturelles, morales et politiques.

3. Quelques-uns de ces peuples ont obtenu leur indépendance et sont devenus aussitôt, dans le concert des nations, d'actifs éléments de paix et de civilisation. D'autres souffrent encore d'être incompris et de traîner le boulet humiliant imposé par des régimes périmés. Ce sont des États, ce sont des hommes qui ont le souci de leur dignité, qui nourrissent des aspirations légitimes et qui ne peuvent accepter d'être traités en Etats et en individus inférieurs à qui est refusé le droit d'être respectés, indépendants et libres, et de jouir des bienfaits d'une vraie civilisation.

4. Les peuples arabes, qui, chacun dans sa sphère, ont apporté à la cause des Nations Unies toute l'aide en leur pouvoir, à la fois pour faciliter la victoire et collaborer à une paix juste et durable, ont envisagé comme une impérieuse nécessité la formation de l'Union arabe en sérieuse voie de réalisation. Par cette Union ils ont la certitude qu'un équilibre qui manquait à l'organisation d'un monde meilleur sera trouvé et qu'entre l'Orient et l'Occident sera enfin close l'ère des malentendus.

5. Aussi bien, cette Union serait incomplète et ne produirait pas ses meilleurs effets si les peuples arabes de l'Afrique du Nord s'en trouvaient exclus et continuaient à vivre sous des régimes contraires à leurs droits et à leurs aspirations. L'Algérie, le Maroc, la Tunisie et la Libye entendent bénéficier, à leur tour, des principes pour lesquels se battent les Nations Unies. Il semble qu'on ne saurait, sans injustice, leur refuser un droit naturel et il serait profondément regrettable qu'ils soient les seuls à être tenus à l'écart des peuples libres et indépendants.

6. La Grande-Bretagne, l'Amérique et l'Union des Républiques socialistes soviétiques, autant par leurs actes que par leurs déclarations, ont encouragé et aidé la libération et l'indépendance des peuples. La France ne peut pas faire moins et nous apprécions les efforts du Comité d'Alger de modifier la politique coloniale française. Les dirigeants de sa politique ont déjà prouvé qu'ils sont pénétrés de l'esprit nouveau en reconnaissant l'indépendance de la Syrie et du Liban. Cependant, quelle que soit la bonne volonté des autorités d'Alger, les événements exigent également ailleurs des mesures définitives et des décisions complètes. La glorieuse France d'hier, qui redeviendra la glorieuse France de demain, se doit de n'être pas la dernière à manifester en actes son libéralisme et son esprit de démocratie.

7. En accord avec tous les peuples arabes, l'Égypte accomplit un élémentaire devoir de solidarité en soumettant à la France et aux Nations Unies les desiderata des peuples de l'Afrique du Nord. Loin de voir son prestige diminué, la France se grandirait en négociant, dans le cadre des principes alliés et de l'esprit de la Charte de l'Atlantique, les modalités de l'indépendance de l'Algérie, du Maroc et de la Tunisie. Elle trouverait, dans la reconnaissance de leur indépendance, la justification de sa politique nouvelle et établirait, en même temps, avec ces pays, des rapports d'amitié et d'alliance beaucoup plus sincères et productifs que les rapports de dépendance qui sont cause aujourd'hui, et le seront davantage demain, de bien des frictions et de troubles.

8. C'est désormais l'esprit de compréhension, de justice et d'humanité qui devra présider aux relations entre peuples et individus. La vraie paix, la seule paix durable, est à cette condition. Devant l'Occident et l'Orient un avenir particulièrement fécond s'ouvrira si les droits et les intérêts mutuels sont respectés et si la justice est égale pour tous. Une paix qui ne tiendrait pas compte des réalités nouvelles, qui, dans l'organisation du monde futur, ne donnerait pas à l'Orient toute la place qui lui revient et qui ne reconnaîtrait pas ses droits, serait une paix dangereuse. Les peuples espèrent mieux et davantage, l'Orient comme l'Occident, l'ancien monde comme le nouveau.

9. Comme prélude à l'ère nouvelle, les peuples arabes attendent des Nations Unies et plus particulièrement de la France que, revenant sur le passé, il soit mis fin au régime de vexations et de persécutions, que les leaders emprisonnés soient libérés et qu'il soit permis aux représentants authentiques de l'Afrique du Nord d'exprimer, sans crainte de représailles, leurs légitimes aspirations. Ainsi la France nouvelle donnerait une courageuse mesure de son libéralisme et mériterait l'amitié et le respect de tout l'Orient arabe.

Veuillez agréer, Excellence, l'assurance de ma haute considération.

Le Président du Conseil,
Ministre des Affaires Étrangères.

Appendix 9 Memorandum of Mr. S.R. Jordan, Chief of the British Delegation in Jeddah of 3 August 1944.

FO 371 | 39989

8368

Registry Number } E 4840/41/65

FROM Mr. S.R. Jordan (Jedda)

No. 72 (1485/653/77)

Dated 3rd August

Received in Registry } 12th August 1944

E : General

Arab Unity Conference.

Refers to his telegram No. 271 of 27th August (E 4512/41/65) and transmits a copy of an aide memoire which he drew up for the Saudi Acting Minister for Foreign Affairs following a discussion regarding the invitation received from Nahas Pasha to send a delegate to preliminary discussions to be held in Cairo.

Copied Ambassador, Cairo and Minister Resident Middle East)

Last Paper.

E 4839

References.

(Minutes.)

In view of last sentence of 2nd. para. off we should perhaps tell Mr. Jordan that we approve.

Ibn Saud has not put us in the cart in any way.

R M A Hankey.
Aug 15.

19/8

21.8.

(Print.)

(How disposed of.)

C.O. Aug

Tel/ Jedda 105 Aug 23.

(Action completed.)

(Index.)

Next Paper.

No.72.

(1485/653/77)

British Legation,

Jedda.

3rd. August, 1944.

Sir,

E 4512/41/65

With reference to my telegram No.271 of 27th. July, 1944, I have the honour to transmit to you herewith copy of an aide memoire which I drew up for the Saudi Acting Minister for Foreign Affairs following a discussion with him of Ibn Saud's attitude towards the invitation received from Nahas Pasha to send a delegate to preliminary discussions to be held in Cairo.

2. I should explain that after my discussion with His Excellency Shaikh Yusuf Yasin he drew up and handed to me an aide memoire covering our talks. I did not consider that the document drawn up by him represented the true facts of the case and I therefore drew up the attached aide memoire. I should perhaps explain that in the course of the discussions he mentioned the King's desire that any proceedings in the preliminary meeting, which was being held basically to draw up an agenda for a plenary conference, should be kept secret and, moreover, that a plenary conference should only be held if the vote of the delegates were unanimous. As it appeared to me that both these suggestions served His Majesty's Government's purpose I agreed with them, more particularly as you will remember that when the idea of this preliminary meeting was mooted in the beginning of the present year it was understood that the proceedings would, in fact, be kept secret. In the aide memoire which I presented to Shaikh Yusuf for His Majesty's information I therefore incorporated these two suggestions and I hope that my action in so doing has your approval.

The Right Honourable Anthony Eden, M.C., M.P.,
etc., etc., etc.,
Foreign Office.

3. Furthermore, I took advantage of the authority contained in your telegram No.88 of 3rd. July, 1944 to lay before Ibn Saud the fullest possible information and I also used the information contained in paragraph 3 of Cairo telegram No.34 of 10th. July, 1944 from which it appeared from Amin's statement that if one or two Arab States were to refuse Nahas' invitation the latter would not call a preliminary meeting.

4. This aide memoire was presented to His Majesty in Riyadh when Shaikh Yusuf visited him with General Giles and Mr. Moose, and after considering it closely Ibn Saud instructed Yusuf Yasin to inform me that he had decided definitely, as he had always been inclined to do, to refuse the invitation of Nahas Pasha to send a delegate to the preliminary meeting. Enclosure No.11. of this despatch is a memorandum presented to me by Yusuf Yasin resulting from his visit to Riyadh and enclosure No. 111 is the draft of the letter which Ibn Saud proposed at that time to send to Nahas. At the same time Ibn Saud despatched communications to the Imam Yahia of the Yemen, Shukri Kutwatli and Riyadh al Sulh informing them of his decision, and he was confident that the Imam Yahia at least would follow his lead.

5. Unfortunately, soon after Shaikh Yusuf Yasin had communicated His Majesty's decision to me, the United States Democratic Party's announcement regarding Palestine and the Jews was made public and I advised Shaikh Yusuf Yasin immediately that perhaps in view of the agitations which this manifesto would surely produce in Arab countries His Majesty might wish to consider withholding his reply to Nahas for ten days or a fortnight until the situation became clearer.

6. I understand that Shaikh Yusuf communicated this view to His Majesty when he visited Riyadh with Mr. Moose and myself on 1st. August, 1944. There seems to be little doubt that the Democratic Party's manifesto has perturbed His Majesty and

although I had not the opportunity of discussing the matter with him since I never visited him except in company with Mr. Moose, he nevertheless took the opportunity towards the end of one of our interviews with him to inform me that he had decided to send Shaikh Yusuf Yasin to Cairo immediately with his reply and had instructed him to discuss the matter first with Nahas Pasha.

7. Shaikh Yusuf Yasin afterwards informed me that he had been instructed to proceed to Cairo and to endeavour to point out to Nahas Pasha His Majesty's conviction that it would not be in the best interests of the Arabs to hold a preliminary meeting at the moment since it would surely embarrass the Allies in the prosecution of the war and lead to heated statements, the repercussion of which could not be foreseen.

8. I believe that the above represents the truth, but not the whole truth, because Ibn Saud's refusal in the first place was so definite and his disappointment at not being consulted by Nahas before he called the preliminary meeting was so acute that he would not have sent Shaikh Yusuf to Cairo unless the statement of the United States Democratic Party had caused him some anxiety. I feel sure that it is to enable him to judge the full reaction of the Arabs towards this statement that he has sent the Minister to discuss the matter with Nahas in Cairo.

9. While in Cairo, Shaikh Yusuf Yasin will keep in touch with Sir Walter Smart at the British Embassy and with the Office of the Minister Resident in the Middle East, and inform them of the trend of his conversations.

10. My impression is that Ibn Saud is still firmly convinced that the moment is not opportune for the holding of a preliminary meeting but he anticipates that the American statement will produce such a sharp reaction in all Moslem countries that he would be placing himself in an invidious position were he to refuse outright Nahas's invitation

without taking into full consideration the effect that such a refusal might have on an excited and even fanatical Moslem population in the Middle East. He has chosen, therefore, to send his delegate to Egypt to judge the depth of that feeling after which he will no doubt decide whether he can with justification refuse to send a delegate to the preliminary meeting and to counsel its postponement until such a time when the holding of such a meeting would not seriously prejudice the Allied war effort, without being accused of being in American pockets.

11. A copy of a communication sent to Shukri Kuwatli and to Riyadh al Sulh appears as enclosure No.IV to this despatch; copies of telegrams sent to the Imam Yahia appear as enclosure No.V.

12. I am sending copies of this despatch to His Majesty's Ambassador in Cairo and to the Minister Resident in the Middle East.

I have the honour to be,
with the highest respect,
Sir,
Your most obedient,
humble servant.

S.R. JORDAN.

ENCLOSURE I

AIDE MEMOIRE.

In his conversation with Mr. Jordan, His Excellency Shaikh Yusuf Yasin referred to the talks he had had with Mr. Ellison regarding the question of the holding of a preparatory meeting in connection with the Arab Unity Conference in Cairo. His Excellency Shaikh Yusuf Yasin declared that His Majesty adhered to his original views on the subject and that he had delayed sending Nahas Pasha a final refusal of his invitation in view of Mr. Jordan's return and his desire to ascertain the views of the British Government. Mr. Jordan thanked His Majesty for the friendly consideration which he had shown to His Majesty's Government and reviewed the circumstances, in so far as he saw the situation. He stated that in the opinion of His Majesty's Government the present time was not propitious for the holding of this Committee Meeting and it was likely that such a meeting if allowed to get out of hand might do more harm to the Arab cause than good. Mr. Jordan has reason to believe that if one or more of the Arab States were to inform Nahas Pasha that the present moment is not an opportune moment to hold the conference he would drop the idea until some measure of unanimity was reached between all Arab powers.

2. Should, however, a sufficient number of Arab powers signify their willingness to send delegates to the preparatory meeting to induce Nahas Pasha to proceed with his idea of calling it on 25th. September next, Mr. Jordan considers that it would be advisable for His Majesty the King of Saudi Arabia to send a representative to the preparatory meeting in order that he could be able to make his views known and in order also that the Committee should enjoy the benefit of his moderating influence. His Majesty's Government, however, would request in these circumstances that discussions about Palestine and the past or future of the French in the Levant States should be kept within proper limits and that there should be no unsuitable resolutions and no tendencious public speeches on either of these points. Mr. Jordan pointed out that of course discussions cannot be foreseen and the failure of delegates to achieve a substantial measure of agreement amongst themselves would be more harmful than if a preparatory meeting had not been called.

3. Mr. Jordan stated that he considered that if a preparatory meeting became inevitable and His Majesty agreed to send a delegate, its main duty when it meets would appear to be to discover whether in fact sufficient agreement exists to justify the holding of a main conference. From records of previous meetings there does not appear to be much liklihood of agreement on the political side though something might be done on the question of economic and cultural relations between the Arab powers, such as a closer coordination of monetary systems of the Governments concerned, the communications between their territories, of their passport regulations or any matters relating to customs or commercial exchanges. There may also be scope for greater co-ordination in educational questions, research and technical activities and perhaps also in codifying their legislation. Unless the preparatory meeting can discover a sub-

stantial measure of common agreement on these points and draw up actual resolutions for subsequent approval by the formal conference it would be useless and even harmful to the cause of Arab Unity to hold a formal conference at all.

4. Mr. Jordan added that when the question of an Arab conference was originally mooted it was suggested that the deliberations of the preparatory meeting should not be made public. Mr. Jordan suggests that it is for His Majesty's consideration whether he should insist on this condition should he eventually decide to send a delegate to the preparatory meeting and also to insist that any decision taken by the preparatory meeting to call a formal conference should be unanimous.

5. Mr. Jordan, in conclusion, stated that, as His Majesty was aware, His Majesty's Government are not opposed to the idea of some reasonable form of Arab Unity, but they do feel - and on many occasions have expressed to him their idea - that the present time is not suitable for the holding of such a conference since unless public utterances are strictly controlled it may give rise to a situation which would embarrass the Allies in the prosecution of the war and in their efforts to bring freedom and peace to a sorely-tried world. Their ideas may therefore be summed up as follows:

(i) Postponing of preparatory meeting until after cessation of hostilities.

(ii) If the preparatory meeting is held, the discussion about Palestine and the past or future of the French in the Levant States willbe kept within proper limits.

(iii) That the preparatory meeting discussions should be confidential.

(IV) That a decision to hold a formal conference should be taken only by a unanimous vote of the delegates.

6. Mr. Jordan added that he felt that if His Majesty could arrange with some other Arab territory to concert with him in refusing to send delegates to the conference as proposed by Nahas Pasha it would probably have the effect of causing Nahas Pasha to abandon the idea of holding the preparatory meeting in the near future.

ENCLOSURE II

Yusuf Yasin has already explained to Mr. Jordan what the views of His Majesty are regarding the meeting to which His Majesty's representative has been invited. As regards the holding of the proposed meeting regarding Arab Unity Yusuf Yasin would like to add that His Majesty is firmly determined not to participate in the preliminary committee meeting which Nahas Pasha has called for the 25th September.

The main reason which prompted His Majesty to take this decision was the knowledge that in no case would the participants refrain from discussing the question of Palestine, Syria and the Lebanon and that they would indeed raise issues directly affecting the friendly British Government. In view of His Majesty's desire to avoid this he prefers that there should be no meeting. His Majesty does not yet know who will join him in his refusal to participate, but it is thought that the Yemen and the Lebanon will do so.

Attached is the text of the telegram sent by His Majesty to the Imam Yahia and of the letters which he has sent to the Syrian President and the Lebanese Prime Minister; also, the text of the reply which His Majesty will be sending to Nahas Pasha.

<u>ENCLOSURE III</u>

We received Your Excellency's envoy on 26th Rajub 1363 and informed you on 3rd Shaaban 1363 that we would let you know our views regarding the preliminary committee meeting which you were so good as to call for 25th September 1944. We have already expressed to you our opinion and our agreement with your view that the meeting should be postponed either until after the War or until we and Your Excellency had reached an understanding with the Allies, in particular the British Government regarding the two main issues, namely, Palestine and relations of the Arabs with the Allies. As regards Palestine, this is a most difficult problem and the Arabs cannot discuss the matter among themselves unless an understanding is reached on a genuine settlement which will guarantee their aspirations and rights and clarify their position in relation to the Arab world. As regards an understanding with the Allies or at any rate with the British Government, agreement must be reached as to their attitude vis-a-vis the Arab States. There is no doubt that the holding of a preliminary committee meeting or an Arab conference cannot lead to satisfactory results so long as no decisions have been reached which guarantee a suitable solution of the above two issues. If a meeting is held and these two questions are not raised or if divergence of opinion as to a suitable solution occurs then the result would be extremely prejudicial to the Arab cause. This point must be borne in mind before proceeding with the holding of a meeting. In addition, we are not yet in a position to know what the attitude of the Egyptian Government is regarding the matters which were discussed. Your Excellency's silence on this subject during this long period, as we have already pointed out in a previous letter has convinced me that we share the same views and agree on general lines and principles. Your Excellency has, however, not raised the matter again before seeking an understanding on the points above-mentioned and contrary to our original agreement. We therefore regret that we have to state with all frankness and clarity that so long as we do not know the true position and are sure that it conforms to the policy which we have stated above, we do not see that our participation would serve any useful purpose. We therefore regret that we are unable to appoint representatives to attend the meeting in question.

ENCLOSURE IV

HIS MAJESTY'S LETTER TO THE PRESIDENT OF THE SYRIAN REPUBLIC.

His Majesty has written a similar letter to the Lebanese Prime Minister.

I have studied and taken due note of the letter which Your Excellency sent to me through my Minister on 30th. Rajab 1363. Your Excellency is aware that, so help me God, I have not changed nor will I change. The purpose of our brotherly affection and understanding is to serve the common interest, particularly the interests of Your Excellency and of the people of Syria. Your Excellency knows best what my aims are and knows best my sincerity. The communication which I made to you and which may have appeared ambiguous can be interpreted in the words of the saying, namely, that every situation has its explanation and every statement its answer. You informed me that Nahas Pasha had asked you to appoint representatives to attend the meeting to be held in Cairo. You added that you had appointed such and such persons and that you had informed Nahas Pasha of their names. By your action you faced us with a fait accompli and we have nothing to say except that you are the best judge of your own affairs. The truth, however, is that Nahas's invitation was a surprise which took me very much aback. The reason is that before the conclusion of the discussions which took place in Cairo I had informed him what my views were regarding this matter and that there were two essential issues at stake; Palestine, and the need for an understanding with the Allies as to what course they were prepared to follow regarding Palestine and their relations with the rest of the Arab world. I pointed out that before this could be achieved new steps would have to be taken regarding these two issues. Nahas Pasha pointed out that he was in agreement with my views and I informed Jamil Bey thereof when he visited me. The last assurance which Nahas gave to me regarding his agreement with my views was when my Chargé d'Affaires in Egypt handed him my letter of the 14th. Rabi Ath. Thani 1363. I was therefore greatly surprised when I learned from you about the receipt of his invitation and the appointment of your representatives. I myself intended to refuse sending representatives in the event of receiving a similar invitation. Such an invitation did in fact reach me, albeit late. I next received a message from Nahas Pasha about the postponement of the date of the meeting until after the Id al Fitr and informing me that the date had been fixed for 25th. September 1944.

As regards my personal opinion of this matter I have three observations to make.

First, if I were to make weighty utterances or to remain silent in certain councils then I would be doing myself an injustice, and if I held forth with pomp and circumstance on a matter which then proved a failure I should not know what to do and my position would be most difficult, for I am not like Cabinets which resign and whose place is taken by others. I therefore prefer the second course, namely, to refrain from clamouring for something which is profitless.

Second, I am until now unaware why a meeting has been

called, what its basis is, on what principles it rests, whether its purpose is to unite the Arab countries like Egypt, Iraq and Syria or whether each party has its own individual plan which it will endeavour to execute; nor am I aware what their attitude is with regard to Palestine which is the most difficult of all problems and without which no satisfactory results can be achieved for the Arabs.

Third, the question of precedence and who shall preside over the meeting. Are all to be equal or will there be one person who desires to dominate the remainder on any particular matter? Moreover, if the intention is to unify the Arabs and bring them together what would my position be and that of certain Arabs who have tried to come to a friendly understanding with them. You yourself are well aware of this and have used your good offices to accomplish it. However, nothing was achieved. Shall I therefore remain silent and leave the matter or try to make bricks without straw?

This is what I wanted to tell you secretly and in confidence so that you should know the truth. I have communicated these observations to you on account of the firm friendship uniting us and you will now be able to judge what we can keep silent about and what we cannot. Whatever the case I wanted you to know what my attitude was and that it cannot be changed. I intend with all the strength at my disposal to work for the interests of the Arabs but I must make it perfectly clear that I cannot agree to any action prejudicial to the British Government, with whom I strive to co-operate and whom I have informed of the true interests at stake in the course of my consultations and discussions with them. This has been my practice with them in the past as regards Syria, Palestine and the Lebanon. I am not one of those who make propaganda for themselves and who try to enlist the support of Zaid or Omar; my true purpose is only to serve all Arab nations and to work for the welfare of them all.

In conclusion I have to state that I do not agree to one party dominating another or one country ruling another but strive to bring about collaboration among all those of good faith in the service of the common interest. I therefore intend to refrain from participating at the meeting and from appointing representatives. have in fact written to Nahas in this sense and wished to explain to you the position so that you would be fully aware thereof and could adjust your attitude accordingly: it is not, however, my intention in any way to influence any decision you may take, my purpose being only to explain that the holding of a meeting would do more harm than good.

ENCLOSURE V

TEXT OF THREE TELEGRAMS SENT BY IBN SAUD TO IMAM YAHIA.

I. I have sent Your Majesty my brother a telegram setting out in detail my views on the invitation of Nahas Pasha to attend the Meeting, which is now being postponed until 25th. September. I trust that you will find them sufficient.

II. I have received Your Majesty's telegram in answer to my telegram of 24th. Rajab and was overjoyed at the mutual agreement existing between our two countries on all matters. I pray God to prolong his blessings on you and grant you long life. I have studied the copy of the invitation which Your Majesty received from Nahas Pasha and which is identical with the invitation which he sent to me. I would like to explain to Your Majesty what my views are on this matter. My representative had already spoken to Nahas on the subject and I also wrote to him pointing out that there were two vital problems on which an understanding had to be reached before discussions could assume the form of a public meeting. The first problem is that of Palestine and the participation of Palestinians in these discussions, as also the question of the validity of their demands. The second problem is that of an understanding between the Arab Governments and the Allies regarding Palestine and the course which the Allies are prepared to follow in their relations with the Arabs. Nahas Pasha informed me that he agreed with my views and supported my opinion regarding the necessity for a solution of these two problems before continuing negotiations. The last thing that passed between us on this subject was a letter which I sent to him dated 4th. Rabi Ath Thani 1363 in which I re-affirmed our agreement on the necessity for postponing meetings and discussions until these problems had been settled by diplomatic consultation preceeding a general conference. His Excellency informed my representative that he was in complete agreement with my views but I suddenly learned from my Minister in Syria that the Syrian Government had received an invitation from Nahas to send representatives to attend a meeting. After about ten days I received a letter from Nahas similar to the communication sent to you. I was greatly surprised and taken aback that Nahas should have sent this new invitation after our mutual agreement on the subject and without even explaining the reasons which prompted him to change his attitude. The fact is I had intended not to accept the invitation and to refuse it as it conflicted with everything which we had agreed upon. I do not know what new factors persuaded Nahas to change his attitude. On 3rd. Shaaban I received a notification to the effect that the meeting had been postponed until 25th. September and until now I have not replied to Nahas either positively or negatively. However, in view of the explanations which I have given to Your Majesty as outlined above, namely, the need to reach an understanding on the two essential points, which in fact has not yet been reached, I intend to approach Nahas and study the position with him once again. I will keep Your Majesty informed of developments.

III. Pray God that Your Majesty my brother and Your Majesty's family are all in good health. I received Your Majesty's reply to the two telegrams which I sent to Your Majesty regarding the invitation which Nahas sent to you with the request to appoint representatives for the proposed meeting on 25th. September. I trust that the observations which I communicated to Your Majesty were sufficient to enable Your Majesty to ascertain what my views are and toact accordingly. I have decided notto accept theinvitation and to refrain from participating in the meeting and I would like to reiterate some of the detailed observations which I communicated to Your Majesty and some of the points which arose from my correspondence with Nahas and some of the Arab Governments. I pointed out to them that there were many factors on which an understanding had to be reached before embarking on discussions. Firstly, an agreed solution of the Palestine problem which would guarantee the rights of its Arab inhabitants, for if this problem is not settled fairly any meeting on the subject would be profitless and no agreement or unity could be achieved between the Arabs. Secondly, an understanding with the Allies, in particular with the British Government, regarding their relations with the Arabs as a whole. Thirdly, an understanding between the Arabs themselves that the purpose of their meeting should be to serve their joint interests and not to lead to the domination of one party at the expense of another or one country by another. Fourthly, I know the attitude of Egypt from (groups undecypherable in original text). I have furthermore pointed out that if a meeting were held and no reasonable decisionswere reached by the participants, and if, moreover, they kept silent on certain vital issues similar to those which I have outlined, or, alternatively, if they raised these issues and differed as to the proper solution thereof, then the meeting would do far more harm than if it had never been held. As these points have not yet been discussed and no agreement has been reached I cannot see that the meeting would be of any use and I myself therefore refuse to participate and do not intend to appoint representatives to attend it.

I have explained the foregoing to Your Majesty not with any intention of influencing you in any way whatever. I do not ask Your Majesty to follow the course I have adopted but felt that in view of the brotherly friendship and affection existing between us I had to tell you in detail of all my actions in this matter. It is now for Your Majesty to act as you think fit.

References

Books

Abāẓah, Fārūq ʿUthmān. *ʿAdan wa al-Sīyāsah al-Bariṭānīyah fī al-Baḥr al-Aḥmar 1839–1918*. Cairo: al-Hayʾah al-Miṣrīyah al-ʿĀmmah li-l-Kitāb, 1976.

ʿAbdul Raḥmān, ʿAbdul Raḥīm ʿAbdul Raḥmān. *Al-Dawlah al-Saʿūdīyah al-Ūlā 1745–1818 AD/1158–1233 Hijri*. Cairo: al-Maṭbaʿah al-ʿĀlamīyah, 1969.

ʿAbd al-Raḥmān. *Min Wathāʾiq al-dawlah al-Saʿūdīyah al-Ūlā fī ʿAṣr Muḥammad ʿAlī, 1222–1234 Hijri/1807–1819 AD*. Cairo: Dār al-Kitāb al-Jāmiʿī, 1983 (Min Wathāʾiq Shibh al-Jazīrah al-ʿArabīyah fī al-ʿAṣr al-Ḥadīth, vol. 2).

ʿAbd al-Raḥmān. *Muḥammad ʿAlī wa Shibh al-Jazīrah al-ʿArabīyah, 1234–1256 Hijri/1819–1840 AD*. Cairo: [n.pb.], 1981.

Cromer, Evelyn Baring. *Modern Egypt*. New York: Macmillan, 1908. 2 vols.

Fahmī, William. *Al-Hijrah al-Yahūdīyah ilā Filisṭīn al-Muḥtalah*. Cairo: al-Hayʾah al-Miṣrīyah al-ʿĀmmah li-l-Kitāb, 1971.

Gerard, B. S. *The Encyclopaedia of Economic Life in Egypt in the Eighteenth Century: a Description of Egypt*, translated by Zuheir al-Shayeb. Cairo: [n.pb.], 1978.

Ghonaim, ʿĀdil Ḥasan. *Al-Ḥarakah al-Waṭaniyah al-Filisṭīnīyah min Thawrat 1936 ḥattā al-Ḥarb al-ʿĀlamīyah al-Thānīyah* (Cairo: al-Khānjī, 1981).

Ghonaim. *Al-Ḥarakah al-Waṭaniyah al-Filisṭīnīyah 1917–1936*. Cairo: al-Hayʾah al-Miṣrīyah al-ʿAmmah li-l-Kitāb, 1974.

Ghorbal, Shafic. *The Beginning of the Egyptian Question and the Rise of Mehmet Ali: A Study in the Diplomacy of the Napoleonic Era Based on Researches in the British and French Archives*. With a Preface by Arnold J. Toynbee. London: Routledge, 1928.

Ghorbāl. *Muḥammad 'Alī al-Kabīr*. Cairo: [n.pb.], 1944.

Al-Ghūrī, Emille. *Al-Mu'āmarah al-Kubrā, Ightīyāl Filisṭīn wa Ḥaqq al-'Arab*. Cairo: Dār al-Nīl, 1955.

Gibb, Hamilton Alexander and Harold Bowen. *The Islamic Society and the West: A study of the impact of Western civilisation on Muslim Culture in the Near East*. London; New York: Oxford University Press 1950–1957. 2 vols.

Grant, A. J. and Harold Temperley. *Europe in the Nineteenth and Twentieth Centuries (1789–1932)*. New York: Longman, 1984.

Ḥajjār, Joseph. *Urūppā wa Maṣīr al-Sharq al-'Arabī: Ḥarb al-Isti'mār 'alā Muḥammad 'Alī wa al-Nahḍah al-'Arabīyah,* translated by Buṭrus al-Ḥallāq and Mājid Ni'mah. Beirut: al-Mu'asasah al-'Arabīyah li-l-Dirāsāt wa al-Nashr, 1976.

Ḥussayn, Fāḍil. *Mushkilat al-Mūṣul: Dirāsah fī al-Diblumāsīyah al-'Irāqīyah-al-Inglīzīyah-al-Turkīyah wa fī al-Ra'īy al-'Ām*, 2nd ed. Baghdad: Maṭba'at As'ad, 1967.

Laqueur, Walter Zéev (ed.). *The Israel-Arab Leader: A Documentary History of the Middle-East Conflict*. Rev. ed. Harmondsworth: Penguin, 1970. (A Pelican Book.)

Lorimer, J. G. *A Guide to the Gulf: Geography*, vol. 2 [n.p]: [n.pb.], 1978]. 7 vols.

Lorimer. *A Guide to the Gulf: History*, translated by the office of translation in the Dīwān of the governor of Qatar, vol. 1. Qatar: Maṭābi' al-'Urūbah, 1967. 7 vols.

MacCallum, Elizabeth P. *The Arab Nationalist Movement*. New York: Foreign Policy Association, [n.d.].

Mnassā, Maḥmūd Ṣāliḥ. *Al-Ḥarb al-'Ālamīyah al-Thānīyah*. Cairo: [n.pb.], 1989.

Mnassā. *Al-Mashriq al-'Arabī al-Mu'āṣir*. Cairo: [n.pb.], 1995, Section 1: al-Hilāl al-Khaṣīb.

Montefiore, Moses (Sir). *Diaries of Sir Moses and Lady Montefiore*. London: 1891. 2 vols.

Naẓmī, Wamīḍ Jamāl, Ghānim Muḥammad Ṣāliḥ and Shafīq 'Abdul Rāziq. *Al-Taṭawwur al-Sīyāsī al-Mu'āṣir fī al-'Irāq*. Baghdad: Baghdad University, Faculty of Law and Politics, Political Science Department, [198-].

Qarqūt, Dhūqān. *Taṭawwur al-Fikrah al-'Arabīyah fī Miṣr 1805–1936*. Beirut: al-Mu'asasah al-'Arabīyah li-l-Dirāsāt wa al-Nashr, 1972.

Qāsim, Jamāl Zakariyah. *Tārīkh al-Khalīj al-'Arabī al-Ḥadīth wa al-Mu'āṣir*, vol. 1. Cairo: Dār al-Fikr al-'Arabī, 1996.

Qāsim. *Dawlat al-BuSa'īd fī 'Umān wa Sharq Afrīqīyā, 1741–1861.*

Al-Qasimi, Sultan Muhammad [Ruler of Shariqah]. *The Myth of Arab Piracy in the Gulf*, 2nd ed. London; New York: Routledge, 1988.

Al-Rāfi'ī, 'Abd al-Raḥmān. *'Aṣr Muḥammad 'Alī*, 2nd ed. Cairo: Maktabat al-Nahḍah al-'Arabīyah, 1947.

Ramsauer, Ernest Edmondson. *The Young Turks: Prelude to the Revolution of 1908*, translated by Ṣāliḥ Aḥmad al-'Alī, foreword and editing by Nicola Zīyādeh. Beirut: Dār Maktabat al-Ḥayāt, 1960.

Rendel, George (Sir). *The Sword and the Olive: Recollections of Diplomacy and the Foreign Service, 1913–1954*. London: J. Murray, [1957].

Rizk, Younan Labib. *Azmat al-'Aqabah al-Ma'rūfah bi-Ḥadithat Ṭābā*. Cairo: [n.pb.], 1983.

Rizk. *Ḥawādith 1935 fī Miṣr 'alā Ḍaw' al-Wathā'iq al-Bariṭānīyah: Buḥūth fī al-Tārīkh al-Ḥadīth*. Cairo: [n.pb.], 1976.

Rizk and Muḥammd Muzayn. *Tārīkh al-'Ilāqāt al-Miṣrīyah-al-Maghribīyah mundhu Maṭla' al-'Uṣūr al-Ḥadīthah ḥattā 'Ām 1912*. Cairo: [n.pb.], 1990.

Rodinson, Maxime. *Israel and the Arabs*, translated from the French by Michael Perl. Harmondsworth: Penguin; New York: Pantheon Books, 1968 (Penguin Special Series; 263.)

Ṣadaqah, Najīb. *Qaḍīyat Filisṭīn, introduction* by 'Abdul Raḥmān 'Azzām and Sayyid Jamāl al-Ḥusaynī. Beirut: Dār al-Kitāb, 1946.

Ṣāyyigh, Anīs. *Al-Hāshimyūn wa al-Thawrah al-'Arabīyah al-Kubrā*. Beirut: [n.pb.], 1976.

Al-Shalaq, Aḥmad Zakarīyah. *Ḥizb al-Ummah wa Dawruh fī al-Sīyāsah al-Miṣrīyah*. Cairo: Dār al-Ma'ārif, 1979 (Dirāsāt fī Tārīkh al-Aḥzāb al-Miṣrīyah).

Shārubīm, Mikhā'īl. *Al-Kafi fī Tārīkh Mīsr al-Qadīm wa al-Ḥadīth.*

Waḥīdah, Ṣubḥī. *fī Uṣūl al-Mas'alah al-Miṣrīyah*. Cairo: Maṭba'at Miṣr, 1950.

Periodicals

Al Ahram: 13/3/1896; 9/6/1909; 20/6/1909; 6/7/1909; 8/7/1909; 12/7/1909; 22/4/1910; 2/12/1931; 5/12/1931; 7/12/1931; 18/12/1931;

27/12/1931; 6/10/1938; 11/10/1938; 12/10/1938; 8/10/1944 and 8/1/1945.

Al-'Aqqād, Ṣalāḥ. 'Najīb 'Āzūrī and his Political Views'. *Economy, Policy and Trade Magazine* (Cairo): 1960.

Ḍīyāb, Tawfīq. In: *al-Jihād,* 7 November 1937.

Magnes, J. L. 'Palestine and Arab Union'. *Bayot Hayom*, 25 July 1941.

Al-Maṣrī, 17 November 1937.

Al-Muṣawwir, 24 January 1944.

Journals

Al-Qāsimī, Nūrah Muḥammad. 'Al-Wujūd al-Hindī fī al-Khalīj al-'Arabī, 1820–1947'. (unpublished Master's dissertation, Kullyat al-Banāt, 'Ayn Shams University, 1984.

Documents

F.O. 371/9007, Peace Conference: Paris Memorandum by the Emir Faisal.

F.O. 371/5066, Foreign Office Memorandum on possible negotiations with the Hedjaz, Appendix B.

F.O. 371/5067, Report of a conversation between Sir J. Tilley, K.C.M.G., C.B., reporting the Secretary of State for Foreign Affairs, and His Highness Emir Faisal representing the King of the Hejaz (held at the Foreign Office on Thursday 23 December 1920).

F.O. 371/9001/39977, Secretariat – Government House – Jerusalem, 22 December 1922.

F.O. 371/9001, From Herbert Samuel to the Duke of Devonshire.

F.O. 371/9001, From the Duke of Devonshire to the Marquis Curzon of Kedleston, 16 January 1923.

F.O. 371/9053-39804, Consul Smart to the Marquis Curzon of Kedleston, Aleppo, 31 May 1923.

F.O. 371/10851, Telegram from Lord Crewe to Mr Chamberlain, Paris, 4 November 1925.

F.O. 371/11436, Vice Consul Jordan to Sir Austen Chamberlain, Jeddah, 17 April 1926.

F.O. 371/11445, Consul Smart-Damascus to Foreign Office, 16 March 1926.

F.O. 371/11436, Enclosure in no. 1, Précis of Munshi Ihsanuallah's Report.

F.O. 371/40064, Memorandum on the political situation in North Africa by F. R. Rodd, 21 June
F.O. 371/15282, Weekly Appreciation Summary no. 7, 18 February 1931.
F.O. 371/15282, The Residency, Cairo, to the Right Honourable Arthur Henderson, 27 February 1931.
F.O. 371/15282, The Residency, Cairo, to Sr. L. Oliphant, 12 June 1931.
F.O. 371/15282, Cypher Telegram from the Secretary of State to the Government of India, dated 18 November 1931.
F.O. 371/15283, Italian Chargé d'Affaires (Conversation), 16 December 1931.
F.O. 407/221, Enclosure in no. 25 – Egyptian Personalities.
F.O. 371/15283, From the High Commissioner in Palestine, to the Secretary of State for Colonies, 17 December 1931.
F.O. 371/15283, From Foreign Office to the Italian Embassy, 18 December 1931.
F.O. 371/16009, The Pan-Islamic Movement.
F.O. 371/16009, The Residency, Cairo, to Sir John Simon, 26 November 1931.
F.O. 371/16009, Colonial Office – Moslem Conference in Jerusalem, 21 May 1932.
F.O. 371/15364, Sir P. Gunliffe-Lister to Sir F. Humphreys (Baghdad), 27 November 1931.
F.O. 371/15364, Morgan to Sir John Simon, 23 December 1931.
F.O. 371/16011, Extract from Palestine Police Secret Appreciation Summary, 2 December 1932.
F.O. 371/10611, Sir F. Humphreys to Sir John Simon, 21 December 1932.
F.O. 371/16855, Proposed Conference, 13 June 1933.
F.O. 371/16855, Position of His Majesty's Government towards the question of Arab Unity, 13 June 1933.
F.O. 371/16855, Memorandum – Points under discussion with King Faisal and his Ministers at present in London.
F.O. 371/16855, Conversation between Secretary of State and King Feisal, 22 June 1933.
F.O. 371/16855, From Sir F. Humphreys (Baghdad) to Mr Sterendle Bennett (Colonial Office), 5 October 1933.
F.O. 371/19980, Clark-Kerr to Eden, 24 February 1936 – Arab Unity.
F.O. 371/19980, Enc. Movement-Sudan Agency, Cairo, 14 February 1936.
F.O. 371/19980, Sir M. Lampson to Mr Eden, 24 February 1936.

F.O. 371/19980, Enc. Report on the Pan-Islamic Arab Movement, Report on the Pan-Islamic Arab-Sudan Agency, Cairo, 28 March 1936.
F.O. 371/19980, Sir M. Lampson to Mr Eden, 2 April 1936.
F.O. 371/19980, Sir M. Lampson to Mr Eden, 8 April 1936, Pan-Islamic Arab Movement.
F.O. 371/19980, Sir M. Lampson to Mr Eden, 28 May, Pan-Islamic Arab Movement.
F.O. 371/19980, Sir A. Clark Kerr to Mr Eden, 3 April 1936, Arab Unity. Visit of Iraqi notables to Syria, Palestine and Egypt.
F.O. 407/19980, Sir A. Clark Kerr to Mr Eden, 28 May 1936 – Arab Unity.
F.O. 371/19980, Consul MacKereth to Mr Eden, 15 May 1936; Memorandum on Pan-Arabism.
F.O. 371/20780 Pan-Arab Conference; note by Samuel Bey Attiya, 13 January 1937.
F.O. 371/20786, Sir M. Lampson to Mr Eden, 9 January 1937 – Arab Unity.
F.O. 371/20786, Sir R. Bullard (British Legation, Jeddah) to Foreign Office, 7 December 1937.
F.O. 371/21872, Saudi Minister, Conversation, 7 January 1938.
F.O. 371/21883, Lampson to Halifax, 24 October 1938 – Arab Parliamentary Conference and Arab Women's Conference.
F.O. 371/23239, Memorandum on Arab Federation, 28 September 1939.
F.O. 371/23195, Major Todd (War Office) to Mr Baggallay, 3 November 1939 – Arab Federation.
F.O. 371/23195, Havard (Beirut) to Mr Baggallay, 14 November 1939, Arab Federation.
F.O. 371/23195, Notes by Gilbert MacKereth, British Consulate, Damascus, 15 November 1939.
F.O. 371/24584, Stonehewer Bird to Baggallay, 8 April 1940.
F.O. 371/27043, British Embassy, Washington D.C., to Charles Baxter, 9 May 1941.
F.O. 371/27043, Arab Policy Memorandum by the Secretary of State on the whole question of our policy in Palestine, Syria, Iraq and Saudi Arabia, 27 May 1941.
F.O. 371/27043, From Sir M. Lampson, Cairo, 3 June 1941, Secretary of State's Speech of 29 May on the Middle East, 4 June 1941.
F.O. 371/31337, War Office – Arab Federation Report, 9 January 1942.
F.O. 371/31337, Text of declaration proposed by General Catroux.
F.O. 371/31338, High Commissioner in Palestine to His Majesty's principal Secretary of State for the Colonies, 7 June 1942.

F.O. 371/31338, Cassia (Foreign Office) to Boyd (Colonial Office), 9 June 1942.
F.O. 371/31338, Plan of Arab Federation by Professor Gibb (Royal Institute of International Affairs), 21 December 1942.
F.O. 371/31338, Minutes by Mr Caccia, 10 February 1943.
F.O. 371/31338, From Baxter (Foreign Office) to Sir Kinahan Cornwallis (Baghdad), 23 February.
F.O. 371/31338, From Edmond (Colonial Office) to Foreign Office, 23 December 1942.
F.O. 371/31338, A Note on the Proposed Equity into the Possibility of Closer Economic Association between the Arab Countries, 23 April 1943.
F.O. 371/34955, Egyptian proposal for a cultural bureau of Arab countries, 22 February 1943.
F.O. 371/35537, Weekly Political and Economic Report, from 29 July to 4 August 1943.
F.O. 371/35537, Weekly Political and Economic Report, from 12 to 18 August 1943.
F.O. 371/35537, Weekly Political and Economic Report, from 14 to 20 October 1943.
F.O. 371/3537, Weekly Political and Economic Report, from 4 to 10 November 1943.
F.O. 371/34975, Resolutions adopted by the Middle Eastern War Council.
F.O. 371/34958, Council of Ministers, Baghdad, to Viscount Halifax, 15 February 1943.
F.O. 371/34959, Memorandum on Arab Unity by the Naval Intelligence Department, 4 June 1943.
F.O. 371/35537, Weekly Political and Economic Report, from 18 to 24 March 1943.
F.O. 371/35537, Weekly Political and Economic Report, from 25 to 31 March 1943.
F.O. 371/34957, From Mr Wikeley (Jeddah) to Foreign Office, 26 April 1943.
F.O. 371/34957, From Foreign Office to Jeddah, 4 May 1943.
F.O. 371/34958, Ibn Saʿūd and the Proposed Conference, from Mr Wikeley (Jeddah), 29 May 1943.
F.O. 371/34958, From Wikeley (Jeddah) to Foreign Office, 27 April 1943.
F.O. 371/34958, From Wikeley (Jeddah) to Foreign Office, 20 July 1943.
F.O. 371/34960, From Wikeley (Jeddah) to Foreign Office, 20 July 1943.

F.O. 371/34960, From Wikeley (Jeddah) to Foreign Office, 27 July 1943.
F.O. 371/34961, Arab Unity Conversation between Colonel Hoskins and King Ibn Sa'ūd at Riyadh, 30 August 1943.
F.O. 371/34960, From Wikeley (Jeddah) to Foreign Office, 29 July 1943.
F.O. 371/34960, From Wikeley (Jeddah) to Foreign Office, 3 August 1943.
F.O. 371/34955, Cornwallis to Foreign Office, 12 March 1943, Emir Abdullah's proposals for a Conference.
F.O. 371/34957, Colonial Office to Foreign Office, 21 April 1943, Emir Abdullah's manifesto on Arab Federation.
F.O. 371/34957, Colonial Office to Foreign Office, 29 April 1943, Emir Abdullah's manifesto on Arab Federation.
F.O. 371/35538, Weekly Political and Economic Report, from 2 to 8 September 1943.
F.O. 371/34963, From Sir H. MacMichael (Palestine) to Colonial Office, 3 November 1943.
F.O. 371/35538, Weekly Political and Economic Report, from 9 to 15 September 1943.
F.O. 371/34962, Record of Conversations between Ibn Sa'ūd, Sheikh Yūsuf Yāsīn and His Majesty's Minister on Arab Unity, 20 September 1943.
F.O. 371/35539, Weekly Periodical and Economic Report from 14 to 20 October 1943.
F.O. 371/35539, Weekly Political and Economic Report, from 28 October to 3 November 1943.
F.O. 371/35539, Weekly Political and Economic Report, from 21 to 28 October 1943.
F.O. 371/35539, Weekly Political and Economic Report, from 4 to 10 November 1943.
F.O. 371/39987, Parliamentary Question by Mr Gallagher, 23 January 1944.
F.O. 371/39987, Sir K. Cornwallis (Baghdad) to Foreign Office, 8 February 1944.
F.O. 371/39987, From Foreign Office to Baghdad, 18 February 1944.
F.O. 371/39987, Arab Unity: Nūrī Pāshā's talks in Damascus, 21 February 1944.
F.O.371/39987, From Lord Killearn (Cairo) to Foreign Office, 24 February.
F.O. 371/39987, Projected Arab Conference in Cairo from Lord Killearn (Cairo) to Foreign Office, 17 March 1944.

F.O. 371/41317, Weekly Political and Economic Report, from 23 to 29 March 1944.
F.O. 371/41317, Weekly Political Report, from 1 to 7 June 1944.
F.O. 371/39988, From Mr Spears (Beirut) to Cairo, 22 April 1944.
F.O. 371/39988, Participation of North African countries in Arab Union discussions, Killearn to Foreign Office, 22 April 1944.
F.O. 371/41316, Weekly Political and Economic Report, from 20 to 26 January 1944.
F.O. 371/41316, Weekly Political and Economic Report, from 10 to 16 February 1944.
F.O. 371/39988, from Mr Eden to Lord Killearn, 5 May 1944.
F.O. 371/39988, Arabic Union project – Sultan of Muscat's interview with Naḥḥās Pāshā, from India Office to Foreign Office, 1 May 1944.
F.O. 371/39988, From Lord Killearn (Cairo) to Foreign Office, 5 June 1944.
F.O. 371/39988, From Lord Killearn (Cairo) to Foreign Office, 22 June 1944.
F.O. 371/39988, From the Foreign Office to Cairo, 3 July 1944.
F.O. 371/41318, Weekly Political and Economic Report, 6 to 12 July 1944.
F.O. 371/39989, From Mr MacKereth (Beirut) to Foreign Office, 8 August 1944.
F.O. 371/39989, From Peterson (Foreign Office) to Mr MacKereth (Beirut) 12 August 1944.
F.O. 371/39989, From Jordan (Jeddah) to Sir Anthony Eden, 3 August 1944, Enclosure I, aide-memoire.
F.O. 371/39989, From Lord Moyne (Minister Resident in Cairo) to Foreign Office, 11 August 1944.
F.O. 371/39990, From Lord Moyen (Cairo) to Foreign Office, 31 August 1944.
F.O. 371/39990, From Mr Jordan (Jeddah) to Foreign Office, 4 September 1944.
F.O. 371/39990, From Lord Moyne to Foreign Office, 7 September 1944.
F.O. 371/39990, From Foreign Office to Jeddah, 11 September 1944.
F.O. 371/39990, From Mr Jordan (Jeddah) to Foreign Office, 14 September 1944.
F.O. 371/39990, From Resident Minister (Cairo) to Foreign Office, 19 September 1944.
F.O. 371/39990, From Mr Ellison (Jeddah) to Foreign Office, 25 September 1944.

F.O. 371/39990, From Colonial Office to Foreign Office, 13 September 1944.
F.O. 371/39990, From Mr Thompson (Baghdad) to Foreign Office, 13 September 1944.
F.O. 371/39990, From Mr Eastwood (Colonial Office) to Mr Baxter (Foreign Office), 3 October 1944.
F.O. 371/41318, Weekly Political and Economic Report, from 28 September to 4 October 1944.
F.O. 371/39991, Foreign Office Minutes, 30 December 1944.
F.O. 371/39991, From Mr Shone (Cairo) to Foreign Office, 1 November 1944.
F.O. 371/39991, From Mr Jordan (Jeddah) to Foreign Office, 14 November 1944.
F.O. 371/39991, From Foreign Office to Jeddah, 28 November 1944.
F.O. 371/45930, Weekly Political and Economic Report, from 25 to 31 January.
F.O. 371/45930, Weekly Political and Economic Report, from 8 to 14 February 1945.
F.O. 371/45930, Weekly Political and Economic Report, from 15 to 21 February 1945.
F.O. 371/45930, Weekly Political and Economic Report, from 22 to 28 February 1945.
F.O. 371/45737, Lord Killearn (Cairo) to Foreign Office, 9 March 1945.
F.O. 371/45737, From Foreign Office to Cairo, 10 March 1945.
F.O. 371/45737, Lord Killearn (Cairo) to Foreign Office, 17 March 1945.
F.O. 371/45930, Weekly Political and Economic Report, from 15 to 21 March 1945.
Maḍābiṭ Majlis al-Shyūkh al-Maṣrī-Jalsat, 29 February 1944.

Index

'Abd al-Ḥamīd II 17, 24–5
Aden 2, 6, 34, 72, 95, 97, 108–9
aeroplanes 32
Afghanistan 58, 87
agriculture 12–13
airports 113
Al-Ahram 17–18, 24–6, 59, 65, 153
Alexandretta 31, 35, 97
Alexandria 13–15
  Alexandria Protocol 137, 156
Alī, Muḥammad
  economic plans 12
  imperial plans of 11
  reforms by 10–11
  retreat from Arabian Peninsula 5, 6, 21, 120
  sends troops to Arabian Peninsula 5–6, 55
  wars conducted by 11
'Ali, Shawkat Mawlāya 54–7, 60
Allenby, Viscount Edmund 2, 38
Arab Confederation 40–9
  and Arab race 42–3
  Britain proposes 41
  and Jewish race 43
  and Palestine 61
  secret history of 40
  suitability of Arab countries to join 42
  Syrian reaction to 42, 45–6, 61
  three-step plan to create 43–4
  western objections to 44–6
Arab Conference in Baghdad 66–75
  agenda 69–72
  British interference in 69
  British report from 69–75
  location for debated 67, 68, 69–70, 74
  Palestinians at 68–9
al-'Arabīyah al-Fatāh vii, 17
Arab Federation
  Islamic character of 156
  proposal for 45, 116, 125, 133, 139, 149, 156, 181–205, 206–15
Arab League
  Antoniadis Conference 142
  British concerns over 143–4
  Charter 137, 153–9
  and Egypt 137–8, 140–1, 143, 150, 154–5
  Foreign Office reaction to 144–6
  General Conference announcement, reactions to 146
  Gulf countries participate in 144
  and Iraq 139–40, 141, 144, 146, 149, 151, 152, 154–5, 157
  and Lebanon 139, 141–2, 146, 152–4
  and Libya 143

and North African countries 143
origins of vii–ix, 133, 137
and Palestine 140–3, 146, 147–8, 152, 154, 156, 158
Preparatory Meeting 137–42, 147
and Saudi Arabia 137–9, 146–9, 151, 154–5, 156
and Syria 139–42, 144–6, 148–53, 157–8
and Trans-Jordan 146, 152–3
Arab nation, proposals for 33–6, 40–49
British U-turn over 36–40, 53–4
provinces exempted from 35
Shawkat 'Alī proposes 54–6
see also Arab Confederation; Arab Conference in Baghdad; Arab Federation; Arab nationalism; Arab Parliamentary Conference; Arab Women's Conference
Arab nationalism
Arab Nationalist Movement 31–40, 48, 67, 87–8
British memoranda on 89–91, 95–101
in Egypt 17–18
in First World War 33–6
Muḥammad 'Alī plans 11–12
Persia fears 67–8
precedents for 33
support for 32–3
technology aids 32
see also Pan-Arabism; Pan-Islamism
Arab Parliamentary Conference 93–4
Arab Resistance Movement 79
Arab Union 32
Arab Women's Conference 93–5
Arabic 11, 31, 90, 95, 123
Axis powers 101, 124
al-Azhar university 5, 56–7, 85, 92, 94
'Azūrī, Najīb 17

Badawī, 'Abd al-Ḥamīd Pāshā, 158
Baghdad
British interest in 35
and Egypt imperial plans 12
see also Iraq
Bahrain 6, 8, 71, 95, 98, 108, 116
al-Bakrī, 'Abd al-Ḥamīd 20, 54
Balfour Declaration 27, 36, 48, 94
Basra 12, 35–6, 118
Bedouin 107
Beirut
Great Mosque 15
boycotts of European goods 54, 78
Boyd, Ken 53, 56
British East Africa 4
al-Buraymī oasis 6

Caliph, Islamic 38, 46, 58–9, 87
Caliph, Ottoman 17, 19, 34, 46, 84, 87
Catroux, Georges 105–6, 112–13
Cavendish, Edward 44–5
Centre for Arab Unity Studies viii
Christianity 35, 81–2, 85, 100, 114, 118, 142–3
Churchill, Winston 40, 44, 73, 119–21
Clark Kerr, Archibald 79–81, 86–9, 178–80
Colonial Office viii
and Arab Confederation 44–5, 49, 53–4
and Arab conferences 69–70, 121, 153
and Arab unity 65, 113
commissions study of Islam in Palestine 60–3
constrained by post-war negotiations 3
growth in power after Second World War 2
'gunboat diplomacy' 6
overlapping responsibilities of 4
and Palestine 2, 56–7
and Syria 64–6
and Trans-Jordan 2
communications 32, 38, 43, 82, 96–7, 111, 114
Cromer, Evelyn Baring 14, 22–3
currency 8–9, 114
Curzon, George, Marquis of Keddleston 6–8, 38–40

Daily Express 1–2

Damietta 13–14
Darfur 33
Deedes, William Henry 41–4, 167–71
Devonshire, Duke of *see* Cavendish, Edward
Dubai 8

Economic Cultural Unity 121–5
economics 110, 112
  Arab, British imperial control of 5, 35
  currency 8–9, 114
  and Egypt 14
  and the India Office 8
  see also trade routes
Eden, Anthony
  and Arab League 139–40
  and report of Archibald Clark Kerr 79–81, 86–9, 178–80
  declaration on Arab unity vii–viii, 77, 101–2, 105, 112, 113, 126
education 33, 44, 48, 67, 70, 81, 82, 110–11, 114, 124, 125, 145, 154
  westernisation of 5
Egypt
  Africa, relationship with 3, 4, 12, 15–17
  anti-British movement in 81, 90–5
  Arab Nationalism in 17–18
  al-'Ahd vii, 19
  and Arab League 137–8, 140–1, 143, 150, 154–5
  Arab union, suspicion of 108
  al-'Arabīyah al-Fatāh vii, 17
  borders 4, 16–17
  British High Commissioner 2, 14, 20, 34, 56, 38–9, 56–7, 78–9, 81–4, 86, 126
  British intervention in 5, 19–20
  causes wars between Britain and France 3
  Decentralisation Party vii
  economics 14
  empire-building 11–12
  European imports to 14–15
  Free French Government 102, 105, 109, 110–12
  Foreign Office control of 2–3
  French campaign in, 1798–1801 3, 17
  and *ḥajj* 15, 91, 155
  independence granted 17, 19–20, 84
  invites Arab cooperation 123
  and Islamic Conference in Jerusalem 58
  London Treaty, 1840 1, 5, 12
  under the Ottoman Empire 10–12, 15, 19
  and Palestine 17, 21, 82
  and Pan-Arab conferences 90–5
  and Pan-Arab movement 83–7
  and Pan-Islamism-Arabism 84–7
  relationship with other Arab states 3, 10–20, 54–5, 93–5, 105, 122–4
  relationship with Sudan 3, 4, 12, 81
  Revolution 1919 20
  and Sinai peninsula 16
  student demonstrations in 78–9
  Sudan agency in 81, 83
  and Suez Canal 13
  and Syria 18, 65, 82–4
  trespasses on Omani territory 6
  Turkish advance on 19
  Ummah Party 18–19
  al-Wafd party 59, 94, 123, 137
Emirate of Trans-Jordan *see* Trans-Jordan, Emirate of
'Entente Cordiale' 4, 163

Federal Council of Arab States 114–15
First World War
  United States enters ix, 31–2
Foreign Office viii
  and Arab Confederation 44–5, 49, 53–4, 72, 92–3
  and Arab League 140–1, 144–6, 151, 154–5, 157
  'Arab Nationalism' memorandum 89–90
  control of Egypt 2–3
  'gunboat diplomacy' 6
  memoranda on Arab unity 95–101, 173–7, 181–205, 216–26

overlapping responsibilities of 4
and Palestine 2
'The Political Situation in North Africa' 48
reacts to Hamilton Gibb's plan 118
reacts to Harold MacMichael's plan 114–15
seeks opinions on Arab unity 105
and Sudan 2, 4, 81
see also Sykes-Picot Agreement
France
campaign in Egypt, 1798–1801 3, 17
as imperialist nation vii, 6, 82–3, 120, 122, 163
Lebanon, mandate in 27, 97, 100, 106, 163
opposes Arab unity 97, 107
and Ottoman empire 21–2
presence in the Arab world 4, 35–6, 61, 64, 112
and proposed Higher Supervisory Council 115–15
Syria, mandate in 42, 46–7, 63, 72, 73–4, 77–8, 82–3, 97, 163
see also Sykes-Picot Agreement
Free French Government 102, 105, 109, 110–12
Fu'ād, Aḥmad 54–5, 123

Gallipoli 34
gender *see* Arab Women's Conference
Germany
Confederation of German States 44
seeks power in Gulf states 6
Gibb, Hamilton Alexander 117–19
Great Arab Revolt vii, 19, 70
and British Foreign Policy 1–2
Greater Syria 12–13, 55, 109, 120, 124–5, 130–2, 141, 145, 152

ḥajj
control of pilgrimage sites 37, 113
and Egypt 15, 91, 155
encourages Arab unity 5
and Kingdom of Ḥijāz 37
overland route of encouraged 15–16
and Suez Canal 5, 15–16
Hashemites 47, 65–71, 88, 97, 107
Hennell, Samuel 6
Ḥijāz, Kingdom of 1, 2
and Arab Confederation 42
British subjects in 38
and Islamic Conference in Jerusalem 58
Ottoman Empire recognises 37
railway in 61–2, 60
Saudi-Hashemite conflict in 47
Saudi Arabia annexes 47, 71
and Syria 31
and United Kingdom 31, 33–7
Hinduism 9
Home Office
European Department 53–4, 84
Humphreys, Francis 67–9, 74
al-Ḥusaynī, Ḥajj Amīn 54, 56, 60
al-Ḥussayn, Emir Fayṣal bin 31, 33, 36, 38, 46–7, 88
and Arab Conference 64–6, 69, 73–5
death 78, 82, 88
Ḥussayn, Sharif bin 'Alī 1–2, 19, 32
Ḥussayn-McMahon correspondence 33–6, 39
Hyamson, Almert M. 20

India
and Egyptian retreat from Gulf states 6
'Indianisation' of Arab States 3, 7
Muslims in 71
Rupees 8–9
see also India Office
India Office viii, ix, 2, 6–10
and Arab Conference in Baghdad 70
assumes responsibility for British administration of Gulf states 6–7, 49
claims to have stabilised Gulf states 7
and economics 8
'gunboat diplomacy' 6–7
opposes Arab unity 115–16
overlapping responsibilities of 4
power of 7–8

social impact on Gulf states 9–10
territories controlled by described 2–3
Iran 6, 36, 94, 96, 98
and Islamic Conference in Jerusalem 58, 62
Iraq
seeks access to Mediterranean 73–4
and Arab Confederation 42
and Arab Conference in Baghdad 64, 69
and Arab League 139–40, 141, 144, 146, 149, 151, 152, 154–5, 157
British assessment of 32
British embassy in 79–81, 84, 131
British rule in 2, 4, 42
coup of Bakr Ṣidqī 78–9
and Egypt 123
independence 42, 49, 64, 72, 107, 124–5
interest in anti-British movement in Egypt 81
international position 68
and Islamic Conference in Jerusalem 58
mineral wealth 115–16
nationalist sentiment in vii, 32
oil 67, 98
and Ottoman coup, 1913 19
relationship with Saudi Arabia 80, 128
relationship with Syria 64, 83, 96
Islam *see* Caliph, Islamic; *Ḥajj*; Pan-Islamism; Shīʿites; Sunnis
Islamic Conference in Jerusalem 57–63
British researchers at 61
concerns over voiced 58
conclusions drawn from 63
decisions taken during 61–3
demonstrations over 60
Executive Committee appointed 62–3
long telegram concerning 57–8
media reaction to 58–60
Italy
and Islamic Conference in Jerusalem 58, 59
occupies Libya 4–5
Jamāl Pāshā 19
ʿal-Jarīdah 18
Jews 43
and Arabs 33, 43–4, 106, 112, 122
and Bolshevist Revolution 27
British Jews 27
commercialism 122
in Egypt 14
German 23
Iraqi 122
Jewish Federation 25
and Ottoman Empire 24–5
relationship with Britain 43
Russian 24, 26–7
Syrian 122
Zionist conferences 23, 79
see also Palestine

Kāmil, Muṣṭafā 17, 18
Kenya 4
Khurshīd Pāshā, Aḥmad 6, 11
Killearn, Baron *see* Lampton, Myles
Kuwait 8, 71, 73, 95, 108, 116

Lampson, Myles 81–5, 91, 93–5, 101–2, 140–5, 157–9, 227–8
see also Eden, Anthony
languages 9, 11, 31, 90, 95, 123
Lausanne, Conference of 41, 44, 46
Lawrence, Thomas Edward ('Lawrence of Arabia') 1–2
League of Nations 4, 37–8, 40–1, 58, 64, 74, 86
Syria and 61
Lebanon 64, 68, 81
at Arab Conferences 61, 93, 151
and Arab League 139, 141–2, 146, 152–4
and Arab unity 95–6, 106, 109–15, 118, 124–6, 132, 139, 141–2, 146, 152–4
Christians in 81, 100, 118
French mandate in 27, 97, 100, 106, 163
independence proposed 106
see also Greater Syria

Libya
Italian occupation of 4–5
Ottomans expelled from 4–5
Sanūsī Revolt 33
Lloyd George, David 2
Loraine, Percy 20

MacKereth, Gilbert 89–90, 99–100, 146
McMahon, Henry
Ḥussayn-McMahon correspondence 33–6, 39
MacMichael, Harold 113, 115, 119, 133
Mecca 31, 37
and ʿAbd al-ʿAzīz Āl Saʿūd 47
see also Ḥajj
Media 2–3, 17–19, 54, 56, 58–60, 79, 82, 91–2, 111, 153
Medina 37
Mersina 35
Mesopotamia 2, 4, 31, 37, 39, 82, 88, 90
migration
to Egypt 3, 14
from Palestine 25
to Palestine 23–5
see also Jews
Montefiore, Hugh 21
al-Moqaṭṭam 17
Morocco 15, 93, 99, 143
Muscat 7–9, 12, 71, 80, 95, 109, 144
Muslim Brotherhood Association 85
Muslim Youth Association 20, 55, 61

Nasīm, Tawfīq 54, 78
Najd 1, 32, 47, 66–7, 88, 117

oil ix, 32, 67, 96–8, 111, 113–14, 116–17
Oman 6, 8, 17, 71, 108
Ottoman Empire
ʿAbbās I, reign of 15–16
Caliph, Ottoman 17, 19, 34, 46, 84, 87
and Egypt 10–12, 15, 19
coups 19, 24
decline of 17–18, 24
domination of Arab race, history of 32
and Egyptian border 16
encouraged Arab unity 5
end of 38–9, 84
former provinces of settled 46
National Empire 17, 20, 55
as Pan-Islamism 1, 5, 17
recognises Ḥijāz empire 37
retains power in Gulf states 6
and Sinai 22
Unity and Progress Party 24
Oxford University
consulted over Economic Cultural Unity 121–5

Palestine
and Arab Confederation 61
and Arab League 140–3, 146, 147–8, 152, 154, 156, 158
Arab political parties in 69
Arab Resistance Movement 79
as arms depot 79
Arab–Jewish relations in 40, 42, 44, 48, 74, 109, 111, 118
asked for opinion on Arab unity 105–6
banned from discussing Jewish question at Arab Conference 68
British assessment of 33, 36–7
British Commission in 69–70, 74, 113
British mandate over 3, 17, 20–2, 40–3, 48–9, 71, 109
British reports on Pan-Islamism from 41–4, 55–7, 167–71
British troops in 40
Colonial Office commissions study of Islam in 60–3
Colonial Office control of 2, 56–7
conferences concerning 40, 128
Criminal Investigation Department 53–4, 55
and Egypt 17, 21, 82
Foreign Office control of 2
fosters Arab division 3, 20
Islamic university in planned 56
Jewish control of 81

Jewish immigration, open door policy implemented 20–3
Jews granted land in 25–6, 43, 59, 78–9, 111
as national home for Jews 3, 37, 41, 43, 118, 125
nationalist sentiment in vii
Palestine National Movement 40
as potential arena of conflict 55–6
requests referendum on leadership 40
rights of non-Jews in 37
strikes in 79
and Suez Canal 22
and Syria 128
uprisings in 48, 54, 61, 71, 101
violence in 40, 42, 44, 48, 61
see also Greater Syria; Islamic Conference in Jerusalem
Palmerston, Henry John Temple 12, 21
Pan-Arabism
Britain examines 70–3, 87–95, 117–19
Christianity and 82
Egypt and 83–7, 90–5
as misleading term 87
origins of vii, 81
and Pan-Islamism 17–19, 35, 84–8
and Pan-Islamism-Arabism 84–7
see also Arab League
Pan-Islamism-Arabism 84–7
Pan-Islamism 54–5
British officials in Palestine report on 55–7
compared to Arab Nationalism 87–8
and Ḥijāz railway 62–3
and Ottoman Empire 1, 5, 17
and Pan-Islamism 17–19, 35, 84–8
and Pan-Islamism-Arabism 84–7
and Pan-Touranism 19
Pan-Touranism 19
Paris Peace Conference 31–3
pearls 8–9
Persia
fears Arab Nationalism 67–8
Picot, George *see* Sykes-Picot Agreement
pilgrimage *see ḥajj*

al-Qarawīyīn university 5
al-Qassām, 'Izz al-Dīn 79
Qatar 71, 95, 108, 116

railways 13, 32, 61–2, 70, 113–14
Roman Catholic Church 21
Rothschild, Edmond James de 25
Royal Navy 6–7, 34
and memorandum on Arab unity, text of 217–26
Russia
Bolshevist Revolution 27
and Jews 24, 26–7
seeks power in Gulf states 6

Sa'īd, 'Abd al-Ḥamīd Bey, 20, 55, 86
Samuel, Herbert 40–1, 44
Sassanian Empire 67
Sa'ūd, 'Abd al-'Azīz Āl 1–2, 44, 55, 62, 89, 91, 93, 96–101
advises Preparatory Meeting of Arab League 138–42, 147, 150–1, 153
annexes Ḥijāz 47
Britain sidelines 127
Egyptian suspicion of 123
and King Fayṣal 66–9, 71
as President of proposed unity council 108, 118
relationship with Britain 47, 106, 108, 118, 127–31
relationship with Iraq 128–9
relationship with other Arab leaders 107
takes control of holy Muslim sites 47
see also Saudi Arabia
Saudi Arabia
and Arab League 137–9, 146–9, 151, 154–5, 156
and Arab unity 42, 126–8, 130–1
independence 107
Iraq, relationship with 80, 128–31
origins of 42
see also Hījāz, Kingdom of; Sa'ūd, 'Abd al-'Azīz Āl

secularisation 35
  see also Pan-Arabism; Pan-Islamism
schools *see* education
Shī'ites 107, 118
Simon, John 69, 73–4
Sinai 16, 22
Spain 58
Stack, Sirdar Lee 81
Sudan
  agency in Cairo 81, 83
  borders 4
  Egypt, relationship with 3, 4, 12, 81
  Foreign Office control of 2, 4, 81
  Sudan Intelligence Bureau 53, 81
Suez Canal 97–8
  and *ḥajj* 5, 15–16
  opening of 4, 5, 13, 22
  and Palestine 22
  Turkish troops at 33–4
Sunnis 26, 107, 118
Sykes, Mark *see* Skyes-Picot Agreement
Sykes-Picot Agreement 27, 36
  text of 165–6
Syria
  and Arab Confederation 42, 45–6, 61
  and Arab League 139–42, 144–6, 148–53, 157–8
  British assessment of 32, 36–7, 65–5
  British consulate in 89
  Christian state in, possibility of 81
  closeness to Europe 81
  constitution 63
  and Egypt 18, 65, 82–4
  and Federal Council of Arab States 114–15
  French mandate in 42, 46–7, 63, 72, 73–4, 77–8, 82–3, 97, 163
  Great Syrian Revolt 20, 46, 63, 71
  independence proposed 106
  and Iraq 64, 83, 96
  and Jewish migration 23
  and Kingdom of Ḥijāz 31
  and League of Nations 61
  National Movement 18, 63, 83, 88
  nationalist sentiment in vii, 32
  and Ottoman coup, 1913 19
  and Palestine 128
  Republic in proposed 65
  strike in 82–3
  student demonstrations in 63
  see also Greater Syria

Ṭābā crisis 16, 18, 22
Tilley, John 38–9
trade routes 4–5
  and British imperialism 5, 8
  from Mashreq 5
Trans-Jordan, Emirate of
  and Arab Confederation 42, 72
  and Arab League 146, 152–3
  and Arab unity 106, 110, 119–20, 131–3
  British mandate over 3, 42
  Colonial Office control of 2
  and Federal Council of Arab States 114–15
  Jewish settlements in 69
  see also Greater Syria
transport *see* railways; aeroplanes; airports
Treaty of Arab Brotherhood 107, 110–11
Treaty of Sèvres 37
Tripoli 15, 19, 58, 64, 95, 98, 113, 158
Trucial Coast 71, 95, 108
Truman Doctrine ix
Turkey
  advances on Egypt 19
  imperial ambitions of 97
  and Islamic Conference in Jerusalem 58
  and Persia 67

Uganda 4
Ummah Party 18–19
United Kingdom
  actively disrupts Arab unity viii, 2–5, 47, 71–2, 90, 163
  Aden, invasion of 6
  and Arab Confederation 43–5
  Arab Conference in Baghdad, report from 69–75

and Arab unity, reports on 79–83, 95–102
British subjects in Gulf states 7, 38, 43
competition to dominate Arab states 6
Criminal Investigation Department 53–4, 55
decline in international influence ix
discourages Egyptian influence in Gulf states 5–6, 19
Eastern Arab states, focus on 4
and Egyptian border 16
encourages Italian occupation of Libya 4–5
European Department 53–4, 84
fears growth of Egyptian power 11–12, 122
foreign policy, external criticism of 43
foreign policy, internal criticism of 2
and Kingdom of Ḥijāz 31, 33–7
military presence in Arab states 106
observation, policy of 53
and Pan-Arabism 70–3, 87–95, 117–19
and proposed Higher Supervisory Council 114–15
research at Islamic Conference in Jerusalem 61
and Saudi Arabia 105–7,
self-interest in Arab states viii, 107
suggests Federal Council of Arab States 114–15
as superpower viii
Sudan Agency 81, 83
Sudan Intelligence Bureau 53, 81
trade route, Eastern, importance of 4
War Cabinet viii
War Cabinet Arab Federation Committee 105, 106–12
see also Colonial Office; Foreign Office; India Office
United Nations 124, 154
United States
decline in international influence ix
entry into Arab political arena ix, 31–2
growth in power ix
and oil ix
and proposed Higher Supervisory Council 114–15
universities *see* education
urbanisation 33, 107
see also westernisation

Versailles Conference viii, 20, 37, 163

Wauchope, Arthur Grenfell 60–1
Westernisation 5, 37
Eastern Arab states denied access to 3
of Egypt 13–14
Wingate, Francis Reginald 53
World War I 19, 26, 33, 59, 71
aftermath of ix, 3, 32–3, 36, 97
Arab Nationalism in 33–6
World War II 77, 95–102
Axis powers 101, 124
see also Arab League
Yemen 32, 34
independence 107

Zanzibar 4, 9

www.ingramcontent.com/pod-product-compliance
Lightning Source LLC
Chambersburg PA
CBHW061438300426
44114CB00014B/1734